PENGUIN BOOKS

PET SHOP BOYS, *LITERALLY*

Chris Heath is a journalist who has known the Pet Shop Boys ever since their first hit, *West End Girls*, went to number one all over the world.

PET SHOP BOYS, *LITERALLY*

CHRIS HEATH

PENGUIN BOOKS

PENGUIN BOOKS

Published by the Penguin Group
Penguin Books Ltd, 27 Wrights Lane, London W8 5TZ, England
Viking Penguin, a division of Penguin Books USA Inc.
375 Hudson Street, New York, New York 10014, USA
Penguin Books Australia Ltd, Ringwood, Victoria, Australia
Penguin Books Canada Ltd, 2801 John Street, Markham, Ontario, Canada L3R 1B4
Penguin Books (NZ) Ltd, 182–190 Wairau Road, Auckland 10, New Zealand

Penguin Books Ltd, Registered Offices: Harmondsworth, Middlesex, England

First published by Viking 1990
Published in Penguin Books 1991
10 9 8 7 6 5 4 3 2 1

Printed in England by Clays Ltd, St Ives plc

Contents

List of Illustrations

SECTION I

‘Left To My Own Devices’. Casper as Debussy
‘Rent’. Neil, Casper, Courtney Pine, Robia, Cooley, Tracey, Hugo

SECTION II

Courtney Pine
‘Love Comes Quickly’
‘Heart’
‘Later Tonight’
Waiting to film ‘Nothing Has Been Proved’
‘Nothing Has Been Proved’
‘It’s A Sin’
‘Shopping’. Casper, Courtney, Tracey, Dominic and Chris
‘Domino Dancing’. Neil, Robia and Casper
‘It’s A Sin’
‘Domino Dancing’. Neil, Robia and Casper
‘King’s Cross’. Chris in front of film of himself originally shot for the ‘Rent’ video
‘Shopping’. Neil and dancers
‘Domino Dancing’. Robia, the bank of sequencers and samplers, Chris and Neil
‘West End Girls’. Cooley’s backflip
‘Heart’. Neil in front of one of the dancers from Derek Jarman’s accompanying film
‘Paninaro’. Cooley and Chris
‘It’s A Sin’. Neil’s famous twirl
‘West End Girls’. Hugo, Cooley, Tracey and Robia
Pet Shop Boys
Neil Tennant
Chris taking his applause

All photographs by Lawrence Watson

Introduction

When we undertook our first ever tour in June and July 1989, we asked Chris Heath to accompany us with the idea of eventually producing some sort of picture book with a short text. For several weeks, in Hong Kong, Japan and back home in Britain, he followed us – and the other forty-odd people on the tour – around with a notebook, jotting down everything of interest he witnessed. In the end we agreed that he would write a more detailed account than we first imagined. The book you are holding is the result.

Although we have never been keen on most of the publicity and self-promotion that inevitably accompanies a successful pop group, it seemed a worthwhile notion to produce a book through the close access to its subject that the normal 'official' biography gets, without the starstruck blandness that usually results. Reading the manuscript for the first time, we were, to be honest, more or less horrified. Are we really that horrible? Is Neil really, by popular agreement, 'like a schoolteacher'? Does Chris always complain so much? Are we that self-obsessed, so frequently rude? Do we discuss money, snipe about other pop stars quite so much? Apparently, yes.

Perhaps we will learn as much as anyone else who reads this book about the Pet Shop Boys.

Neil Tennant   Chris Lowe

Acknowledgements

Chris Heath would like to thank the Pet Shop Boys for their help with this book, and would also like to thank the following: Michael Braun, Murray Chalmers, Rob Holden, Ivan Kushlick, Pepa Misas, Jonathan Riley, Derrin Schlesinger, William Shaw, Gill Smith, Jill Wall, Lawrence Watson and Johnny Wright.

Pet Shop Boys:
A Brief History

Neil Tennant (b. 1954) grew up in Newcastle. In 1970 and 1971 he played acoustic guitar and sang in a folk group called Dust. In 1972 he moved to London to study history at the Polytechnic of North London. His first job was as British editor of the American firm Marvel Comics. He subsequently worked at Macdonald Educational Publishing (1977), ITV Books (1981) and at *Smash Hits* magazine (1982).

Chris Lowe (b. 1959) grew up in Blackpool. He briefly played keyboards in a school heavy metal group, Stallion, then became trombonist in the school orchestra and in a local seven-piece jazz band One Under The Eight. In 1978 he moved to Liverpool and studied architecture at Liverpool University.

In 1981, during Chris's year of work experience at Michael Aukett Associates in London, the two struck up a conversation in a King's Road hi-fi shop and were soon writing songs together. In 1983 they persuaded a cult American disco producer called Bobby O (full name Bobby Orlando), whom they idolized, to make records with them. The first result, a song called 'West End Girls', was a modest club hit. In 1984 they signed a management contract with Tom Watkins. In 1985, after lengthy legal negotiations to extricate them from their contract with Bobby O, they signed to EMI Records' subsidiary, Parlophone Records. Their first single, 'Opportunities (Let's Make Lots Of Money)', was a flop. The next, 'West End Girls', reached number one all over the world.

They have since released four LPs – 'Please' (1986), 'Disco' (a collection of dance-floor remixes, 1986), 'Actually' (1987) and 'Introspective' (1988) – and have had twelve British hit singles: 'West End Girls' (1985), 'Love Comes Quickly', 'Opportunities

(Let's Make Lots of Money)' (a re-recorded version) and 'Suburbia' (all 1986); 'It's A Sin', 'What Have I Done To Deserve This?', 'Rent' and 'Always On My Mind' (all 1987); 'Heart', 'Domino Dancing' and 'Left To My Own Devices' (all 1988); and 'It's Alright' (1989). They have also written and co-produced: a single for Patsy Kensit – 'I'm Not Scared' (released under the artist name Eighth Wonder, 1988); two singles for Dusty Springfield – 'Nothing Has Been Proved' and 'In Private' (both 1989); and a whole LP for Liza Minnelli – 'Results' (1989). Aside from making records they have also released two video collections: 'Television' (1986) and 'Showbusiness' (1988) and have made a full-length feature film, *It Couldn't Happen Here* (1988), directed by Jack Bond and co-starring Barbara Windsor, Gareth Hunt, Neil Dickson and Joss Ackland.

In 1986, then again in 1987, they scheduled and subsequently cancelled major concert tours in theatres. Both times they had planned to collaborate with people from the English National Opera and both times the economics proved forbidding. Thus their only live performances before June 1989 had been at the Brixton Fridge to backing tapes (1984, six songs), at the ICA (1985, three songs), on the TV programme *Whistle Test* (1986, two songs), on the televised American MTV awards (1986, two songs) and at Before The Act (an anti-Clause 28 benefit at London's Piccadilly Theatre, two songs, 1988). In early 1989 they received an offer from a Japanese promoter, Mr Udo, generous enough to allow them to tour as they wished as long as they played venues with audiences of around 8,000. They agreed. Soon afterwards Hong Kong dates were added at the beginning of the tour and at a late stage they agreed to add dates in July in Britain.

Chapter One

In an article entitled 'Thinking the possibility of realization for their live', issue three of the Japanese Pet Shop Boys fanzine, *Out of Order*, chews over the Pet Shop Boys' predicament. Would they ever play live? Could they? It begins by summarizing the situation as the writers see it. The Pet Shop Boys have mentioned playing live since their inception, but to their readers' disappointment ('the resigned voice came from fans') it hasn't happened. The Pet Shop Boys are quoted as saying that their dance-floor twelve-inch remixes are their equivalent of playing live and the article deduces that 'that makes the live realization doubtful'. Their earlier theatrical touring plans are described but the commentary tartly notes 'the plan stops at thinking step, and after action doesn't reported'.

They then reveal how, in an earlier issue of *Out of Order*, they had polled the fans on their hopes. They were given four options: 'a) we'd like to see it immediately; b) we like to see them play in their own good time; c) we don't mind – it's up to them; or d) we don't want them to do it because, by the looks of their videos, they'd be tragic live.' Predictably the fans mainly plumped for a) or b). The piece closes with a more optimistic quote from Neil ('Mr Tennant', as they deferentially refer to him), plainly translated into Japanese and then back into English:

'Please look forward to it! We won't make it ordinally pop concert. We're planning gaudily show 'cause we want to give our impression strongly. At first, we're thinking to use theatre instead of proper music fall. It gives you different atmosphere. Well, take a look. We'll make you think our's not average concert.'

★

The first I hear of the tour is in mid-May when Rob Holden from Massive, Tom Watkins' management company, telephones me. The Pet Shop Boys are to tour Japan and Hong Kong in late June and early July. Would I like to come? Some sort of book perhaps? He is vague, obviously trying to do the Pet Shop Boys' bidding without being precisely sure exactly what that bidding was. I said that I was very keen.

The next week I see Neil and Chris. I have been asked to interview them, off-camera, for various Far-Eastern TV programmes to promote the tour. (The programmes would either just use chunks of the Pet Shop Boys' conversation or dub their interviewer's voice over mine.) There is a side of the Pet Shop Boys that treats explanation as a chore and a burden foisted upon you whenever you do anything. In the weeks to come Chris will claim wryly that they only decided to tour because they got bored with explaining to people why they didn't tour. Today, after the second interview, they declare that they are already bored with their spiel about it.

There are four interviews to do (two for Japan, one for Hong Kong, and one general, all-purpose one) and a long list of Japanese TV Station IDs (Chris: 'Hello, we're Neil and Chris, the Pet Shop Boys . . .' Neil: '. . . and you're watching Funky Music Tomato!' and so on). Lucy Campbell from EMI's international department tells me beforehand that they probably won't do the IDs and highlights three she'd like me to push for if possible, but they actually run through the lot without any fuss. As the camera is reset for the Hong Kong interview, Chris tells Neil, 'Apparently all our fans in Hong Kong are little girls. You'd better book your facelift now.'

Asked to introduce the interview Chris begins, breezily, 'We're currently rehearsing our show and it's going to be really good . . .'

He breaks off. 'I can't do this sort of rubbish. I'm not a salesman.'

But they soon get going, presenting a persuasive description of 'a very special show, we hope not like any other rock show'. Again and again they hammer home that the show is to be unusual: 'not a traditional rock'n'roll show which doesn't cost very much money'. They run through the costs and effort going into the backing singers, the six American dancers, the special lighting; the programming that allows them to transmit all the programmed music at the push of a button from a small computer set-up on one side of the stage; Courtney Pine, Britain's most famous young jazz musician in his own right, playing saxophone; and, most of all, the role of Derek Jarman both in shooting the films to be projected behind the performance and in directing the whole show.

'It's directed,' explains Neil, 'in the same way you direct a play or a musical, whereas a rock'n'roll show is supposed to be "spontaneous, maan", even though it's exactly the same every night.'

They harp on the differences between this and a normal rock show. Neil points out that they 'find normal rock concerts boring. Actually I think a lot of people do if they have the honesty to admit it. It's always great when the group comes on, then five minutes later you're thinking . . .' He mimes boredom.

'Also,' Chris expands, 'rock shows are really embarrassing. The audience can be embarrassing and the performers I find cringeworthy. You light your lighter during the ballad . . .' He frowns. 'It's the way it's meant to have some kind of importance when it evidently hasn't – that's what I find embarrassing . . . If I go to a concert and I'm genuinely thrilled or excited I'll automatically stand up and start dancing, but what you don't do is the standard thing. I think you've got to feel it. I don't think a lot of these reactions in rock concerts are genuine, either from the performer or the audience. I just think they're going through the motions.'

They explain how, to their surprise, most of the guidance they have received has been to make their concerts like everybody else's. 'There's a whole industry around rock concerts in London,' explains Neil, 'and the whole idea seems to be you do exactly what anyone else does. It took us a while to get across to a lot of people exactly how un-rock'n'roll our idea for the show was. There was a specific moment when the lighting designer realized and he was quite shocked.'

Chris says they couldn't do that sort of show anyway. 'The type of personality you have to have, I don't think me or Neil have. We're not in your Bon Jovi mould, when you get down on your knees and start shoving your crotch in the air at people. We're basically not male bimbos.'

And if they are making this effort to be different, Chris makes clear, their audience should do the same: 'I'd be very disappointed if they start going through the rock audience clichés – the cigarette lighters. I'll probably have to turn the keyboards off and tell them to stop. It's embarrassing.'

'Of course,' says Neil, who looks as though he'd be more embarrassed by Chris causing a scene on-stage than by cigarette lighters, 'I quite like that.'

In between each interview we gossip. Chris declares that the interviews are boring and that 'it'd be better if we just gossiped'.

'Yes,' concurs Neil. 'Let's just gossip about Bros.'

But they carry on none the less. Chris explains over and over about the music being generated from a computer bank. He says how this will leave most of the stage free and enthuses about how fantastic electronic music sounds played live: 'The best concert I've ever been to was Kraftwerk.'

When I ask them if they'll be playing all their hit singles Chris says, 'We haven't got enough time' and laughs. Neil explains that they chose the song list and order in a couple of hours round his flat and haven't changed it since. Chris sarcastically suggests that for his solo spot, 'Paninaro', he will split the audience into two halves 'where you get one half to singalong and then tell the other half to be louder'. When I ask about the six-track CD 'In Depth', being released just in Japan to coincide with their visit, they bluff endlessly. Finally Neil grins, the tape still rolling, and says, 'Actually I don't know what to say about this because it's the record company's idea and I have no idea why we're doing it, to be honest. Unfortunately I haven't been able to think of any rationalization whatsoever.'

During the interviews I ask them several times why they have chosen the Far East in which to tour. To begin with they mention that the offer from a Japanese promoter was the first to make touring in the manner they wanted a financial possibility. Once Neil also confesses that 'If your first concert is in London or New York I would have this paranoid feeling that they're out to knock you.' It is Chris who adds the third reason:

'We wanted to do it a long way from home in case it was an absolute disaster so no one would really know about it over here.'

'Frank as ever,' sighs Neil.

In fact the Far East is chosen by many artists to begin their live careers. It is highly lucrative, thanks to the strength of the Japanese economy and the severe exchange rate. The audiences are famously uncritical. Also, as Neil points out, it is a long way from London or New York. When the cameras aren't rolling the Pet Shop Boys slip into talking about it as if it was a remote practice, a rehearsal for an American tour in 1990.

Today however they have just been presented with a proposal for a British tour, to follow directly after the Japanese dates. They seem impressed – shocked, I suspect – by the financial terms: another two weeks of concerts would turn round a projected small loss into a substantial profit. They tell me that they're not going to accept it, but I suspect that they will change their minds. Not just because of the money, but because as the tour draws closer and the cast of performers they are assembling grows more impressive, it's obvious they're beginning to think it might be a waste, all this effort, if they don't show it off at home.

They don't mention anything about me coming or about a book, so neither do I, but in the days that follow I get promising phone calls from the management office. Am I vegetarian? Do I prefer window or aisle seats? I also hear that the British tour is happening. One morning Mark Farrow, the designer responsible for nearly all of their artwork, who works in the same office as the management, telephones me about 'the tour programme we are doing together'. Of course no one has mentioned this, but I wanted to do it anyway. Mark tells me their suggestions for the content: an interview with them, a piece on Derek Jarman, a chronology of the Pet Shop Boys and 'the Simon Frith article', an analytical piece written for the *Village Voice* in early 1988 which Neil wants included.

A few days later, while Mark Farrow and I are working on the programme proofs, Chris comes in. He has just been learning some dance moves at a rehearsal studio. He is working with six American dancers, brought over for the tour by a dancer and choreographer, Casper, who had worked on the 'Left To My Own Devices' video. Chris bounds around, showing off his new steps. He leans over Mark Farrow to see what he's working on. 'Neil's bloody Simon Frith piece,' he moans.

I phone Derek Jarman to interview him for the tour programme. He is in a London editing suite, finishing off the films that are to be back-projected during the show. In the background I can hear an instrumental version of 'It's A Sin' playing over and over and every now and again he interrupts a train of thought to declare that this is 'some of the best Super-8 imagery I've ever done . . . *well* up to scratch . . . The film is often brilliant, even though I say it myself.'

He first met the Pet Shop Boys when they asked him to direct the video for 'It's A Sin', a dark, rather confused drama in which Neil and Chris played prisoner and gaoler. 'I thought of it initially as another pop video – it always is until you meet the musicians.' He is frank that one of the main roles a tangential involvement in music has had over the years has been to keep him solvent while he worked on his own film projects (*Sebastian, Jubilee, The Tempest, The Angelic Conversation, Caravaggio, The Last of England, Requiem*). Though he professes to have little idea about music – 'I'm pushing fifty now . . . I live in my own mad world in Dungeness' – he found them straightforward and nice. He was pleased that, having decided to work with him, they let him do what he does.

'I can honestly say, of all the music people I've worked with, they've put the most trust in me. Neil, and Chris too I think, has a knowledge of the theatre and knows that having asked people to do something you have to leave them free to do what they want to do if you're going to get good results. They seem to understand this and they seem to stick by what's done.'

They worked together again on the 'Rent' video then asked him in April if he would get involved in this tour. They had about six meetings, just throwing ideas around. He explains that the most similar thing he's done before was a modern Italian opera called *Inspiration* by Silvano Bussotti in Florence, but this back-projection is the first time it has ever been done with 70mm film.

It's strange hearing how he has jumped from the songs to the ideas for staging them: the process seems to be a mixture of odd logical leaps, lateral thinking and bizarre puns. 'I just improvise these things . . . there's no point in illustrating the songs.' They are simply, he explains, 'a taking-off point for the imagery'. 'Paninaro' takes its name from an Italian youth cult – his film is like 'old washed postcards of Italy, of statues and clouds and ceilings and Italian hustlers from another age'. Most of the scenic footage is from an Italian holiday he took in 1985: several of the films plunder his private film library, 400 hours of imagery ('no one else,' he murmurs proudly, 'could have done this'). There is also a Dalmatian dog in the 'Paninaro' film and from that the black-and-white polka dot motif is transposed back on-stage for the dancers' costumes.

'There's definitely an element of musical in it,' he says. 'When we came to the finale for "West End Girls" we were saying, "Well, what *are* West End girls? We can't put a whole lot of people in West End modern fashion – it's got to be a musical ending, hasn't it?" And the musicals that were going through our mind were things like *Red Shoes* from the fifties, or *American in Paris* . . . dancers . . . music . . . bright, bright colours.'

He talks about the tour with a refreshing, but also rather frightening, devil-may-care 'well, it might be a complete disaster, I haven't the foggiest really' attitude. He talks of the first dress rehearsal as 'a moment of reckoning when we'll have to throw everything together'. He says he hasn't been to any rock shows recently – 'I actually rather hate crowds' – but when he has been to them he's always surprised 'how audiences accept things that look dull'. This, at the very least, will look different: 'There really hasn't been anything like this one . . . If it doesn't work, it doesn't work – we'll have a bash. That's how I think about it.

'They asked for a theatrical concert,' he concludes, 'and that's what we're doing. I suppose some people think pop music and theatre shouldn't mix but I think pop music *is* theatre and I don't see why it shouldn't be so. To my mind there's two ways of doing it – you either just sit there and sing on a stool and do it the simple way or you go for it.'

They finally mention to me my inclusion in the tour party when I go down to rehearsals in Nomis studios to interview them for the tour programme. 'You're coming, aren't you?' they inquire in a friendly but vague way, as if it was no bad thing that I was joining them, but little of their business.

I talk to Rob Holden some more times to try to sort out the details, but without result. At one stage he phones to suggest a financial arrangement suggested by the Pet Shop Boys which I agree sounds fine, but the next time I talk to him he says that when he'd tried to go through the detailed budget with them and Chris had queried the figure, Rob had had to point out that it was their suggestion. In the end nothing is arranged: no financial deal, no contract, no proper discussion of what the book might be or what they expected or what I might or might not be allowed to do, though it is tacitly understood that they will have control over the result. No one ever officially tells me that I'm going, but *Smash Hits* contact me after talking to EMI Records and ask me to write a piece on the first part of the tour, so I presume I must be. Anyway, I see my name on tour personnel lists in the management offices. I have a bag number: 45. Sometimes next to my name it says 'journalist'. Sometimes it just says 'tourist'.

I invite myself down to the final dress rehearsal at Brixton Academy. There I see the show for the first time.

The synthesizer sequence which begins 'One More Chance' pumps out from the darkness. To the left of the stage flashlights shoot round. On the back screen, simple, sloping, black-and-white images of tenement blocks, a New York skyline, appear. The four singers – left to right as you look from the audience: Jay Henry, Carroll Thompson, Juliet Roberts and Mike Henry – hold torches under their chins and begin singing: 'one more, one more chance'. The dancers appear: three men (Casper, Cooley and Hugo) and three women (Jill, Tracy and Robia). They throw themselves around the stage in *West Side Story*-style choreography. From the left and right wings stride Neil and Chris. Chris is in all-over leather and wears a spherical 'ruby'-studded helmet: he looks down, doesn't smile and seems to try to look as if he's playing as little as possible. Neil wears a long overcoat; he illustrates the words with occasional exaggerated gestures.

'Opportunities'. On the screen, the first of Derek Jarman's films begins: an oriental woman with a fan and an evil, enticing stare bends her index finger in a sinister 'come hither' gesture. While the on-stage lighting has been down, Chris has taken his helmet off – he places it on the ground, next to his keyboard – and Neil has removed his overcoat to reveal a black suit studded with 'diamonds'. He is wearing a bow tie. At one point he walks near the backing singers and Mike Henry grabs a piece of cloth dangling from Neil's back trouser-pocket. As he walks away a string of four large handkerchiefs resembling American dollar bills streams behind him.

As 'Opportunities' finishes a screen is carried on and placed stage-centre. Neil disappears behind it. The orchestral beginning to 'Left To My Own Devices' swells up. Two of the dancers, Casper and Hugo, position themselves in front of either edge of the screen. Casper is dressed as a classical conductor with a baton; Hugo is in khaki military garb and beret: the allusion is to Debussy and Che Guevara in the lyrics. They move robotically, then, when the drums burst in, dance across the front of the stage. All the while clothes are tossed up on to the top of the screen. (In fact Alan, the head of wardrobe, is behind the screen helping Neil change.) Just in time for the song's first line, Neil appears in a turquoise-and-green dressing-gown with pink pyjamas underneath: 'I get out of bed at half-past ten . . .' At the end of the song he strolls off and Courtney Pine steps forward for a solo, accompanied by Chris and Dominic Clarke, their keyboard programmer, playing the chorus's chords on keyboards.

Neil enters for 'Rent' wearing a large white fake-fur coat. Midway through the song he takes it off, to reveal a black-and-gold waistcoat over a white shirt, and drapes the coat over Juliet Roberts' shoulders. The dancers are dressed as ballroom dancers and act out a ghostly routine in three pairs.

'Heart' begins with the backing singers scat-singing around the tune that repeats through the chorus, then a Derek Jarman film begins: first a bright pulsating light, then lots of ecstatic dancing in what appears to be a suburban disco. The camera is clearly mounted so that it swings in a circle, its subject at any particular moment dancing around with it in a wider circle. The dancers are young and old. A ginger-haired girl, almost hysterical, features most. Near the end Derek Jarman himself glides rather regally across the screen. Beneath this, on-stage, Neil acts out the song's declarations of affection with some very formularized hand movements.

The stage is bare at the beginning of 'Paninaro', then out runs Cooley in a Dalmatian-spot jacket. Behind him a film starts, Derek Jarman's old holiday footage, in front of which a good-looking Italian youth, with a broad, confident smile that shows off a glistening brace, caresses a Dalmatian dog. Cooley acts out a love scene with Robia, then Chris strides on, in pink peaked cap, sunglasses, lime-green t-shirt and jeans. He speaks a few of his lines, then dances in time with Cooley. Next Cooley does an amazing dance including a backflip, after which Chris is supposed to address the audience on his likes and dislikes (in rehearsal he says nothing). He ignores the attention of Robia and Tracy (who has joined the action as Robia's rival) and strolls off. Cooley acts a tug-of-love between Robia and Tracy, then positions himself on the left side of the stage away from both of them. They pull out knives and fight, and Tracy kills Robia. Cooley, horrified, pretends to greet Tracy lovingly but has palmed the knife Robia lost in the fight and, in full embrace with Tracy, stabs her in the back. Cooley surveys the pitiful carnage, picks up the other knife and, with great drama, on the precise beat with which the song ends, drives both knives into his stomach and buckles over, dead.

For 'Love Comes Quickly' Chris wears more casual wear (usually a purple-and-black striped Issey Miyake top) and Neil is in another suit. Blue light pulses and washes over the stage in time with the song.

'Love Comes Quickly' is followed by two completely unprogrammed songs. Two old stand-up lamps are placed either side of Chris's keyboard and Neil sits next to him on a stool. Dominic remains on-stage, playing extra keyboards. Mid-song one of the lights is swivelled round to shine on Courtney Pine, mid-stage, who solos.

During 'Nothing Has Been Proved' the set is littered with people – the backing singers and dancers, sitting on-stage reading newspapers proclaiming SCANDAL. Casper and Jill act out a scene between a proud showgirl and a cool, selfish, sharp operator. Behind them all, Derek Jarman's film plays around with images from the Profumo affair – endless pictures of Christine Keeler doctored and moved round the screen. In the end it becomes a fantastic playpen of rotating and receding colours. The song finishes with everyone leaving the stage and the dissonant acid disco of 'The Sound Of The Atom Splitting' begins to ricochet round the theatre. Smoke puffs everywhere and lights rotate not just round the stage but into the auditorium. In the actual performance a special device is fixed to the mixing desk so that the sound itself encircles the arena as if it is circling the audience. After a few minutes billows of smoke seep on to the stage and, within it, dim outlines can be discerned. The lights slowly fade with the opening bars of 'It's A Sin', revealing the dancers in huge, grotesque costumes, representing different deadly sins. One is a horrific primitive face, mostly just one huge, dangling tongue. Another is a rotund British bulldog Winston Churchill-type figure in a Union Jack waistcoat. Another has huge long pointy fingers. Another is ugly and bald and has deformed ears; it is wearing a skimpy bra and panties. Chris appears, like the singers, in hooded robes. Neil enters grasping a trident, a crown on his head, in flowing, red, almost papal vestments: at first he holds a mask on a stick over his face as disguise. In mid-song he twirls, the red cape following him round and round in a decaying spiral. Behind is a nightmarish film sequence: birds pecking away, strange, fuzzy creatures feverishly enacting mysterious rites, gluttony . . . Cut between this are two boys, wallowing in luxury, rubbing oil over each other, then kissing. The overall effect is quite shattering, quite unlike anything one's used to seeing at a pop concert.

'Shopping' follows sharply. Chris is in a t-shirt and straw hat but everyone else is dressed as city business types. Neil has a blue striped shirt and red tie and comes on talking into a portable phone. The dancers act out a caricature of yuppies. Cooley is carried about, stiff as cardboard, and then at the end moonwalks backwards followed by a spotlight.

A Spanish dancer appears on the screen, clicking her fingers as 'Domino Dancing' begins. She twists and turns to the Latin rhythm while behind her bullfight scenes are shown – smiling, heroic faces interspersed with gorings, matadors being tossed, fearful little Spaniards scurrying across the sand to someone's rescue. On-stage Neil sings in an embroidered black shirt while Casper dances a fake flamenco, then trails a cape. After one pass near the right of the stage he whips it up and Robia appears behind it. They dance. At the end strange psychedelic lights play on the screen as Chris and Courtney mess about with a strange Acid House snippet Chris has come up with in rehearsal.

As 'King's Cross' begins a black-and-white grainy film starts, footage set around King's Cross station, somehow just as sad and hopeless and beautiful as the music. Later on Chris appears in it, in scenes originally filmed for the 'Rent' video two years ago, looking joyless and resigned, a woollen hat on his head, a dufflebag over his shoulder.

The last song of the main set is 'Always On My Mind'. Neil wears leather. Behind, a paintbox of shuddering oranges and green is superimposed, near the end, by a picture first of Neil, then of Chris, first hidden by his cap then looking up to face the audience. At the very end they are shown side by side, Neil facing the camera, Chris away. They turn to face each other, stare sternly, move just very slightly, then, as the song echoes away, turn back.

Two encores are planned. First is 'West End Girls'. In true encore etiquette Neil returns in his 'Opportunities' suit. The dancers each do little solo turns, and dance around using three chairs set centre-stage. Before the second encore Neil introduces everyone one by one as they come back on to the stage, as one might at the theatre, his spoken introductions leading into the slow beginning of 'It's Alright': 'dictation being forced in Afghanistan . . .' As the song speeds up the show ends in exuberant celebratory mayhem.

The small crowd allowed into the dress rehearsal – Derek Jarman, the entire Massive management office, their press officer Murray, Chris's sister Vicki, Neil's sister Susan and his brother Simon, a few friends – applauds rapturously. Beforehand, those who hadn't seen any rehearsals were extremely apprehensive: afterwards, they are not just relieved but extremely impressed. Everyone celebrates with champagne in the dressing-rooms.

Mark Farrow gives me a lift home and on the way we stop at Neil's flat. We meant only to pick up a book, but there are a few people there, nice red wine is thrust in our direction and Neil – a little drunk and somewhat euphoric after the dress rehearsal – is in full flow, dominating the company so that it is less like a conversation, more like a performance. Just before he launches into the evening's *tour de force* – Neil Tennant on the subject of Cliff Richard, a rambling and deeply hilarious discourse on 'the Peter Pan of Pop' – I notice, on the table next to me, a chronicle of the Rolling Stones' 1972 America tour, *Stones Touring Party* by Robert Greenfield, which a friend, journalist Jon Savage, has lent to Neil to get him into the touring spirit. Seeing me peering at it, Neil says, half-jokingly, that it might give me some suitable ideas. I read the flyleaf: 'Its style matches the subject, the crazy exhausting enormously brutal punishing life of a rockbiz tour.' Like that? I ask.

I know little more when the cab arrives to pick me up and

take me to Gatwick airport, so I decide to go wherever I'm able and note down whatever I can until somebody stops me. As it turns out they rarely do, and people get used to me wandering around in dressing-rooms, at receptions, over smart dinners, in nightclubs with my notebook open, scribbling. Sometimes, when something slightly embarrassing happens, someone will triumphantly bellow, 'It's in the book.' Sometimes – not often – something will happen and someone will say, either hopefully or threateningly, depending on who they are, '*That's* not in the book.' Mostly, after the first few days, no one takes any notice.

Chapter Two

Sunday, *25 June 1989*

In the car to the airport the tour photographer Lawrence Watson and I are entertained by a non-stop monologue of great rock'n'roll tour stories from the make-up artist Pierre La Roche. The best is the famous Rolling Stones 1975 tour when the entourage would line up each morning, backs to the 'doctor', and drop their trousers for their daily vitamin shots.

When we arrive, Neil and Chris are already there, relaxing in the first-class lounge. They are always famously early on occasions like this – one of their frequent gripes is that, as pop stars, they are frequently assumed to be incapable of simple time-keeping. After some persuasion – for only Neil, Chris and their assistant Pete have first-class tickets – we are all ushered in. 'Isn't it exciting?' says Neil, greeting us, meaning the tour. He browses through the small booklet giving all the dull day-to-day touring details and mutters, 'How real it makes it all seem.' In the book is a list of rules set by tour manager, Ivan Kushlick. Rule 2 reads: 'Fines will be imposed at the rate of £1 per minute by me by my watch for persons late for calls, departures etc. All proceeds will be donated at the end of the tour to the Lighthouse Trust (a charity).' When Pierre sees this he goes round telling people that it is their duty to be late: 'It is such a good cause.'

Chris enthuses about 'the rave' called Sunrise that he and Pete went to the previous night. He describes their journey through the countryside, joining a long convoy of cars, 10,000 searching for a venue whose location has only been revealed that evening. They had danced and talked all night, only interrupted by the announcement in the middle of the night that the front gate had

had to be sealed because it was being attacked by people from a rival firm with axes. It had been brilliant, they gush, when the doors had been opened before dawn and the party had stretched over the fields as the sun rose. Chris has had two hours' sleep; a deliberate ploy, he says, to make him sleep on the plane.

Rob Holden diverts us by revealing his dream the previous night. Massive also manage Bros and he had 'woken up' – still, in fact, in his dream – to discover that he was not, as he would normally expect, in bed with his girlfriend but with Bros singer Matt Goss. 'I thought, "What on *earth* can I do?"' he splutters.

Chris moans about how useless the shopping is here in Gatwick. Last time he was here he wandered round for half an hour vainly 'looking for one of those women doing questionnaires' so that he could register his disgust. Today he gives them another chance, but they have neither Polaroid film nor the Victor Bokris biography of Andy Warhol that Neil has recommended to him. Instead he buys *The Orton Diaries*. Neil chooses the book on the Australian 'dingo baby' case, recently filmed as *A Cry in the Dark* which he has recently seen, and enjoyed.

As we queue for our flight a middle-aged businessman recognizes Neil and engages him in conversation. It is only a few weeks since Chinese troops killed thousands of students in Peking's Tiananmen Square and the British media has been full of the fury and resentment in Hong Kong towards the British government. In 1997 Hong Kong will be ceded to China and Britain is seen as washing its hands of the responsibility for the people there. The crisis has badly affected the Pet Shop Boys ticket sales: people have other things on their mind and aren't disposed to go out and enjoy themselves. The Hong Kong promoter, Andrew Bull, had suggested, a week or so earlier, that the Pet Shop Boys publicly dedicate the concerts 'to democracy'. They decided that it would be a cheap and tasteless stunt and refused.

'Is there much resentment towards the British?' Neil asks.

'Not yet,' says the man. 'There may be, but not yet.'

'A bottle of Jack Daniels!' hoots Chris, propelling himself into the Duty Free shop. This is part of a familiar, long-running Pet Shop Boys game – Let's Play At Being Tragic Rock'n'Roll Stars. The point of it, apart from being funny, is of course to emphasize how far removed they really are from all that. 'He always buys skincare products,' predicts Neil, accurately.

As Chris pores over the cosmetics counter a trickle of fans recognize him and ask for an autograph. Dainton, the security man – soon to be described, with some exaggeration, by one British magazine as a 'six foot six Mike Tyson lookalike' – intercepts them and hands them a postcard of Neil and Chris, ready signed. Throughout the tour he will make them do brief signing sessions to replenish his stock.

On this plane there are nine of us: Neil, Chris, Pete, Dainton, Pierre, Lawrence, Rob, Lucy from their record company and myself. The others – Ivan, the six American dancers, the four backing singers, Courtney Pine, Dominic the keyboard player, the wardrobe department etc. – are flying separately on a flight that stops over in India. We were all originally booked on that flight but Neil and Chris refused to do the extra take-off and landing.

They are both dreading the flight. They've had bad experiences in the past and hate flying. Chris has even investigated the possibility of getting to Hong Kong by rail across Russia but went off the idea when he discovered that it took days and was 'really boring anyway'. In fact the flight passes quietly, without incident. They sleep through most of it. When I interview them in Hong Kong for my *Smash Hits* piece, Neil mentions the dream he had on the plane – driving down the Fulham Road on the bonnet of a car, going to see Stephen Ward, the man who committed suicide in the tragic aftermath of the Profumo scandal. Several weeks later he tells me that this wasn't the whole story. He had also dreamt that Chris had been on top of the car as well, and as they sped down the road Chris had been trying to push Neil off.

The first time I interviewed the Pet Shop Boys was for their first *Smash Hits* cover feature in February 1986. 'West End Girls' had just been number one and they were recording in Advision studios in the West End, putting the finishing touches to the follow-up, 'Love Comes Quickly'. Neil had left *Smash Hits* less than a year before. (I joined the staff during his last few months as deputy editor and worked there full-time until December 1987.) When Neil worked there, Chris would often come in near the end of the day, hanging around, sitting on the photocopier, talking, dancing to records.

Before the interview we sniggered at the tacky pomposity of the BPI Awards on the studio TV: the next year Neil would be there, accepting the best single award from Boy George after being pressurized into turning up. Chris stayed at home and watched it on TV.

We went to the nearby health food snackerie Cranks to talk. The tape begins with Chris announcing, 'Actually I may not answer some questions because . . .' long pause – '. . . I might not have an answer.'

It seemed a bit preposterous interviewing them, difficult to take them seriously as pop stars, and they seemed to find it all a big strange too. In the few other interviews they'd done already they'd messed about a lot. Their last *Smash Hits* piece – involving them talking as they normally would, about the rest of the charts – had helped earn them the *Sun* nickname THE RUDEST MEN IN ROCK. In another article they had lied about their ages, taking five years off each for a laugh – a lie that would chase them round for years. They joked about the tragic nature of the interviews they'd been doing. 'Someone asked us,' said Neil, '"did you always dream of being a pop star?" It's the favourite question I've been asked. I love the idealism of it.'

And he said?

'I sniggered.'

'In Europe,' he said, 'they endlessly ask you what it feels like to have a number one record, and of course it feels like vaguely nothing. It feels like having a cup of tea.'

I mentioned that Chris is getting a reputation for looking miserable – only just beginning then, thanks to some remarkable surliness on Top of the Pops and in the 'West End Girls' video. 'Well, it isn't just an image,' said Neil, 'I think *Smash Hits* readers should be aware.'

They announced that they are preparing a live show for that September, 1986.

'It's not going to be a rock show,' claimed Neil.

'It'll be very theatrical,' amplified Chris. 'Entrances and exits. If we have backing musicians they're not going to be on-stage. They'll be in the orchestra pit.'

Neil said they have a long-term plan 'which everyone thinks is a joke but is serious'. It is that 'The Pet Shop Boys are going to carry on but we are actually going to leave being the front men of the Pet Shop Boys and we're going to change the line-up every year or so. Suddenly we've got four sixteen-year-old boys as one Pet Shop Boys and the next thing you know it will be two thirty-five-year-old Elaine Paige types. We'll be fed up with it by then. We'll write the music and do all the nice things like go to bed really early. We won't have our photograph taken or be asked why we're called the Pet Shop Boys. We can just make the records. And make lots of money.'

To which Chris muttered, 'We want to write stage musicals'; odd because they still say that now, but it is usually presented as an ambition of Neil's.

After, I talked to them separately, about each other. Neil says Chris is moody and picks his nose too much, is funny, hates people smoking, being embarrassed and being pretentious, is better-looking than Neil, and has got a not-very-nice flat. Chris says Neil is brainy, talented, stylish, generous and musical ('I'm going to be dead nice actually'), a bit bossy, too tidy, too obliging, a good judge of people, hates incompetence, is quite snooty, has a more homely flat and has an Action Man dressed in combat uniform on his bookshelf.

Neil says that when they get their money he'd like to buy a flat of his own. Chris says he'd like a car, 'but I don't feel like spending money because it just feels like I'm frittering it away'.

Monday, *26 June*

Before getting off the plane Neil and Chris make themselves presentable; a photo opportunity has been arranged at the airport. They are directed down a walkway and stand as ten or fifteen local photographers snap away. Then they walk back up the walkway, as this isn't the way we'll actually leave the airport. We take some other stairs to the car pick-up point and the photographers, for whom this is obviously a slightly farcical routine, join us there and snap away some more.

The following day a piece appears with a walkway photo in the main English-language newspaper, the *South China Morning Post*. Under the scrupulously accurate headline 'Pet Shop Boys arrive for gigs' they are welcomed and the promoter is quoted as saying that a fortnight earlier they had considered calling off the concerts because of the political situation (not true, at least as far as the Pet Shop Boys were concerned). Andrew Bull then adds: 'But we decided to go ahead because we thought Hong Kong needs something like this. It needs a lift,' as though a couple of verses of 'It's A Sin' will be adequate compensation for a nearby massacre. To the Pet Shop Boys' amusement next to their arrival the paper notes the arrival of Courtney Pine, who rates both more words and a larger picture and is raved about as 'the best thing to happen to British jazz in a very long time'.

After we have checked into the Ramada Renaissance Hotel, Neil phones me and suggests we go shopping. At a book-store he buys a book about Hong Kong by Jan Morris. We stop to look at training shoes but concur that shopping for training shoes is far too confusing for us alone. In the world of fashion some training shoes are fabulous and some not, but the rules change by the week and we haven't a clue. 'Pete knows these things,' he says. 'I'll come back with him.' He never does – in fact a few days later he declares, as if it was a weight off his mind. 'You know, I don't think I really like training shoes.'

In a small empty restaurant down a side street we stop for tea, then a beer. Neil leafs through *TV Times & Entertainment*, a local magazine he's just bought because they're on the cover. The article – a straightforward band history – is fine, but Neil is more impressed, thrilled even, by a piece about the problem of mounting hysteria at Hong Kong concerts because it suggests that security will have to be especially good to cope with the response to the Pet Shop Boys. He reflects that the group's management and publishing contracts expire soon and that they are undecided what to do, and mentions how pleased he is that a German group are recording a Pet Shop Boys B-side, 'Do I Have To?'. He says that the other day he made a tape of all their slushy ballads and hopes that one day they will put out 'The Slush Album'.

That evening promoter Andrew Bull takes the whole en-tourage out to dinner. We are told that we are to eat on a boat floating in the harbour and indeed we do, though the boats – three, for about ten people each, pulled together – only move about twenty yards from our embarkation point down a narrow avenue of moored boats. The sea has a stagnant smell. As we sit there, smaller boats pull alongside and we are offered a choice of as yet uncooked foods, paraded before our eyes in full gory biological horror. We indicate our choices and a succession of squashed ducks, squid, sea shells and noodles are cooked, then handed up. When we have finished and pushed our paper plates piled with empty shells and bones to the centre of the table a waitress daintily stacks them, lifts them off the table and then, with a deft flick of the wrist, tosses them into the water behind us. Soon we are surrounded by a flotilla of plates and prawn shells.

To go to the toilet you simply climb through a curtain to the back of the boat where some timber has been removed and pee into the water. Chris, alone, decides that he doesn't like the sound of this and clambers on to a moored boat and disappears to find some greater privacy. The dancers, getting restless, start tipping one of our boats from side to side. 'Don't rock the boat,' titters Neil.

Then a music boat arrives: musicians, a singer and a list of songs that it hands up to us as if it were the pudding menu. Someone plumps for 'Sealed With A Kiss' – number one in Britain for Jason Donovan as we left – and a sweet Cantonese version follows, chased by an impenetrable distant relation of the Beatles' 'Can't Buy Me Love'. Then Pinkie, one of the wardrobe department, jumps up. She is dressed – as she will be on every day of the tour – in amazing pink finery and is immaculately made up; when she lived in Los Angeles she was on an agency's books as a Betty Grable lookalike. On this tour she will be forever stared at and often assumed to be the star of the party. The Pet Shop Boys take a strange pride in the attention she attracts, though once, when Murray, their British press officer, suggests that they are photographed with her, Neil, only half-jokingly, snaps, 'We're not in the business of making Pinkie a star, you know?' Tonight, hearing it is someone's birthday, she serenades the boat with a deliberately fragile and trembly Marilyn Monroe version of 'Happy Birthday'.

Afterwards we try some discos called Hot Gossips and Boobs. Everyone is drunk; everyone dances. Most people slink away from Boobs at about 3 in the morning but a few stay. One of the crew is enticed to take a girl back to the hotel despite warnings from a sober Dainton that she looks like trouble. He is woken at 11 o'clock the next morning by a call from the venue. He had been due there hours before. The girl has gone. So has £400 in various currencies and £60 of spirits from the mini-bar in his room. He suspects he was drugged and later it turns out that he isn't the first to be similarly duped. 'I don't even remember what she looked like,' he sighs.

Tuesday, *27 June*

The Pet Shop Boys don't give press conferences as a rule. They're happier doing what interviews they do face to face with individual journalists, aware that it's the only way they can encourage articles about them to be more than general information and vague chatter. Press conferences are one of the great modern media tools, by which, under the pretence of giving access and information, a lot of people learn a very little. But at the start of their tour they are keen to show willing, especially as the two Hong Kong concerts are far from sold out, and so at 11 o'clock this morning about fifty journalists and a couple of TV crews gather in one of the hotel's reception rooms. Many of them are from Chinese-language papers and speak little English, but there is no interpreter. Some gold and platinum discs are stacked in the corner, but a few minutes before the Pet Shop Boys appear they are mysteriously carried away again. The Pet Shop Boys are to sit at a table and speak through microphones, connected to the sort of battered old speaker usually seen at school discos, but for the first ten minutes of the conference it refuses to work, and as they talk an elderly man in overalls beavers away wearily trying to fix it. There is lighting too – one intense yellow-white bulb – but before they arrive there is a bold *ker-puff* and it blows. Neil and Chris appear about twenty minutes late – slightly outrageous rock'n'-roll behaviour to the punctual locals. Perhaps they imagine that the hectic business of being a celebrity has delayed them. In fact Chris has been sorting out his dry-cleaning.

After the photographers have been allowed a couple of minutes Andrew Bull introduces them. 'On behalf of myself, EMI . . .'

The list goes on and no one pays much attention.

'. . . Levi's . . .'

The reaction is instantaneous.

'Levi's?' exclaims Chris, furiously. The Pet Shop Boys are deeply particular about sponsorship. In principle they oppose it completely, but like many artists outside their home country they relax their rules a little. Nevertheless they are still painstaking about what they will or will not allow, and Levi's small-scale sponsorship of the advertising of the Hong Kong leg of the tour has been very carefully negotiated – no direct or public endorsements, no banners at the concerts and so on. And most certainly no announcements like this at their press conference. They are livid. For the moment they merely fume and meaningfully exchange 'there'll be hell to pay for this' looks.

'I want a retraction,' Chris spits afterwards. Neil looks at Chris in utter disbelief. A retraction? They have just been publicly associated with Levi's in front of a nation's press and Chris wants 'a retraction'.

'I want one thousand dollars,' says Neil.

For the rest of their visit the promoter will hear of little else. He has almost certainly, they speculate, 'made promises he couldn't keep'.

'I don't know why anyone wants to do sponsorships with us,' Neil says, 'because you get nowt in return. You get absolutely nothing. *Literally* nothing. You're not allowed to meet us or anything.'

It's a policy that – in theory at least – they take to extremes. Though Neil is wearing a pair of black Adidas training shoes that he was given by the manufacturers in Los Angeles, as a rule they say they'd rather not accept things. Chris typically says that if they were sponsored by someone whose products he already used, he'd stop using them immediately.

'There's no such thing as nothing for nothing,' sighs Neil.

'I don't like anyone to feel they've got a hold on me,' agrees Chris. 'They always want something.'

'The Pet Shop Boys,' announces Ricky Fueng, head of EMI Records in Hong Kong, introducing them a second time, 'are one of the biggest artists to emerge, after Madonna, in Hong Kong.' This is something that we shall hear again and again during our stay, that in Hong Kong the Pet Shop Boys are 'second only to Madonna'.

Once Ricky Fueng sits down there is silence. Everyone waits for everyone else to ask the first question.

'Where's Rick Sky then?' asks Chris. Rick Sky is the main pop writer on the *Sun* and over the last couple of days they have been speculating whether he, or one of his ilk, will turn up and begin hounding them in search of scuzzy stories. They are relieved that he isn't, though I suspect they're also slightly disappointed, because they thought a Fleet Street contingent would be there anyway.

Eventually the questions start, to begin with all the obvious ones about the tour, why they chose Hong Kong to start in, how the show will be and so on. Neil plays his role as diplomat on these questions, patiently talking through the explanations that the two of them are already long bored with, while Chris fidgets and occasionally scowls as if to say, 'Well, this is dull, isn't it?' The press conference has been going less than ten minutes and Neil has just tried to explain their success in the Far East (an earnest account of the popularity of 'European dance music' here followed by the observation 'It's always difficult to explain your own popularity. Someone told me that because our first album was called "Please" everyone thought we were very polite') when Chris first says, 'Is that it then?'

He perks up when the questions get more interesting. As the minutes pass one journalist with a Liverpool accent more or less commandeers the press conference as a private interview. He has read *Annually*, a Pet Shop Boys annual that I had written with them the previous year and which had been photocopied and given to all Hong Kong journalists for biographical information, and refers to an article where they list and comment on their ten favourite records as of the summer of 1988. He reads out part of Chris's approving comments on Kylie Minogue's 'I Should Be So Lucky': 'I like the bit where she goes "I-I-I-I-I-I-I-I should be so lucky" and I just love the line "I should be so lucky, lucky lucky lucky". If that's banal it's a strength. It's just a mark of pure genius.'

'Are you being serious,' he asks Chris, 'or are you taking the mickey?' He is cockily confident it is the latter.

'No, I'm being serious,' answers Chris truthfully. 'It's like my favourite line in that other record is "uh-uh-oh".' That other record, after some discussion, is identified as Paula Abdul's 'Straight Up'. 'That's a classic line as well because it's a no-nonsense . . . it's just pure ecstasy.'

A little baffled, the journalist nods and turns to Neil. He reminds Neil that he likewise raved about the original-cast recording of Lerner and Loewe's *My Fair Lady*.

'*Shame* on you,' laughs Chris, turning to Neil.

'Rex Harrison speaks rather than sings,' says the journalist earnestly. 'I was wondering if you'd taken that singing style into your records.'

Neil looks pleased as punch by this question. 'Actually no one's ever picked up on that before, but it's true. I've always liked stage musicals and I think you'll see the influence of that on Thursday night. Rex Harrison does have a speaking singing voice and I think songs like "Opportunities" have the same kind of recitative quality.'

He has earlier observed that the first three songs ('One More Chance', 'Opportunities' and 'Left To My Own Devices') share this quality. This isn't entirely by chance. Though they are both appalled at the suggestions that their failure to tour before has been because of stage fright – the unwelcome implication being that their normal reticence isn't for a reason but is just timidity – it is true that Neil has been worried about his voice. As he had put it back in England, 'The good thing about the first three songs is I don't really have to sing.'

Neil: We were always going to get another singer. I was only singing as a holding operation. In fact at one point we thought about asking Jimmy Somerville to sing with us, because we saw that video he was in, that famous gay video.

Chris: Revenge Of The Teenage Perverts.

Neil: He sang a song on it ('Screaming') that ended up on Bronski Beat's first album and we thought then, because Chris vaguely knew him, that we might ask him to sing because we thought he was so good.

Chris: How fortunate we were.

Neil: Exactly. *That* wouldn't have lasted. But I became the singer by default. We often used to discuss having a singer. When we went to see Sharon Redd at the Embassy Club there were these two black girls singing along who were a real laugh and we nearly asked them, but we decided not to.

When did you stop looking?

Neil: When we started making records. Then it was too late. But I never liked my voice.

Did you change your mind when you heard it on record?

Neil: It just seemed too late.

The questions turn back to the show. Will they dance?

'I do a bit of a dance routine,' nods Chris, 'which is dead good.'

Neil explains once more about the Los Angeles dancers. 'I just sway in front of them,' he says.

Someone asks how much of the show is programmed. Perhaps the majority of large pop shows these days have a lot of programmed material: the standard answer to this question is to mutter that a couple of things are but that it won't affect 'the live feel'.

'Virtually all of it,' chirps Chris. He painstakingly explains how the music is generated live on-stage from pre-programmed linked sequences that trigger computer-memorized banks of samples, talks about how this means that the sounds are first- not second-generation sounds as they would be if they were on tape and how they could change an arrangement whenever they want to, and about how the best thing about this is that it brings on to the stage the very same technology that they used to make records in the studio. It's an impressive, coherent speech and one of which no one seems to take a blind bit of notice. Later when they write reviews, favourable or not, to a person they mention 'the Pet Shop Boys' backing tapes'.

'I can't really think of anything like it,' says Neil, asked once more to pontificate about the show. 'Maybe the Grace Jones One Man Show . . .'

'But Andy Warhol did things in the sixties with the Velvet Underground,' objects the journalist with the Liverpool accent.

Neil takes this objection seriously. 'That was in a more experimental way,' he counters.

So is it, the journalist responds, a show with much room for audience participation or is it purely a spectacle for people to view?

Neil turns to his side. 'Chris?' He is perhaps unwilling to choose an answer to this as he knows that Chris has been declaring for weeks that if their concerts turn into chummy clichéd participation affairs where people wave their hands or punch their fists or – the worst sin of all – hold up flickering lighters during slow songs he is to storm off stage. But his response is conciliatory.

'Do what you want to, I suppose,' he grunts.

Do they expect to see the stadium rockin'?, the journalist persists.

Neil wrinkles his face, disturbed by the terms used. 'I don't know about "rockin'",' he says, carefully pronouncing the offensive word as you would pick up something rather unpleasant and put it by the side of your plate, 'but I hope they'll be moving slightly.'

Have they got any guitars on stage? they are asked.

'Don't be *ridiculous*,' Chris huffs.

Several weeks later, after this response has been quoted in *Smash Hits*, they print a letter from an Alison Taylor, objecting to this:

'. . . Chris explains "don't be ridiculous!" Oh, very sorry, sir. What a ridiculous notion right enough. Guitars are dreadfully unfashionable, aren't they? Best just stick to being a crap twinkling synth duo because it's so very "eighties", early eighties, to be precise. Plus you can't play a guitar with one finger, can you? . . . what a pillock!'

When he reads this, Chris is upset. At the time his comment about guitars gets a laugh and he is asked to explain further.

'Just because of its rock'n'roll connotations. I don't like the look of them either.'

A lot of people, continues the Liverpool accent, have criticized lyrics like 'We're S-H-O-PP-I-N-G . . . we're shopping' for being too banal. Neil looks a little narked. 'Shopping' is actually a relatively straightforward anti-privatization song. 'Well,' he sighs pointedly, 'they've also been criticized for being too intellectual.'

Finally the Liverpool accent lunges at the conclusion he's been edging towards throughout the press conference. 'Is the whole thing tongue in cheek?' he asks. 'A lot of it seems . . . you are perfectly aware that the pop business is a very one-dimensional one, that it's very easy to influence people . . . but on another level what you do does seem to verge on the pretentious. What is the Pet Shop Boys' view on this?' In other words are the Pet Shop Boys, as is often assumed, more often by critics who like them than by those who don't, just making pop music as some sort of superior, clever clever, ironic joke, forever secretively tapping their noses to those smart enough to be in the know?

'Well,' says Neil, 'firstly the Pet Shop Boys genuinely love pop music, which makes them quite rare in the music business. The music business itself, particularly in Britain, tends to despise pop music. So if Chris says in an interview that he genuinely likes a Kylie Minogue record people assume that he's taking the mickey for some reason, whereas we appreciate the real ecstatic response that a really good pop or dance record can generate, and I think that's probably our favourite thing about pop music.

'There's also a kind of assumption that if you're writing pop music it's not an important kind of music, whereas rock music – you mentioned U2 earlier – is perceived as being an important kind of music. And I don't really like the idea of people projecting themselves as being important humanitarian figures, which is the tendency for rock personalities nowadays. At the same time it doesn't mean that when you're writing a pop song it can't have some kind of serious meaning, and if people want to discover that for themselves that's great. At the same time if they don't want to . . . if they don't notice it . . . I think that's great as well, because they're just responding to pop music in different ways.

'Having said that, I think that's one of the reasons why the Pet Shop Boys have a strangely wide audience. In Britain, for instance, we get the whole spectrum from primary school children through to people's parents and kind of . . . *NME* readers and all the rest of it. So, although we present ourselves in a kind of pretentious way sometimes I don't think we're really at all pretentious. I think we're one of the few honest groups in our approach that there are nowadays, because I don't think many groups nowadays are the remotest bit honest. I think there's a lot of hypocrisy in the rock business which you don't find in the pop business . . . in pop music. People now pose as humanitarian figures – they're all Mother Teresa of Calcutta or someone, and at the end of the day they're only pop stars, normally singing fairly uninterestingly banal things.'

There's little obvious interest in what Neil has said from his audience and none of the above is printed in the newspapers the next day.

Neil: For eight or nine years all pop music lived in the shadow of punk. Punk was the first time for a long time that music – *popular* pop music – came out that had an ideology to it, that said it was about something, not just entertainment. And the New Romantic thing was just an extension built out of it – they took certain punk attitudes and made it more fun or glamorous. Groups like Duran Duran, Spandau Ballet and Culture Club wouldn't have existed if punk hadn't existed.

But they had the ideology that persists now, didn't they, that music was for entertainment?

Neil: No, I don't think so. Boy George was a mass market creature and he was a man who wore women's clothes. I think that was a very powerful thing for teenagers. At the very least it makes them more broadminded. And the idea of Culture Club, as a mix of cultures and sexuality, of male and female, was a very strong idea. It was basically an intellectual notion, if maybe a feeble one. Nowadays you get a group like Wet Wet Wet and they just want to be 'quality'. It's like the mid-seventies, when all anyone tried to be was 'quality'.

So what do you think is the implication of just being 'quality'?

Neil: It means they have no aspirations whatsoever beyond immediate consumerist ambitions.

And does that change the audience that listens to them?

Neil: I think it does. Apart from anything it's larger now.

Are you determinist enough to bèlieve that pop music actually creates an audience with the same values that it espouses?

Neil: No. Actually I think it's the other way round. I think the values of the people tend to create the pop music that, at the end of the day, they like. What people don't want to have thrust at them nowadays – almost for the first time in the history of pop music – is aggressive sexuality of any kind. If you look at pop music nowadays it's almost totally sexless. Look at Jason Donovan. Bros are the first group to be sold on the size of their crotches for a long time, but they are kind of sexless too, because Matt tells everyone how he doesn't have sex. It seems to me it's all got Doris Day-like.

So where has the ideology of Doris Day pop come from?

Neil: I don't know really. I think it comes from people's aspirations being totally consumerist nowadays. People want to be like their parents. This is the first generation for ages who wants to be like their parents. That, by the way, involves being quite a nice person – it doesn't necessarily involve liking Mrs Thatcher. This girl who writes to me says she's going to university and she doesn't want to go somewhere too far away from home. It's a generation that isn't rebelling. To be honest, people coming to see the Pet Shop Boys aren't making a rebellious statement on any level. Some of them might be a bit, because there's a side to us a lot of people don't like: the notion that we never smile, the way we behave on television . . .

Though of course that's also a large part of your commercial appeal.

Neil: Yes. It filters through to the audience and once people know what you're like they want you to always be like that. But we were always under pressure at the start, from EMI and Tom, to be more . . . *nice*. And we deliberately took care to be the opposite.

What do you think about all this, Chris?

Chris: I like to do something that I feel like . . . if someone might want you to do something I'll automatically do the opposite. People have got to like it or lump it, really. Anyway if we were to contrive looking . . . you know, bouncing up and down, happy, good-looking pop stars . . . it wouldn't work.

Neil: One of the things the Pet Shop Boys are always trying to do is always to be mass market without watering down anything we've ever done, without 'selling out' or whatever. I still have the sixties idea that you can 'sell out' and I don't regard the Pet Shop Boys as having sold out to get where we are now. I don't think that we've fundamentally watered down anything we've wanted to do to make it palatable to people.

What, the Liverpool accent would like to know, do the Pet Shop Boys think of Sting's work to promote opposition to the deforestation of South America?

'Actually as it happens I think what Sting's doing about that is very good,' says Neil, 'and the reason I like it is, as he said himself, he hasn't got a record out about it. Also, as it happens, I think he's done a lot to publicize that.'

So if they were asked to play a concert with him to spread the word would they do it?

Neil and Chris exchange dubious glances. Their answer is perfectly obvious – no. But how can they explain this? Neither of them answers for a while, then finally Chris speaks.

'We're not a live band really.'

There is confused laughter. The next day's *South China Morning Post* opens its report of the press conference by saying, 'It's a rare old thing when a pop act promoting a forthcoming concert describes itself as "not a live band, really".'

The press conference closes with the first question for some time from an oriental journalist. Are they serious, he asks hesitantly, about the clothes they wear? Again there is a silence as they try to restrain themselves from giggling – somehow this question seems incredibly funny. Afterwards they worry that, after waiting so long for other people to join in the questioning, they seemed to be ridiculing the question, but a sensible answer is beyond them. Chris turns to Neil.

'Are you serious about those shorts, Neil?'

Neil is wearing knee-length Indian-style shorts from Emporio Armani that fade in colour towards the knee. 'I don't know really,' he confesses.

It seems a good moment to finish. 'Is that it then?' askes Chris again. It is.

Chapter Three

We convene in Neil's room. It looks over the harbour. 'You've got a brilliant view,' grumbles Chris. He mutters that Neil always gets the best view. They briefly reflect on the press conference, as if it were a necessary chore to be rid of so that they can get out and enjoy themselves.

'When the going gets tough,' they say – Chris begins but by the fourth word Neil has joined in – 'the tough go shopping.'

They have heard that Hong Kong markets do a good line in cheap fake Rolex watches. It is a fabulous opportunity to make Bros – who are consumer addicts in general, designer watch fetishists in particular – very jealous.

'I'll phone up Matt and say I've got three Rolexes,' decides Chris.

'I'll phone up Luke,' trumps Neil, 'and say, "I've got two Porsches and I can't even drive."'

Their banter is interrupted by the arrival of Mr Fueng. Their refusal to accept their Hong Kong gold discs in public has ruffled some feathers, but as a compromise they have agreed to accept them in private and so here, in Neil's room, the redundant presentation takes place. They are given platinum discs for 'Actually' and 'Introspective', gold discs for 'Please' and 'Disco'. As they pose for photos with Mr Fueng and the discs Chris conducts a dialogue with the rest of us in the room. He suggests that in all photos from now on they should use cardboard Pet Shop Boys cut-outs. 'It'd look the same in the pictures. We should leave them down in the hotel lobby for people to have their photo taken with.'

'That's a *brilliant* idea,' exclaims Neil, Mr Fueng all but forgotten. 'We'll do it at Wembley – people can have their photo taken with cut-outs of us.' They instruct Rob to arrange it.

'The trouble with all these things,' says Pete quietly, shaking his head, 'is that they never actually happen.' And, indeed, it never does.

Chris turns back to Mr Fueng and now that the diplomatic duties are over amiably chats with him about computer technology. He raves about a new IBM computer. 'It's *orange*,' he proclaims, leaving no doubt that its orangeness is a highly important quality, 'and it slides up.' He notices me laughing at this and addresses me sternly. 'If something looks good,' he proclaims, 'it usually is.'

'We've got to get rid of them,' fumes Chris.

There is a problem with the security people laid on. They are young, mostly British, sporting blue suits and premature moustaches. 'We don't like the look of them,' says Neil. The feeling we all have is that they're far more likely to inspire or invent trouble than to shield us from it.

Rob is dispatched downstairs to lay them off. We wait by the elevator on the thirteenth floor. Chris says he doesn't want to come down until the security people have actually gone. 'I want the lobby cleared!' he laughs.

In the minibus Ivan tells Neil and Chris about the unhappy fiasco of the drugged crew member.

'You can get that disease here,' tuts Neil, 'where your dick swells up like a cauliflower. Apparently.'

Chris chews over the story, settling on the detail of the £500 lost. 'Not *our* money?' he asks.

Everyone roars at Chris's misplaced concern. Neil lampoons his reaction, replaying the conversation: 'Ivan: "They murdered him and took ten pence of your money." Chris: "Ten *pence*!!!"'

We stop at an electrical shop where Neil buys a Polaroid camera: 900 Hong Kong dollars.

'We're S-H-O-PP-I-N-G,' sings Chris sarcastically. 'Is it really banal?' he goads Neil, mimicking the Liverpool accent at the press conference. Neil says nothing. 'I like your answer,' Chris continues. 'Some people say our lyrics are too intellectual . . .' he roars with laughter.

By now the shop assistants have recognized that there are pop stars in their midst and ask them to pose with the staff for a photo. 'That's $50 off,' says Neil, and jokes whether he should negotiate for a bigger discount in return for introducing the concert as 'In Association with Carlton Cameras'.

We drive off. Everywhere there is building work surrounded by bamboo scaffolding, a simple lattice of bamboo poles. It looks incredibly flimsy and unsafe – but also to our eyes mysterious and rather wonderful against the otherwise modern buildings. 'Maybe we can patent it,' murmurs Neil, though he doesn't explain what he means.

Everyone takes Polaroids of everyone else. Neil has not washed his face since the press conference and says, 'I'm the only person who wears make-up for snaps.'

They discuss where to shop. Someone suggests the Jean Paul Gaultier shop.

'The problem with Gaultier,' frowns Neil, 'is that you look like Bros. Whenever you go into a Gaultier shop it's like Matt's wardrobe.' Bros, two twins, Matt and Luke Goss (a third member, Craig Logan, has recently left in inauspicious circumstances), are the biggest teen stars Britain has seen for years. They share the same manager as the Pet Shop Boys: Tom Watkins. The Pet Shop Boys are forever talking about them.

'Tom reckons we're obsessed by Bros,' says Neil.

I say that Tom has a point.

'I'm always obsessed by the current teen idols!' shrugs Neil. 'I was obsessed by the Bay City Rollers.'

*

Neil Tennant and Chris Lowe met on 19 August 1981. Chris thought Neil looked brainy 'because he had glasses on' (these days he wears contact lenses). Neil thought Chris was a little mad 'because he laughed a lot'. They talked about music. Neil liked wordy rock music by people like Elvis Costello, which Chris viewed with suspicion, and Chris liked 'Body Talk' by Imagination, which Neil thought was dreadful, but they also liked a lot of the same things. Chris began dropping round to Neil's flat.

What did you say to each other when you first met up that led to you writing songs together?

Neil: I can't remember us having any specific dialogue. It was more *ad hoc*. It was a gradual thing. I had a synthesizer and Chris used to come round and eventually we started writing a song. (*To Chris*) Can you remember?

Chris: I'm sure you didn't say, 'Let's write a song.'

Neil: I don't think I did either.

Chris: You played me a cassette of something you'd done.

Neil: Yeah. In 1981 I made a demo tape in a recording studio in South London. I'd started writing songs that were slightly punky because it was that sort of era. I went to an audition once, in 1978 or 1979, from an ad in *Melody Maker* to this bedsit in Clapham and the bloke was dead impressed and said, 'You should get your own band.' Then my brother Simon was always saying, 'You should do something with these songs,' and eventually I got a bonus from work and went into this demo studio with Simon and his girlfriend Sarah. One song was called 'The Taxi-Driver' – that was the popular one – and then there was one called 'She's So Eclectic' and another was called 'The Man On The Television'. The chorus was 'There's a man on the television/I don't want a television'.

Chris: You just played me one.

Neil: It was 'The Man On The Television'.

What was it like?

Chris: It had a good bit in.

Surrounded by lots of bad bits?

Chris: No, there was a *good* bit . . . a *special* bit.

Neil: It was like the Clash or something. That's what it was meant to be like.

Chris: It didn't sound like that.

Neil: No, but that was the starting point. It was just a guitar and me singing.

Your Billy Bragg period?

Neil: Yes, it was very Billy Bragg. Me and an acoustic guitar. I'm not embarrassed about these songs. Anyway, I played one to Chris and maybe the idea came up that we should write a song, though I don't think it was as communicative as that, was it?

Chris: No, it just happened.

Neil: We'd go to the pub.

Chris: The Chelsea Potter. (*Laughs.*)

Neil: There we'd probably drink three pints of beer – maybe I drank Pils and Chris drank pints. Anyway, then we'd go back over the road to my flat and Chris would start doodling on the synthesizer. We'd write songs and play them to friends sometimes. They were intrigued.

How did you start talking about music in the first place?

Chris: Well, all I really had to talk about was music.

So you weren't looking for someone to write songs with?

Chris: No. I think Neil had been in a way. But we never talked in terms of forming a group. In fact I still don't think that way. It's never been like that. Quite often you get accused of sitting down – the journalist and the architect – trying to think of some masterplan. It was never ever like that. It was pure enjoyment. We've always said in interviews that we make records to please ourselves, and we still do.

We pass Arsenal Street. Pete and Dainton cheer. They both live in North London and support Arsenal. Early this summer

Arsenal won the Football League championship with a goal against Liverpool in the last minute of the last game of the season and Dainton could be seen on TV, one of the celebrating mob. The cheers turn to boos as we pass the Prince of Wales building.

'They're everywhere,' scowls Chris, meaning the royal family. The Pet Shops Boys are not fans of the royal family.

'You'd *think* we were in a Crown Colony,' says Neil sarcastically.

The Prince of Wales building is square, drab and undeniably ugly.

'What a carbuncle it is,' sneers Chris.

'I presume he's approved it,' says Neil. He adds, outraged, that he has heard that these days if you want to put up a major building in London you must informally present the plans to Prince Charles, a pre-emptive move to head off future criticism.

Today's excursion is, in fact, partly inspired by an architectural motive for, as well as shopping, we are to visit the Hong Kong and Shanghai Bank. Completed in November 1985 to the designs of architect Norman Foster, it is one of the landmarks of modern architecture. Chris had studied the plan for it in his architectural days and in one of the telephone interviews they did as pre-publicity for the tour he claimed that it was his desire to see the actual building that prompted the choice of Hong Kong as the site of their first concert. The bank's management, flattered to read this, subsequently contacted Mr Bull and through him extended an invitation to a private guided tour.

We are all expecting a building that towers gloriously over its overawed little neighbours, but it is actually smuggled within a jumble of hi-tech buildings. It looks nothing very special at all.

'It's a bit drab,' Chris sighs unhappily.

'It's getting the thumbs down,' echoes Neil.

'We've come all this way, just for this,' harumphs Chris.

'The tour's off,' declares Neil, matter-of-factly.

The disappointment heightens when we see the Bank of China next door, which dashes upwards, a topsy-turvy pile of equilateral triangles by I. M. Pie, the Chinese-American architect who built the Louvre's glass pyramid. Chris is far more impressed. 'I love the geometry.'

In the open plaza that runs beneath the Hong Kong Bank we meet our guide. It's like a school trip – brochures are shoved into our hands and she proudly gestures at the escalator that rises out of the plaza into the bank's underbelly: 'the world's largest unsupported escalators'. We are whisked below to the bank vaults where only Neil and Chris are allowed inside the bullet-proof glass screens. They sit framed by the circular opening and as Dainton lifts Pete above the glass surrounding to take a photo armed guards look on twitchily. We are shown a bewildering spaghetti junction of tracks that spread throughout the building carrying sealed boxes, then we're led to a lift and ascend to level 42.

'Level 42,' guffaws Chris. The guide looks puzzled.

We walk round a dining-room that ends in a semi-circular glass window with staggering views both across the bay to Kowloon and up the hills to the richest Hong Kong properties, where – it is pointed out – the head of the bank lives.

'Did anyone fall off while it was being built?' Ivan asks.

The guide shakes her head. She explains that one person died in a fire during the demolition of the old building on this site, one person died in construction and one person was electrocuted.

'Nobody fell then?' confirms Ivan. He seems disappointed: a building this tall and no one has fallen off it . . .

Neil and Chris are ushered towards the visitors' book. There is no suggestion that the rest of us are invited to sign. The last signature is for the 'Taunton girls' school hockey team'. The guide proudly flips the pages back to where Princess Anne – a page to herself – has inscribed her name. The Pet Shop Boys decide that they too should have a page to themselves. Chris carefully reproduces a logo that was devised years ago. Often it is accompanied with a drawing of the two of them, their heads in a box, Chris wearing a cap covering his eyes, his mouth downturned, but this time they simply add the date and sign. Once he has finished they consider whether it looks right.

'Do you think it should have a line over the top?' asks Neil, thoughtfully. If they're going to sign this book, it's going to look fabulous. Chris considers the suggestion, then vetoes it.

Moving off, they reappraise the building.

'Absolutely fantastic,' says Neil, who seems to have changed his mind.

'Disappointing,' murmurs Chris.

'Mmmm,' concedes Neil, swiftly persuaded. 'Not one of your best, Norm.'

'I'm gutted,' says Chris. 'I was so looking forward to it.'

'It's very nice,' says Neil, vacillating. 'But I don't really like modern architecture.'

When you began writing songs did you make jokes about appearing on Top of the Pops*?*

Neil: No, that seemed inconceivable. At the same time I always thought there was definitely something there and I was always keen to carry on. Chris knew things about music that I didn't know. I'd written loads of songs before, but the existence of a bass-line had fundamentally never really occurred to me.

Were you less concerned about carrying on, Chris?

Chris: Well . . . (*shrugs*) . . . if you're sitting in someone's room messing about on a synthesizer you're not really thinking about *Top of the Pops*, are you?

On the contrary, I think a lot of people are.

Chris (*surprised*)*:* Are they? Well, something like that never occurred to me. Even when we recorded with Bobby O I didn't think that. I knew Jimmy Somerville slightly and he went on *Top of the Pops* and even watching him I didn't ever think that we would.

Neil: Eventually we'd written so many songs and some of them we thought were good. One of them, incidentally, is on Liza Minnelli's album ('I Can't Say Goodnight'). We were particularly impressed by a song we'd written called 'Bubadub-adubadubadubadum'. It sounded a bit like early Depeche Mode. Once we wrote a song and Chris said he didn't think the lyrics were very good – he couldn't work out what they were about and that had an effect. Because I used to write deliberately impressionistic – or whatever word you want to use – lyrics and Chris thought we should write direct lyrics, about sex or something like that.

Chris: I can't remember saying that.

Neil: Well you did.

Chris: But your lyrics are pretty obtuse anyway.

Neil: Yes, they've got more obtuse really. They've gone back the other way. But it had an effect then. We wrote 'Jealousy'. Chris wrote the music in Blackpool and gave me a cassette and I wrote the words and sang it to him and we both thought it was unbelievably fantastic. We also had a song called 'Oh Dear'. When Chris lived in a house in Ealing they used to like that one. He used to play it on the piano.

Chris: It was dead funny. What were the lyrics?

Neil: The tune sounded like the Specials and it went:

> *I was walking down the high street in the middle of the night*
> *Someone caught my eye and I nearly died of fright*
> *Crossed the road to whisper something secret in my ear*
> *And now I know I'll never be the same again*
> *Oh dear*

(*They both collapse into hysterics.*)

★

Still on the 42nd floor we make our way outside and saunter along hi-tech walkways. Polaroid cameras go crazy.

'I've taken a happening one!' Neil exclaims, brandishing an image of angular metal shapes and blue sky. 'It's a Depeche Mode album sleeve called something like "The Technological World".'

Chris takes no notice. He is photographing small design details on the handrails and the floor tiling. 'I don't like the height,' he mutters. 'I'm always having nightmares like this. I'm up this thing and I'm going "Help! get me off!" and I'm waiting for a search party and sometimes they don't come and I fall off. Which,' he adds succinctly, 'is *crap*.'

We take the elevator down to a level only 170 feet above ground. We stand at a balcony and beneath us, inside the building, a huge atrium falls away. The room is curved and mirrored – throughout the day the mirrors adjust their angle automatically so that the maximum intensity of natural light is reflected down on those working below. We are quietly impressed.

At either end the metal vertical supports that hold the building are connected by cross-bracing in the shape of an 'X'. Each has a long window box running beneath it, greenery draping from it. It turns out that 'Norm' made a gaff here. The shape 'X' is extremely bad luck for the Chinese and the only antidote is the colour green. Chris tuts. 'He overlooked something quite important there.' Chinese culture is full of such pitfalls for the innovative architect. I. M. Pie's Bank of China building is, I later learn, considered to be misconceived on a much more fundamental scale, to have 'unfavourable *fengshui*'. Triangles are never used in Chinese architecture because the apexes are believed to deflect evil spirits in the direction of onlookers – those in nearby buildings have apparently taken to putting cacti and spirit mirrors in their windows to ward off the bad vibes.

The debate on the building echoes on.

'It's not as imposing as I expected,' admits Chris. 'It's all very grey. It's a bit over-the-top. More science fiction than hi-tech. It seems like typical James Bond.'

'Well,' says Neil. 'The basic premise of hi-tech is a fiction, isn't it?'

The argument carries on for days. Can a building ever really be determined by its function? (In the end they agree it cannot.)

They discuss the Lloyd's building in London.

'The thing is,' says Chris sadly, 'that Norman Foster and Richard Rogers *delight* in architecture. They're quite rare in that respect.' It doesn't take much imagination to realize that when he says this he's not just talking about how he feels about architecture. One wouldn't be unjustified, for instance, in taking that sentence and exchanging 'Pet Shop Boys' for 'Richard Rogers and Norman Foster' and 'pop music' for 'architecture'. 'One of the reasons they don't do much in England,' Chris continues, 'is that no one in England is prepared to put that confidence in modern architecture, particularly when you've got Prince Charles at the helm . . .'

This, I mutter, is almost a parody of what some people think a Pet Shop Boys tour should be like: sitting around earnestly juggling intellectual notions about architecture.

'Actually,' says Neil, 'it's probably me who would spend more time studying architecture than Chris.'

'Yeah,' agrees Chris. 'I prefer to live it, rather than study it.' This is said to sound preposterous.

'I like modern stuff,' he says, suddenly serious again. 'Everything I like is modern. Neil tends to like old stuff. He likes modern as well but I'm more interested in it. Looking round cathedrals!' he splutters to Neil, as if this was the most ridiculous pastime he could think of. 'Neil can wander round all the cathedrals that there are on the planet. To me they all look the same.'

Chris's flat has white walls, polished wooden floors, simple modern furniture, modern art; the latest brilliant twelve-inch dance record booms out from the record player. Neil's has dark old paintings, religious statues, gothic revival furniture, shelves of hardback books, carpet; in the background a classical CD plays.

We go shopping. Brenda, Andrew Bull's assistant, who is showing us round, leads us into an upmarket arcade, looking for the Issey Miyake shop. From about forty feet away Pete spots some sunglasses at the back of a shop called The Temptation Boutique. They are Porsche Carrera ski goggles, just one thin horizontal tinted strip. Chris whoops with excitement and tries them on.

'You've basically got to get them, haven't you?' he asks himself rhetorically.

'It's a photograph,' confirms Neil. The Pet Shop Boys are constantly on the lookout for clothes that constitute 'a photograph'; some of their best photographs work around pairs of glasses Chris has found.

These cost $470 – about £44. This is almost pathetically cheap for a viable fashion item.

'It's a snip,' says Chris, buying them. They won't reappear for the rest of the tour.

While he is paying, Pete sidles over to a watch display. He has something on his mind – back in London he has been giving advice on a watch that Chris might like and the one he has suggested is here on display.

'Chris!' he says, beckoning him over. 'That'd really suit you, wouldn't it?'

Chris considers this and shakes his head. He points to the one next to the one Pete had pointed out. 'I like that one better.'

Understandably I assume that this exercise has been a disaster, but Pete has a sneaky smile on his face. He explains that he knew the best way to find out was to point at another watch – the alternative Chris had suggested was the one Pete knew he'd like.

The in-store muzak is a cheesy selection of instrumental melodies from *The Sound Of Music*. It inspires an animated discussion of the musical's merit. This is no quickly improvised kitsch banter – Chris only recently went out and bought the soundtrack on CD (disappointing, he later admits: 'better as a video'). They discuss the highlights. Neil suggests 'I Am Sixteen Going On Seventeen'.

'Oh,' says Chris, 'but what about when Christopher Plummer sings "Edelweiss"?'

Neil tells the assembled company how he has heard that *The Sound Of Music* is a centrepiece of family life in the Lowe household. 'The whole Lowe family – *en masse*, including Judy the dog – bursts into tears,' reports Neil.

Chris is happy to confirm this. 'That and *The Waltons*,' he nods.

We find Issey Miyake but it is a women's-only branch. We walk off, discussing how we all share the same pathetic habit of saying 'thank you' at the wrong moments, for instance when we give someone something. We also say 'sorry' when someone steps on our foot.

An old woman sits begging on a concrete walkway. Chris, up ahead, quietly slips her some money.

'It does pong a bit in Hong Kong, doesn't it?' he says when I catch him up. 'Someone told me it meant "fragrant water" in Chinese.'

You must get asked to do a lot of things for charity.

Neil: I don't know. Rob always makes us sign things when we come into the office, which he'll endlessly send off to garden fêtes. You get thousands of things like being asked to be on Greenpeace albums, but I think they're just using you.

Chris: I think it's bad that everything depends on charity.

Neil: That's what I think, totally.

Chris: There should be no need for charity.

Neil: Live Aid had that negative effect that it reinforced the whole charity thing.

It's the privatization of charity really, isn't it?

Chris: Exactly. Not only do you have to pay less tax, but you feel good by giving money to charity at the same time.

Neil: And that's the whole point, that you feel good.

Chris: No one should have to think about charity. Everything in the whole world should be taken care of by government.

Neil: I suppose that's not what most people want.

Chris: Well I do. I don't want to feel good giving to charity. I think I should be forced . . . it should automatically come out of your pocket.

Neil: Society should get together and sort out these things. If I was blind I'd be really pissed off having to get hand-outs from charity.

Chris: And then it's nauseating – people who do a lot for charity get commended and everyone gets patted on the back . . .

Neil: . . . and get awards. It's all bound in with the establishment. They'll all get invited to the Queen's garden parties because they've done something marvellous. They've all been Governor General of Mauritius or done something for charity. And everyone in show business is supposed to do this. It's an unwritten rule.

Chris: The Rotary Club! It's right-wing people cutting taxes then having these big *massive* posh dinners where they do something for charity and all make themselves feel good and cleanse themselves.

Neil: And normally it's so they can get to meet celebrities – that's the other thing. They can get to meet Ken Dodd because they've given a Variety Club sunshine bus.

Chris: It's so vile. It's so pathetic and petty.

But of course it's always very easy for people to present your viewpoint as meanness.

Neil: We're not mean, but a lot of people in the public eye want people to think they're a wonderful person. We have never set out to make people think that we're wonderful people. Quite the reverse in many ways. We've never set out to make people think, 'Aren't they warm . . . generous . . . they give such a lot.'

It is hot, we are sweaty and the shopping is unsuccessful so we decide to take tea.

'How about the Mandarin Hotel?' suggests Brenda.

'Is it snooty?' asks Chris.

'I *like* snooty places,' Neil reminds him.

On the stairs up to the hotel lounge a waiter stops us and theatrically frowns at Neil's shorts. (He has changed since the press conference: these are simple, blue and knee-length.) The waiter says he will have to ask for special permission. After a long wait, during which Neil is approached for autographs by several members of the hotel staff, permission is refused. The assistant manager comes up and takes great and obvious pride and pleasure in turning us away. As we leave, Dainton overhears as the assistant manager walks back towards the reception and the receptionist eagerly asks him, 'Did you manage to get the tickets then?'

Outside Brenda addresses the furious party. 'Do you still want tea?'

'We're English!' hoots Chris. 'We want tea and sandwiches!'

The incident has enraged them both. Neil, as Chris teasingly reminds him, is a big supporter of dress codes but he is incensed by the petty delight the assistant manager took in turning us away. A few days later I sit him and Chris down for a taped interview for a piece I am writing on the tour for *Smash Hits* magazine and the fury is still obvious.

'I'm famous for getting annoyed by petty figures of authority,' he reflects. 'It's like when I go through customs I almost *tremble* with rage that I have to do it, because I hate them so much. I went through once and the man was convinced I had drugs on me. He was going through everything and I said, "I know what you're looking for and I haven't got anything. I don't take drugs." He said, "Is that *so*, sir? It's just that you look rather nervous." And I said, "It's like, you know, when you see a policeman you feel guilty?" and he said, "Oh, *do* you sir?" I felt like hitting him.'

Funnily enough the customs person had been right about one thing – he had been nervous because when the case had been opened he'd realized that sitting on the top were a brand new pair of expensive American training shoes that he'd been given and hadn't declared.

'The Mandarin Hotel person annoyed me because I personally felt we were quite nice and signed autographs for the whole staff. It's not like we walked in wearing football kits. What really got me was the way he spoke to me. He took pleasure in it and he had this smile on his face when he said it. I felt like kicking him in the teeth, to be quite honest.'

Later on in the trip our travel plans separate and I don't see Neil for a couple of days, during which I fax my copy back to Britain. There is another sentence he has said, in the heat of the moment, about the shorts incident and next time I see him the very first thing he says – it has obviously been on his mind – is 'You didn't put that bit in, did you?'

I confirmed that I had, though I can't see why he is so embarrassed about it.

'I *knew* that you would,' he says, with considerable annoyance, but said no more on the matter.

He didn't ask me to change the article, but the next time I talked to *Smash Hits* I mentioned, knowing the article was too long anyway, that if it was easy it might be better if they took that out, but if they couldn't, or didn't want to, then it would be no problem. As it turned out they took this as a firm request and – as I would have – rather resented it but removed the phrase.

Later I was surprised to discover that Neil had expected the phrase to be removed for, at the hotel reception when I picked up a fax from *Smash Hits* and muttered something about 'bad news' (about an entirely different matter), he immediately snapped, 'Oh no, don't tell me they haven't taken that bit out.'

'Tea and sandwiches' are suspended while we shop a little more. Neil tries on a multicoloured silk jacket, marked down in the sales from $13,800 to $8,300.

'It's a bit Coco the Clown,' advises Chris.

'I'm not paying $8,300,' agrees Neil.

Finally we successfully adjourn to a rather sweet English-style tea room. The assistant manager of the Mandarin Hotel is far from forgotten. In the show, during Chris's one vocal performance, 'Paninaro', he is scheduled to ad lib a speech about things he doesn't like. He has so far failed to do it in rehearsals, but there is a rough script – endlessly chuckled over and revised – that goes 'I don't like The Cure . . . I hate U2 . . . and I think Malcolm McLaren is a prat.' It is now decided that for the Hong Kong dates an extra line should be added: 'I hate the assistant manager of the Mandarin Hotel.'

This decided, Neil quizzes Brenda about the political climate in Hong Kong. Is everyone planning to leave before 1997, when the country is Chinese once more? She says that she is – in 1991 she emigrates to Canada.

Her choice of destination inspires Neil to tell of their Worst Hotel Experience Ever. One night in Toronto, having flown through a storm, they checked into their hotel suite and went downstairs for dinner. Returning to their suite they discovered that all Chris's belongings had been hurled into the sitting-room of the suite and a camp bed set up there, while an actor had been checked into Chris's room and was busy shaving in Chris's bathroom. 'I went downstairs,' says Neil, 'and just went *bonkers*.'

This is but one of a repertoire of promotional trip stories that they will tell, given the chance. Like all modern pop stars, whenever they release an album they're pressured into travelling the world for months, simply to 'promote' it: 'servicing countries,' as Kylie Minogue once graphically described it. They groan about Germany, where they once had to mime 'Love Comes Quickly' in a swimming-pool, surrounded by German teenagers dripping wet, Neil complaining, 'We're not supposed to be a flamin' pop group.' Then there's France, where they were once asked to mime on the radio – '*mime* on the radio!' – and they agreed, because the show was broadcast live in front of an audience, but then finally blew a gasket when the producer insisted that they *rehearsed* their mimed performance. They both now agree that 'the age of promotion is over'. EMI, they point out, fly people round the world to speak to Paul McCartney or Duranduran in London; so from now on EMI can jolly well do the same for the Pet Shop Boys.

Whether by accident or design the music playing in the café is the Pet Shop Boys 'Actually' CD (probably design; the waitress later brings the CD sleeve to be signed). Neil cocks an ear to Dusty Springfield's performance on 'What Have I Done To Deserve This?' and mutters, more to himself than to anyone else, 'God, Dusty sang this well, didn't she?' Then he looks at a Polaroid of him taken earlier by Pete. 'More chins than the Hong Kong telephone directory,' he sighs.

He congratulates himself for his lack of success shopping today. 'I feel quite virtuous that I haven't bought anything,' he admits. 'I usually feel terribly guilty at this point.' This is a pose that he will build on in the days to come and he will relish announcing frequently that these days he, Neil Tennant, is now officially 'post-shopping'.

As we leave the café, the waiter makes a V sign, palm towards us and says 'good luck'. Neil pontificates on the symbolic meaning of this while we descend the stairs. He says he believes it's an ancient Chinese sign for good luck and asks Brenda whether this is so. She looks a little confused and carefully explains that, no, it's actually a sort of hippie symbol meaning peace.

We have sent the minibus home and so we take the Star Ferry that runs between Hong Kong island and Kowloon. On our journey we continue to enjoy blowing the Mandarin Hotel incident out of all proportion. It is now decided that, as well as denouncing him from the stage, the most fitting means to repay the assistant manager is to invite him to the concert and then turn him away at the door.

Neil: After about a year we decided to make a demo so I got the *Melody Maker* and looked up the cheapest demo studio we could find. It was £6 an hour.

The decision was purely made on the basis of cost?

Neil: Totally.

Chris: I couldn't believe how expensive it was.

Neil: I paid for it with my redundancy money from Macdonald Educational. It all cost about £32 – a lot of money then. We took our equipment – Chris's trombone, my synthesizer and a little Casiotone – but Ray Roberts (*the studio owner*) had a much better synthesizer and a piano so we used those. We recorded 'Bubadubadubadubadubadum', 'Jealousy' and 'Oh Dear'. At that point we decided we needed a name so we could send the tape to people and we chose West End. Actually we always thought it was a really useless name.

What did it mean?

Neil: We just liked the West End of London. We used to spend a lot of time wandering around there.

Was it from the song 'West End Girls'?

Neil: No, that was written slightly later, I think. Maybe the idea of 'West End Girls' came from West End. I can't really remember. Anyway, Ray Roberts liked our songs and liked us, so he said we could use his studio for nothing if he could have a share of our publishing. Chris was back in Liverpool and he'd come down at the weekends and we'd go to Ray Roberts' studio on Friday and Saturday night. That was when we really started writing songs in an organized way. Then Chris heard 'Passion' by the Flirts (*written and produced by New York producer Bobby O*) and made me come over to his flat to listen to it. Our first Bobby O-influenced song went 'Life's hard/it's all you've got/and all you get/is a broken heart/it's . . .' (*here he sings a jaunty instrumental passage*). The Bobby O influence definitely focused us. We weren't just writing songs any more.

Neither Neil nor Chris have grasped hold of the idea – assumed by most of those around them – that there ought to be some kind of consistent hierarchy in operation and so tonight there is no method to their invitations to dine with them in the hotel's smart Italian restaurant. It is simply those people who they have bumped into over the preceding hour: Dainton and Pete, myself, Lawrence, Casper and Jill. Another dress code altercation has been headed off by an agreement that we eat at a table hidden round a corner and that we will enter the restaurant by a back route; consequently throughout our meal we don't see a single other diner.

The evening's brief briskly decides itself: celebrity gossip. Neil and Chris are fascinated by gossip. Perhaps one could say they are fascinated by the way tittle-tattle about the famous reflects on the contradictions of fame, the tawdry preposterousness that reveals itself when you dig away into celebrity life styles. Perhaps they just like a good gossip. It's nothing new: at *Smash Hits*, Neil – having called the office to attention and offered a disclaimer that 'it's probably not true, mind you' – would always be the first person to relate some new 'fact', to toss round news of scurrilous associations between people and to declare 'the *shame* . . .'.

As the starters arrive Chris mentions their dinner with 'Frank' – Sinatra, that is. It was while they were making Liza Minnelli's

LP – she broke off recording to appear alongside 'Frank' and 'Sammy' (Davis Junior) in 'The Ultimate Event' (as it was billed) at the Royal Albert Hall. On her table alongside them was Bob Hoskyns ('just like Phil Collins,' says Chris), on Sammy's table was Lionel Blair, on Frank's Michael Caine and Roger Moore.

Neil tells of the night he met Prince in London at a private party after one of his 'Lovesexy' concerts. Considerably worse for wear, Neil resolved that Prince, he of world-famous reserve and master of the one-word answer, was not going to get away with the silent mysterious routine tonight. In the end they chatted about religion and pop music, Prince's show and 'It's A Sin'.

They ask Casper about Michael Jackson. Casper and Cooley, as legend (and the tour programme) has it, taught Michael Jackson how to moonwalk. Cooley has been muttering to people how Michael also wants to learn his two new moves, a backflip and a gravity-defying trick where he appears to fall sideways, his body vertical, then bounce back upright off his left ankle. Cooley claims that he refuses to teach Michael any more.

All this is recapped – as in 'well, this is what we know already' – by Neil. Casper and Jill exchange glances that clearly mean both that Cooley is prone to exaggerate and that he shouldn't talk so much anyway. Nevertheless Casper slowly tells his side of the story. Michael Jackson saw them both on the American TV dance show *Soul Train* and had also seen an advert Casper had done in which Casper had been imitating Michael. He had asked the two of them over and they had subsequently spent two weeks together. The next time they met Michael blanked him.

Casper entertains us with stories which Neil counters with the tale of when the Pet Shop Boys went to the première of Michael Jackson's Disneyland film *Captain Eo*. To their horror only soft drinks were offered. 'We expected *champagne*. Champagne only, *please*.' They were ushered into an open-top vintage car and then suddenly found themselves without warning being driven down Main Street, Disneyland, through crowds of spectators, while a booming voice announced to the public: 'From London, *England*, please welcome the PET SHOP BOYS!!!' They felt conned.

'Was that the A party or the B party?' asks Casper. Apparently there were two – one posh, the other posher. Casper was invited to the B one. Chris insists that theirs must have been that one too.

'Ours can't have been that bad,' Neil points out. 'Jack Nicholson was there.'

Casper talks about Courtney Pine. He has been astonished to learn in the last day that the saxophonist on stage with him is fairly famous.

'I had no *idea*,' he confesses. 'I was going to say, "Do you want to come and do this gig with me?",' thinking, he explains, that he would be doing Courtney a major favour.

After the meal Neil pours champagne in his room as a nightcap and chatters on . . . about German journalists who ask why German music doesn't sell in Britain (to whom he and Chris always answer, 'Because it's no good. I tell them they make good cars. All Britain is good at these days is pop music') . . . arriving in New York, hearing records like 'Planet Rock' and seeing people breakdancing on the streets . . . how he writes songs from chord changes and how Chris writes from single notes . . . about Depeche Mode and how he thinks Martin Gore writes weak lyrics, but how wonderful 'See You' is . . . about Japan's suicide culture. He repeats a strange story he was once told. A couple's daughter idolized a Western actress, and felt herself so in love that she killed herself. The parents asked the actress to attend the funeral. They said it would be a great honour.

Chapter Four

Wednesday, *28 June*

This morning is the final rehearsal. The bus to the venue is due to leave at 11.30. Courtney Pine, the last of several Rule 2 violators, slides aboard at 11.41.

'First fines of the tour!' crows Ivan.

'How much? How much?' demands Carol to Courtney, but he doesn't reply, just flashes his inscrutable, shy half-smile at her. It's an expression we shall all get used to. At the back of the bus they discuss a jazz notable, James Moody, whom they saw play here last night.

'He was saying, "Y'all can sing?" and just staring at my tits,' laughs Juliet.

'He just got married,' says Courtney.

Before we leave, Ivan calls Neil to say that their special car will be leaving fifteen minutes later than scheduled.

'Oh good,' says Neil from his room. 'I can faff some more.'

The stage is empty, but the backing tracks are already echoing off the empty seats. It's odd to hear this much of the music being generated without anyone on stage to claim responsibility for it. Dominic has been instructed to run through the whole set once a day, just in case. It is one of the great paranoias of the tour that the computers will crash. If they do, no music.

Neil and Chris are met outside by two fans, one of whom cheerfully introduces herself as a satanist.

'She wanted to stand next to *Neil*,' laughs Chris, triumphantly, as if this absolves him of any responsibility. 'I've always said that rock'n'roll has nothing to do with all this devil stuff, but,' he muses, affecting a spooky voice, 'it makes you wonder, doesn't it?'

Before the rehearsal – first things first – there are some pressing problems. The stage is black but the curtain pinned along its front is brown. Chris is raging. He rails about it in a well-for-goodness-sake-how-could-anyone-*possibly*-imagine-we'd-put-up-with-that-for-even-half-a-second voice. It is changed.

Neil likewise has found an object for fury, the huge Diners Club sign that hangs from the venue roof. This is less easily solved – they are firmly told that it cannot be removed or covered. Surreptitious secondhand sponsorship like this is a pet hate and they look furious.

As this is going on the musicians wander on to the stage and begin doing their solo turns. Courtney Pine – with a little help from Jay – careers into Luther Vandross's 'So Amazing'. This sort of thing is pretty impressive the first time you see it – all these talented people, just *creating* . . . how *wonderful*. But it has been happening at every rehearsal and will continue throughout the whole tour; the pleasure soon wears thin. Sometimes – with Courtney for instance – you feel that he does it just for the pure joy of playing (he plays for much of the rest of the day in his room, without an audience). Sometimes it seems as though they're auditioning.

One of the ironies of touring is that now – the day before their first major concert – the Pet Shop Boys have been so busy travelling on planes and giving press conferences and fighting for their right to take tea and sandwiches in bare knees that they haven't rehearsed for ages. In their case it has been particularly long because of their decision to come to Hong Kong a couple of days before the shows to acclimatize and approach their first major concert without panic. The last run-through was six days ago and this afternoon it shows a little. There are a few sticky patches, a few wrong entries on-stage and a few technical hitches.

Chris is quite clearly In A Mood. It's never difficult to notice this. You can tell when Chris is In A Mood not just because of his determined lack of cheer but because he won't talk and he does everything with an exaggerated nonchalance as if to scream, 'What does it matter anyway?' Today he is partly In A Mood because the computers have been doing odd things, but he is mainly In A Mood because of his clothes.

The Chris Lowe Stage Clothes Saga has been bubbling along for a while now. From Neil's perspective Chris had said some weeks ago that he didn't want many clothes changes and he has only recently had a change of heart. From Chris's perspective he has been deliberately ignored and overlooked.

Later, when I ask them about this, they both play it down (perhaps because it's part of a taped interview for *Smash Hits*) and explain it away as a misunderstanding. Neil sorted his clothes out one Sunday afternoon after going to Derek Jarman's, tiddly on champagne after a fulsome brunch at Tom Watkins' house. They whizzed through a list of fanciful costume ideas and Neil had said yes to them all because 'it seemed like a jolly good idea at the time'. Chris didn't because everyone had picked up the idea – they thought he'd said this and he insists they just assumed it – that he would just wear the normal Chris Lowe wardrobe. Perhaps Derek Jarman was partly to blame: when he talks about the Pet Shop Boys he will often slip between the terms 'the Pet Shop Boys' and 'Neil' as if they're synonymous and he often talks about the show as if it is a performance whose core is Neil, not the two of them. (Perhaps that's what Chris is really annoyed about.)

Anyway, this afternoon the clothes situation comes to a head. Chris is not happy with the few things he wears. He storms off-stage at the end of the rehearsal and silently paces furiously from the dressing-room a few minutes later with Neil and Pete in tow. They are going shopping and – they promise – will arrive at this evening's scheduled radio interview under their own steam. This they do – Chris walking in, considerably more cheerful, with a selection of clothes, including an Issey Miyake suit with which he seems very pleased. Tomorrow afternoon he will wear it at the dress rehearsal and decide he doesn't like it, and it will never appear before an audience, but by then the crisis will have passed.

Neil: Writing a song called 'Let's Make Lots Of Money' was Chris's idea. He takes the blame for that one. That was in about June 1983. We thought it was funny. Once Chris had suggested the title I wrote the words in about fifteen minutes: 'I've got the brains, you've got the looks, let's make lots of money.' It's meant to be a satire; it's meant for everyone to hate it. Here was this nauseating synth duo singing a song called 'Let's Make Lots Of Money'. It's basically an anti-rock group song. It was meant to be rather punk. One of the things we always liked about Bobby O was that we thought he sounded like punk disco and this is like that because it's singing about things you're not supposed to sing about. Saying you're only in it for the money is to destroy the rock credibility, the idea that you're in it for the meaningfulness or for world peace or whatever. It's meant to be a bit of a wind-up, really. The two people in the song are supposed to be absolutely hopeless. I was vaguely thinking of the film *Midnight Cowboy* where Dustin Hoffman is the guy who wants to go to Florida and John Voigt is the hustler, the brain and the brawns combination. People have often thought it was about me and Chris but I don't think it was really. I don't know if Chris thought that but I just pictured two people. I've never thought of the Pet Shop Boys as me having the brains and Chris having the looks. I don't think it's true.

They are a little late for the radio interview but it doesn't matter because just before they are due on a bigger story breaks. One of the Chinese student leaders, Wir Xaxi, until now feared dead, has surfaced in the West and given an interview and all other programmes are postponed while they broadcast it. It is in a Chinese tongue. Brenda listens intently, sadly, and says he's talking about how the students died 'like cats and dogs'.

In the car park a hysterical fan gives Chris a bobble hat she has made, blue with his name stitched on in red.

'She said, "Will you wear it?"' reports Neil. 'Of course Chris said, "No".'

'She's crying,' says Pete.

Chris elaborates with theatrical cruelty. This is a private routine that Chris specializes in – being horrible about the fans. One suspects it's an embarrassed reaction to how preposterous he finds having fans. Typically once inside the safety of the radio station the hat he has refused to wear goes straight on to his head and remains there for the next hour.

The station is called RTHK, Radio TV Hong Kong: 'like the BBC,' says Brenda. We wait in a reception area that looks and smells like a hospital corridor and discuss what the Liza Minnelli LP might be called. The deadline is fast approaching and they have not yet come up with a good idea. For a while it was to be called *In Depth* but then they repossessed that as the title of a six-song Pet Shop Boys CD released in Japan to coincide with the tour. Liza has suggested *Pink*, but they're not keen.

The interviewer introduces herself and asks them what they would like the questions to be about. They shrug.

'How about anything personal?' she inquires.

'I don't have a personal life,' answers Neil firmly.

She reconsiders. 'Hobbies?'

'*That's* a good one,' says Chris. It's hard to tell whether or not he's serious.

'We could talk about the political situation in Hong Kong,'

offers Neil. Anyway, he reassures her, 'We'll just rant on once we get started.'

She nods.

'How about phone calls?' he suggests, getting into the swing of things. 'Phone calls are always good. Have some phone calls.'

She looks pleased and relieved, as if this was something she'd wanted but had been too timid to ask about.

In the studio she suggests that they might like to speak some Chinese words to introduce themselves.

'I only know one word,' sniggers Chris, 'and it means two things.'

The word is 'hai' which, depending how you say it, means either 'hello' or something rather rude. As it happens it is included in her suggested sentence 'Ngor day hai Pet Shop Boys': 'Hello, we are the Pet Shop Boys'. They say it.

The interview begins with her playing their new British single 'It's Alright'. As it plays she asks them, off microphone, if they can talk about the song afterwards.

'Yes,' threatens Neil, 'I can talk about it for *hours*.'

In fact he talks about it a bit. Then she teases Chris on air for eating sandwiches while talking, Neil stands up and shows off his shorts while she describes them, Chris announces that he is wearing a woolly hat and 'looks a bit like Blackadder' (a television reference that understandably foxes her) and they are played a Cantonese version of 'It's A Sin' by someone called Danny Chan: rather thin and cheap but fairly faithful to the original. Neil mentions that a Japanese star recorded it and, to their annoyance, changed the words. Neil was told that the reason for this was that in Japan they don't have the concept of sin. They are asked about how they find Hong Kong (they say they like the people and the mountainous skyline, hate the humidity) and then Chris reminisces about playing drums in his school's Combined Cadet Force.

'I was the person who decided the rhythm but I've got a notoriously bad memory so I'd keep changing it.'

'That must be how you learned to compose?' suggests the interviewer, hoping that she has made a fundamental discovery here. Chris looks taken aback.

'Um, *possibly*.'

The interview is given an added bizarre edge by the need to translate it for the Chinese audience. After each section of speech – maybe five minutes' worth – the interviewer launches into Chinese and offers a résumé of what's been said. Whenever proper nouns and untranslatable English words pop out from her speech Chris giggles.

More questions: they explain how 'Domino Dancing' was inspired by a phrase they used on a holiday in St Lucia when Pete would dance after winning at dominoes (Pete obligingly demonstrates the triumphant steps through the glass next door).

As she plays another record Rob anxiously pokes his head round the studio door. This interview has been set up, and been agreed to, largely because the concerts here are far from sold out. 'You haven't talked about the concerts,' he says to them beseechingly. Maybe this is the sort of thing he is supposed to worry about; they nod and after the next record Neil does a spiel about how wonderful the concerts will be. It's an advert everyone's already bored with and as he talks Chris mimes a yawn.

Chris yawns again when the first caller, Gladys, gets through only to ask why they have chosen Hong Kong to begin their tour. It's a question they have already answered on tonight's show. Chris scowls. The next caller, Dennis, asks what the aim of the concert is. Neil and Chris exchange bemused looks.

'To spread love and peace throughout the world,' says Neil with a straight face.

The interviewer takes over again.

'What do you do?' she asks Chris.

'Very good question,' he answers. 'Dunno really.' A few

minutes later he is telling the audience how 'we write songs, just like Rodgers and Hammerstein'.

'What are you doing after the tour?' she asks.

Chris squirms with embarrassment. 'Writing a new LP,' he says. Later he explains how shameful it was to say this: 'writing a new LP' is the pathetic clichéd answer that pop stars *always* come up with when asked what they're doing next. It's not the sort of thing the Pet Shop Boys should say. Even though, of course – and this was the tricky problem that Chris couldn't find a way round – in this case it's the truth. After the tour they *are* writing a new LP . . .

To finish, Neil makes a long, passionate speech about the fabulousness of being here.

'And you, Chris?' the interviewer asks.

He grunts nonchalantly. 'I'd like to say exactly the same.'

Now and again during the interview people have come in and, while records are playing, argued with the interviewer. It seems an inter-radio row is going on between this and another station in the same organization over the Pet Shop Boys. They are now led to another studio, to another DJ, this one older and English. He chats enthusiastically about jazz performers whom we have never heard of and asks the same questions, more or less, polite but fairly uninterested.

It is only later that we note that there were no questions asked about the political situation. Back in Britain we had imagined it would be all anyone here ever talked about – it was all over the British newspapers – and pop stars always get asked questions on thorny issues of the day. Maybe they thought these things were the last things to discuss with a pop group, though I suspect it's simpler than that. People who live here can talk about the situation here any time. The Pet Shop Boys may be more interested in talking about the situation here than about themselves, but Hong Kong is more interested in talking about the Pet Shop Boys.

Back at the hotel Neil has decided he is ill. He has been

muttering all day that he thought last night's Italian meal was dodgy and now he has made his mind up. It is, he officially declares, a drama. 'I'm ill,' he sighs, heading for bed. 'I can spend all tomorrow saying we'll cancel the concert.'

Thursday, *29 June*

'London OK, first Birmingham very poor, Glasgow slow, Japan something like 80, 50, 60, 80, 30.'

Ivan rattles through the latest ticket sales. Neil and Chris aren't too happy – they have accepted advice on where they should play and are worried that some concerts simply won't be sold out. Ivan explains that one reason is that in Britain credit card bookings have fallen way below expectation. Ironically they take some pleasure in this statistic, for it has long been a reluctantly accepted law about the Pet Shop Boys that a large part of their audience are yuppies. Perhaps, this new evidence suggests, this isn't so. There is another plus point. 'You get more money on non-credit card bookings,' Ivan explains to them. They look pleased. Then Chris looks worried.

'I hope it's not all screaming girls.'

Tonight's show isn't sold out. All ticket sales and nightclub attendances have been way down since the Chinese student massacre and between 50 and 70 per cent capacity seems likely. They are cheered a little by the story – happily bandied around though nobody even seems quite clear where it's come from or just how true it is – that American teenage starlet Tiffany recently visited and only managed 15 per cent.

Neil is still feeling ill. 'Maybe it's nerves,' he considers, though he stubbornly adds, 'I don't feel remotely nervous.' He phones me and asks me to his room to discuss the format and content of this book. Nothing is decided. After a while we are interrupted by Ivan. He has a problem. Derek Jarman's films, to be back-projected during six of the songs, had to be sent to the Hong Kong censor for clearance and approval. The censor has requested two changes.

The first is simple. During 'Nothing Has Been Proved', a song about the Profumo affair, written for Dusty Springfield to sing as the theme song of the film *Scandal*, images from the time are superimposed with words and phrases like 'LONDON SWINGS'. At one point it says 'FUCK'. Neil and Chris didn't like this in the first place and had already asked for the film to be re-edited – at a cost of £4,000 to themselves – to exclude the word. Somehow it is still in. Ivan is to instruct Steve, the projectionist, to black out the word on every one of the three hundred frames on which it appears.

The second objection is more problematic. The 'It's A Sin' film builds into a crescendo of images perceived as sinful. 'Lust' is depicted by two handsome boys. At first they run oil over their chests, then one kisses the other on the temple, then they kiss mouth to mouth, deeply. All the kissing – say the censors – must go.

Neil's immediate reaction is simply to show it anyway and to face the consequences. 'If they impose a big fine or cancel tomorrow night, if it causes a big rumpus, it'll probably be good for the tour . . .'

'Well,' says Chris in his I-told-you-it'd-be-a-disaster voice as we pull up outside the deserted venue, 'as usual hundreds of fans screaming outside.'

'They don't have screaming fans in Hong Kong,' insists Neil authoritatively. 'Someone told me . . .'

'There's two,' points out Ivan, clearly feeling that there is a morale problem he must overcome. Characteristically Chris is having none of it.

'They're probably looking for the bus station,' he says.

Inside we meet Mark Farrow, the designer responsible for all the Pet Shop Boys artwork. He has just flown in from Britain via Delhi. He brings with him a copy of the *NME* in which Malcolm McLaren, reviewing the singles, is fairly nice about 'It's Alright'. Neil and Chris are somewhat bemused, for the previous week on Radio One's *Singled Out* review programme he had been horrible about it: indeed it is this, one suspects, rather than any more deep-rooted objection to him that is the inspiration for the 'Malcolm McLaren is a prat' script.

Mark also tells us that the Sunrise party Chris had been to on Saturday night was on the front page of the *Sun* on Monday. Last autumn the tabloid press had whipped up a moral panic about Acid House parties, but throughout this year raves have been growing in number and size without the newspapers knowing it – the furore about the party Chris was at will, it turns out, mark the beginning of a second wave that will continue throughout the year, with the police blocking roads, closing service stations, disconnecting phone information lines and successfully imprisoning organizers. But all that is months away, and here in Hong Kong, so far away, it seems unbelievable that it was even in the papers. For the moment the *Sun* has merely recorded their insincere outrage. They say the landowner was told the venue was being used to film a video and report that there is to be a Home Office inquiry.

After a dress rehearsal, they have a censorship rehearsal. Despite Neil's earlier bravado Ivan has persuaded them that it's not worth deliberately spiting the censors. Steve, the projectionist, simply covers the projector's light beam with his hands during the offending sequences so that the screen behind the stage goes dark. At the end of the film, where the two men simply enjoy a friendly embrace, he lets the film run as normal.

'Hugging's all right, is it?' Chris asks Ivan.

'I'm going to say at the end,' announces Neil a touch regally, 'that it's been censored. I think it's quite exciting. Don't you think I should?'

'*Neil*,' reprimands Chris. 'It was *my* idea.'

★

Do either of you think of one of you as the boss?

Neil: Well, obviously I operate as the boss because I'm the bossy person. But I'm not the boss, because Chris operates in a very different way from that.

Chris: I've never liked the idea of bosses. You can't divide up operations like that. Neil is naturally very good at 'being the boss'. But nothing's as simple as that; that's why I think it's wrong when you have a job and there's a boss. I've basically got a kind of communist attitude towards things where everyone's just as important even if it's the person who makes a cup of tea . . . I've always felt like that.

You encourage people to think that Neil is the boss in business matters, don't you? If someone comes to you you deflect them . . .

Chris: Well, there's no point in asking me because Neil will have a different opinion . . . (*He pauses, realizing this doesn't quite make sense.*) It's got to be run past two people.

Neil: Also Chris doesn't like saying things to people. If we're making a record – and this has been true from day one – Chris will say about someone, 'I don't think they should be playing that' and I say, 'Say something' and he'll start sulking. So I have to say, 'What do you think about that bass-line?' to the producer and then I'll say, 'And what do *you* think, Chris?' . . .

Chris (nodding): . . . and *then* I'll say it.

Neil: I'm Chris's representative on earth half the time.

Chris, do you recognize this scenario?

Chris: Yes. It's true.

Neil: Like, for this tour in a meeting Patrick, the lighting designer, was going on about this model (*a small, three-dimensional model, hopelessly conventional and inappropriate, of how the lights for the show might be*) . . .

Chris: . . . and I'm *furious* . . .

Neil: . . . and I can see, as I interpret Chris to the world, that Chris is in a bad mood about this but he's not going to say anything so we're going to waste the entire meeting. So I have to say, 'Chris, what do you think?' And, by the way, he was totally right about it.

Chris: You see, Neil is very good at saying something diplomatically. If I was to stand up in that meeting I would absolutely *destroy* Patrick. That's why I sit there, because I know I can't say it in a nice way.

Neil: Yes, you'd say something personally insulting.

What would you have done if Neil hadn't been there?

Chris: I probably wouldn't have done anything.

Neil: Actually you're quite good when I'm not there.

Chris: Actually I would have gone up to Derek Jarman afterwards.

Neil: Chris has stronger opinions about things like that. I'm sometimes a bit of an 'anything for a quiet life' merchant, whereas Chris tends to have an opinion which doesn't involve the personality concerned, therefore he has an uncluttered opinion about it.

Do you mind it, Chris, when all the official communication is directed to Neil?

Chris: I don't like it. Sometimes it's fair, but if there's a bias with a team of people we're working with . . . I get a bit ratty when we shoot a video and I'm not in it at all. That can annoy me because it's unfair. (*Pauses.*) I don't like talking about it.

Neil (*to Chris*)*:* But the imbalance is there for the things we're talking about because you very rarely communicate your ideas directly to people. You communicate them through me, therefore sometimes they assume you don't have ideas. Also you have, in my opinion, an inferiority complex anyway.

Chris: Yeah, probably.

Neil: I actually think you have a *giant* inferiority complex, that you fundamentally think inside you that you're not very important. Therefore you get paranoid and think, 'No one thinks I'm important'. In fact people do, but one of the good things about this tour is that they can see what Chris does. Often, because Chris operates so that he doesn't say things to people, they assume that he's not interested, that he doesn't play a major role. And then, of course (*turning to Chris*), when they do ask, you say the biggest put-downs about yourself. (*Chris laughs in recognition of the truth in this.*) It's *you* that originally compared yourself to Andrew Ridgeley.

Yes. It's like during the radio interview where, when they asked what you did, you said, 'Very good question . . . dunno really'.

Neil: Of course that is also a sense of humour, but to most people listening, especially once it is translated, that sense of humour won't come across.

Chris: Well, who in their right minds is going to say that and mean it?

Do you think you do have an inferiority complex?

Chris: I probably have. It's very difficult to judge yourself. Actually I'm a great kind of niggling little-hater-from-behind-the-scenes person.

Of yourself?

Chris: No. Of figures of authority. I've always been like that, from a very low-profile position, rather than someone who says, 'I don't like that.' 'Lack of confidence' might be better than 'inferiority complex'. I've not got much confidence.

Back-stage Courtney Pine wanders the corridor, practising, blowing shrill phrases from his saxophone.

'What time do they let the little people in?' he asks.

The doors open at 7pm. Lawrence and I hurry round to the front entrance, to talk to the crowds of excited fans and to photograph their anticipation before they stream into the hall. We locate what we think is the main entrance but we are obviously wrong because there is no one there. We walk round the building. We return. We meet no one. Our first guess was right: this *is* the main entrance but no one is there. Confused, we ask the security guard. No, he explains, people won't come for a while. This is how pop audiences behave in Hong Kong. If the ticket says 8 o'clock then they're jolly well not going to turn up at 7 and twiddle their thumbs for an hour, getting over-excited. Just as in Britain one might turn up to the theatre or the cinema just a few minutes early, so will they here.

The security guard's confidence is justified. By quarter to eight there is a steady trickle of locals, walking into the auditorium to be met by wafts of classical music being piped through the PA (Schönberg's *Transfigured Night*). In other places, later on the tour, this music will seem an effective antidote to the traditional chomp-a-cheeseburger-and-shlurp-a-coke expectant rock'n'roll bonhomie; here, in a well-lit, clean hall, half-filled with a polite Hong Kong audience, it only heightens the feeling that we all might be waiting for a serious academic lecture, not the first night of the Pet Shop Boys tour.

Behind the blackout curtains friendly chaos rules. The dancers practise their moves – '1-2-3-4 1-2-3-4' – the singers shout 'scrumpity scrumpity scrump' (the significance of which is lost on me), wardrobe tetchily chide people who are using 'It's A Sin' costumes as seats and everyone waits. Neil and Chris are in their dressing-room. To get themselves into the mood they listen to 'In Private', an ecstatic, Motown-style song that they recently wrote for and recorded with Dusty Springfield.

By the side of the stage Steve, the projectionist, mutters about the film for 'Nothing Has Been Proved'. As instructed he has scribbled over the word 'FUCK' 300 times but he is well aware it's a poor disguise.

'You can still see it.'

He is pleased.

'It's a compromise for Derek really. I'll take the blame.'

The whole 'It's A Sin' censorship fiasco has deeply affronted him.

'Friends of you know,' he says angrily. 'It's still banned here.'

The Pet Shop Boys actually go on-stage at 8.25, twenty-five minutes late, a fact that is blackly noted in the local press. The message is clear. The way things are done here is: people turn up on time – not early, not late – and they expect those they come to see to do exactly the same.

Neil awaits his entrance standing in his shiny silver overcoat holding a cup of white wine. (There was to have been a strict no-alcohol-before-the-performance rule but at the very first hurdle it has been deemed unrealistic and has been abandoned.) The house lights go down and he grins. 'We haven't decided who to blame yet,' he says, walking stagewards.

Afterwards, they are happy to blame no one but themselves. The performance is quite clearly a triumph. It's plain on Neil's face how delighted he is to be in front of an audience and everyone who has watched him in rehearsal is shocked by how animated he has suddenly become. Chris stands stock still for most of the show but bounds around delightedly during 'Paninaro'. All his targets – the Cure, U2, the redeemed Malcolm McLaren and the assistant manager of the Mandarin Hotel – escape their planned public vilification: instead he says, 'I don't like rock'n'roll . . . I don't like country . . . I love disco music . . . I love having a good time . . . I like it here' for which he receives a decent cheer.

During 'It's A Sin' the covering-up of the kisses is sloppily done and each time darkness comes a little too late. The censors – who have actually turned up to check that their directions have been followed – smile benignly as if to say, 'Fair enough, you've made an effort, we can live with that.' Neil says nothing to the audience about the censorship – in fact he says nothing much to the crowd apart from several 'thank yous' until the band introductions before the encores when he, with transparent sincerity, says he'd 'like to thank you for being such a great audience'.

There is one disaster. Before 'Domino Dancing' Neil must change very quickly from the striped City shirt he sports for 'Shopping' into an embroidered Latinesque one. He fails and misses his entrance. Then he begins singing the chorus at the wrong place. The rest is chaos. Eventually he sits down at one side of the stage and lets Courtney Pine fill in what has now become a peculiar semi-instrumental. Afterwards this is not seen as tragic, just hilarious. 'I'm rather proud of the disaster,' Neil says. Nevertheless in future it is decided that Danny Cummings will play a percussion solo between the songs. This, of course, they realize with delight, is thrillingly un-Pet Shop Boys. A percussion solo is nothing but a fancy name for a drum solo and the drum solo is the epitome of rock'n'roll naffness. Neil and Chris try to turn this about-turn into a virtue: when you make a stand out of standing against tradition then you can always justify reverting to tradition as a stand against your own new tradition. They say that they '*love* the fact that we've got a drum solo'. Likewise they rave about the intermission.

'After all we've said,' laughs Chris, 'we've got one of the best rock'n'roll light shows ever.'

These same conflicting impulses drive their reaction towards performing for an audience. The standard rock'n'roll pose is to encourage the audience to celebrate your wonderfulness and conspicuously to bask and indulge in their approval: you, the star, and they, the followers, tacitly agree to join together in praising you. Rather problematically – as far as the Pet Shop Boys are concerned – audiences seem rather to like this, perhaps because when a performer responds, when the performer looks as though they're enjoying the acclaim, well, then, the audience is *having an effect*; they are part of the performance, not just spectators.

The Pet Shop Boys' instincts run against that. Their demeanour in performance was established in their second Top of the Pops appearance when 'West End Girls' had just reached number one. As they were introduced Chris, a little concerned, leant over to Neil and hissed, 'Don't look triumphant.' Likewise on-stage in Hong Kong the Pet Shop Boys again do their best not to look triumphant. It's obvious in Chris's nonchalant wave as he leaves the stage after 'Paninaro'; it's obvious in Neil's embarrassed half-waves and quiet 'thank yous'; it's most obvious of all in Chris's habit of standing still during the songs and then, when the lights go down between each, when no one can see him, having a dance in the dark 'because it's so exciting'.

Neil: Whenever we were going to do *Top of the Pops* there were always crisis meetings beforehand between EMI and our management. They always felt we should *do* something on *Top of the Pops*. To be quite honest this still happens now. They want us to have an *angle*.

Chris: Once Tom drew us a diagram of the idea of the layout he thought we should have. The funny thing was, it was the traditional layout, the one that *every* group has on *Top of the Pops*.

Your performance of 'West End Girls' where you – Neil – stood there in a long coat and you – Chris – had a cap over your eyes and played the keyboard with one finger, neither of you moving . . .

Chris: It was a landmark. It had never happened before.

Had you thought out beforehand that doing what you did was probably the most striking thing you could have done?

Chris: We did it because that's what we did in Belgium, when the first version of 'West End Girls' was a hit there. *That* was an accident, the one in Belgium, because we thought we were just doing a radio interview and we had to do a performance. There was one keyboard there and I had a BOY hat so I said, 'I'll play the bass-line' and so, mainly because of that, that's what I got stuck with. It was an accident originally, then I decided to carry it on. I thought it fitted the mood of the song.

It did more than fit the mood of the song in retrospect, didn't it? It established in the public imagination a certain attitude.

Chris: Yeah, it did. But I also wouldn't have felt natural doing anything else. My unreasonable logic (*laughs*) is that I decide which part I'll mime to, and for that the bass-line is the most obvious part of the arrangement so I just used one finger.

And deliberately put the other hand in your pocket?

Chris (*indignantly*): I don't have my hand in my pocket! I'd *never* have *one* hand in my pocket. I've always thought that if you're going to put your hand in your pocket you've got to put both your hands in both your pockets. To put your hand in one pocket looks 'maybe'. (*I look dubious.*) It's *true*! People who walk down the street with one hand in their pocket . . . it's nerdish. You've *got* to have both.

That's a remarkable thing even to hold an opinion about.

Chris: But it's true! Doesn't *everyone* think that?

I don't think so. Myself, I've never thought about it.

Chris (*surprised*)*:* Haven't you? Oh, I do.

And not just recently, since becoming a pop star?

Chris: No, I've always been conscious of that. (*He suddenly switches, without warning, back to the previous topic of conversation.*) Actually, another thing about Top of the Pops, you notice that if you don't move very much you get closer shots on you. A TV presenter told us this. If you're very static the camera will come in very close on you. We didn't know this at the time but one of the things about being static during 'West End Girls' was that you got these close-up shots. I always think that looks good for pop television.

So that the audience feel like they're communicating with your inner soul or something?

Chris: Yeah.

'I'd prefer it to have been a one-off,' Chris announces backstage, forever determined not to appear triumphant. 'Now,' he complains, 'we have to do it again.' It's a theme he will return to several times in the early stages of the tour – that the repetition of something like this is fundamentally pointless, that one should do something once and then move on – though in a few weeks he will grudgingly admit that he's changed his mind. Tonight he doesn't keep it up for long. Soon he has forgotten that he is trying to be very cool about all this.

'I'm just a tragic rock'n'roller!' he hoots, champagne in hand.

This, Neil suggests, is the beginning of the end, that they're on the slope towards self-parody and pantomime. 'By the end of the tour in "Domino Dancing" we'll have split the audience up,' he laughs, 'and we'll have one side of the house going, "All day all day . . ."'

Perhaps.

Rob arrives breathlessly in the dressing-room, full of congratulations. 'There was so much of it,' he raves.

'*Wrong* thing to say,' teases Chris. '*Very* tactful. So it was too long?'

'The manager says: every song dragged on,' adds Neil.

Rob, who was genuinely thrilled by the concert, is embarrassed into silence.

Patrick, the lighting designer, pops his head round the door. '"Paninaro" was good, Chris,' he says.

Chris flashes him an I'll-try-to-look-bashful-but-what-the-hell!-I'm-marvellous-aren't-I? shrug. 'I've worked hard on it,' he says, though he can't resist adding, 'It's the best show we'll ever do – it's all downhill from here.'

Chris is actually obviously a little surprised at how Chris Lowe – the man who has said time and time again 'I don't enjoy performing at all' – felt out on-stage. As we join the band and crew for more champagne he admits to a very strange, unexpected feeling during 'Paninaro' at the back of his eyes. He never mentions it again, ever. People flood round, congratulating him. He laughs. 'Don't you just *love* adulation?'

Meanwhile Neil is having a minor crisis. His right eye has swollen up; some make-up under a contact lens, he later decides. He asks if the venue people have some eye ointment. The remedy round these parts, they tell him, is black beans. He politely refuses.

Outside the stage door are perhaps fifty fans. Neil and Chris leave the party to sign autographs for them. As soon as they appear the fans go hysterical. (Whoever told Neil that this sort of thing doesn't happen in Hong Kong was clearly mistaken.)

'Chris! You're a cool man!'

'Give us a kiss!'

'On the *lips*!'

'Give me some smile, man!'

'Hit the smiling face!'

They sign posters, programmes, records, t-shirts, handbags, anything. Whenever they kiss someone the nearby fans whoop in shared delight. Once they have completed a round they get into a car, the metal barriers are pulled back and they drive off.

The fans loiter a while longer, thrilled by what has happened.

'Chris is a cool man,' says one, 'and he kissed me.'

'Neil is very smart,' offers another, 'and the voice is very good.'

'Tonight I do not wash the face,' says a third. 'Neil kissed me. I dream I get married with him.'

I ask them which other pop stars they like.

'Depeche Mode.'

'OMD.'

'New Kids On The Block.'

'Erasure.'

'Depeche Mode.'

'Martin Gore! Chris is like Martin Gore!'

This assertion is greeted by many agreeing nods.

'They are similar. Chris is stylish, They are both lovely. No sexy.'

'I think Neil is sexier than Chris.'

This causes heated debate.

'Neil has too much hair on the legs,' says one disapprovingly. 'You can *see* it.'

Neil: It only occurred to Chris and me months after we were successful that one reason people liked us was because they liked the way we looked. It took us ages and ages and ages to realize that and we were quite startled by that fact, because it had never occurred to ourselves to look in terms of people fancying us. We never thought we were good-looking like that and we'd never thought of presenting ourselves in a cute way and then we suddenly realized that it was quite a big part of our audience.

Were you pleased?

Neil: Yes. As it happens I like the scream pop element.

Because you like it simply for itself or because you like the idea of it because you have an obsession with teenage hysteria?

Neil: Because I have an obsession with teenage hysteria, and just to find *myself* at the centre of any of it I just find quite thrilling. So the other must be partly true as well.

Ivan has firmly laid down the law: tonight there shall be no group celebration because if we celebrate tonight then tomorrow's show will suffer. Nevertheless by common instinct everyone gathers in the hotel foyer and by the time we reach a Japanese restaurant there are at least thirty of us all sat cross-legged round a low table in our socks. Drink flows.

'Speech!' shouts someone to Neil.

'*Unaccustomed* as I am . . . I'd just like to speak for an hour or so on the situation in South-East Asia,' he mugs, but already everyone's attention has wandered.

Chris – at the other end of the long, thin table – points in disgust at some raw fish in front of him and complains loudly to Neil.

'It's so fishy!' he shouts indignantly.

'Of course it's fishy,' snaps Neil back. 'It's fish.'

'I want meat,' says Chris and stands up. 'I want more food.'

All along the table members of the touring party are getting to know each other. Pinkie talks to percussionist Danny Cummings.

'How did you get your job?' she asks.

'I'm very very famous,' says Danny straight-faced.

'Well,' she says, and considers this assertion, 'I've never heard of you.'

A lobster arrives. It is moving. It is alive. Chris looks horrified – raw fish is bad enough, but *this*. It is sent back and returns a few minutes later, dead and tidily unpacked, lying desiccated within its shell.

Friday, *30 June*

At the afternoon soundcheck everyone japes around. Spirits are high.

'It's madness, isn't it?' says Pete with concern. 'They're too cocky. After one show they think they've toured.' Already, he says, after one night Neil is talking about taking the tour to America.

In the canteen I sit next to Courtney. More than anyone else he seems a little alarmed by this person strolling round taking notes in a big blue book. 'I'm going to burn your book,' he laughs. 'I'll get it banned. I've got cousins in the BBC.'

He plays me some music on his new portable DAT machine. It is him playing a saxophone synthesizer and it is very beautiful. 'My next LP,' he says, and I tell him it sounds good. He looks at me – incredulous – as if to say 'you know nothing' and says that it is rubbish and he just recorded it this afternoon, making it up as he went along.

We are interrupted by the promoter's partner, Steve Beaver. He has something on his mind. He marches up to Courtney as if they have been friends for many, many years and starts telling him about some old harmonica-based instrumental of which he is recording a new House music version.

'I've been thinking,' he says, feigning nonchalance, 'that

maybe you could play saxophone on it and we could make you the featured person on the record.'

He promises to send Courtney a tape – making it sound as if Courtney has twisted his arm into him doing Courtney this one very special favour. Courtney mumbles a few polite 'maybes' and 'we'll sees' then leaves.

A minute or so later Andrew Bull walks in.

'Great news,' announces Steve. 'Me and Courtney are going to be doing some work together.'

Before tonight's concert Neil and Chris give an interview for the London magazine *Time Out*, to be published just before the London dates. As a rule the Pet Shop Boys don't do many interviews for British publications, but they have done an unprecedented number for this tour: *Smash Hits* (twice, including my on-tour piece), *No. 1*, *Just 17*, the *Daily Mirror* and this. Murray, their press officer, has also arranged, with their blessing, a series of interviews to be done by Derek Jarman. In retrospect they explain this activity as them wanting people to know about the tour simply because they are proud of it but, although there's a degree of that, right now one also feels that, faced with a new and unpredictable situation, they are determined to do everything they can to make it go right. Besides, they have had endless arguments to get their current British single 'It's Alright' released and several people have told them it won't do well. They are determined to prove those people wrong.

The interviewer, an ex-*Time Out* staff member called Jon Wall, now living and working in Hong Kong, is friendly and genuinely interested and afterwards they pronounce him perfectly nice, although the interview was a little dull. 'It was one of those "don't mention their sex lives" interviews,' smiles Neil.

Jon Wall had seen the show the previous night and liked it enough to come again tonight, and he told them that the locals he has talked to were particularly impressed at the way the Pet Shop Boys have – they assumed – adapted their performance to the Chinese theatrical style of presentation. Here, in Hong Kong, the habit of Western performers of expecting people to be entertained just by their music and maybe the odd piece of jigging about, with at best one or two costume changes, is considered a little disappointing.

A couple of weeks later when the article appears everyone involved is pleasantly surprised. It isn't dull and in fact is the most lucid account of the tour that will be published anywhere (like most pop stars they are pleased as punch when anyone takes the trouble and bother to find out exactly what they have done). It also has, as is now traditional in almost all pieces about the Pet Shop Boys, a stab at The Point Of The Pet Shop Boys:

'The Pet Shop Boys' ethic, their certain aloof trademark that permeates video, lyric, photoshoot and interview, is an unflappable sense of cool. Coolness is their purpose. Consider their history: they met not at a club but at a music shop; Tennant's vocals are not sung or torched but chatted; lyrics, never strident political tub-thumps, are more often sly, wry personal devices or obtuse anti-Thatcher-brutalism social observations; the duo's buzz marketing word has always been "undersell", Tennant wary of the instant pop bleed he witnessed as a writer on *Smash Hits*.'

The piece finishes like this:

'"Sometimes," says Tennant, "we've been puzzled as to what the entire point of playing live is, anyway."

'"I'm still puzzled, really," says Lowe.'

Shortly before going on-stage Chris has a strop. Their reception in Hong Kong has not been good enough. Tonight's show is still not quite sold out and Chris is furious that they have bothered to tour here – proclaimed as 'second only to Madonna' – and, student massacre or no student massacre, there are empty

Taking a break during the filming of the never-released live video

Arriving at Narita airport, Tokyo, 3 July

After-concert champagne in the Pet Shop Boys' dressing-room at the Tokyo Budokan: (left to right) Kaz, Janet Street-Porter, Chris Lowe, John, Tom Watkins, Alan

A traditional Japanese 3-3-1 handclap in the Pet Shop Boys' honour at the Cavern, Tokyo. Mr Udo is on the right

Neil (in his Down Boy! T-shirt) and Chris consider some fan mail backstage in Osaka while the author (reflected in the mirror behind them) takes notes

Neil being interviewed as the tour bus draws near Birmingham, 13 July

At the back of the bus

Neil gathers drawings and presents before their performance in Nagoya. Chris and Pete look on

Waiting at Nagoya railway station on Neil's birthday

On the bullet train from Nagoya to Tokyo, discussing their fan mail with Juliet Roberts (left) and Carroll Thompson

Chris watches two fans kissing on a bench from the Glasgow dressing-room

Chris and Neil pore with fascination over the celebrity-packed Smash Hits autograph book in the lounge of Airth Castle

The celebrated 'Neil, you're a sex god' banner

Signing autographs through the backstage fencing at Wembley Arena

Chris waves goodbye to the football team who the Pet Shop Boys sponsor

Ivan Kushlick, Tour Manager

'One More Chance'

'West End Girls'. Chris and Courtney Pine

'Rent'. Neil presents Juliet with his fur coat

'Left To My Own Devices'. Neil in a dressing-gown

'Left To My Own Devices'. Casper as Debussy

'Rent'. (Left to right) Neil, Casper, Courtney Pine, Robia, Cooley, Tracy, Hugo

seats. 'They always complain that big groups don't come,' he says, 'and then when they do, *they* don't come.' He announces, categorically, dramatically, that they will never return.

Tonight's concert is like last night's without the mistakes. Chris's speech has shrunk further, just two words: 'Hello everyone.' Huge cheer. During 'It's A Sin' one of the costumes, the one worn by Hugo, a bloated, pink, polystyrene body in bra and panties, is fully exhibited for the first time. It has a penis, last night tucked away out of sight. This evening it is showing in its lengthy semi-erect glory. From now on interested parties will inquire before each show whether it is to be a 'penis in' or a 'penis out' occasion.

At the end of 'Always On My Mind' Neil begins to stride off-stage, then breaks halfway, turns back to the audience and holds out his hands, palms upwards, as if to say 'Well? Weren't we fabulous?'

'You can hear the "hello London's" coming on every night,' says Murray, both impressed and a little flabbergasted by this blossoming showmanship.

Andrew Bull is in a tizz. Tonight, when the 'It's A Sin' film was shown, no one bothered to cover it up. This wasn't by express design as far as the Pet Shop Boys were concerned, but they're happy enough.

'I'm *so* disappointed,' fumes Mr Bull. 'You never even *tried* to cover it up.' One can't help getting the impression that in this matter he is not bowing down to officialdom but expressing his own prejudices, his own disgust.

The Pet Shop Boys take little notice. In fact they are privately rather amused by the excuse given by projectionist Steve – that he couldn't tell when the kissing scenes were until they'd been projected.

'It's getting boring, playing live,' pipes Chris, cheerfully.

Pete, who was taking photos from in front of the stage,

disputes that this is Chris's true opinion. He tells Chris he thought that at one stage Chris had been crying with emotion.

'*Chris? Crying?*' scoffs Neil incredulously. 'You must be joking.'

'I'm sorry,' says Chris, 'but I'm a bit *bored*. I keep thinking "just five more songs". The edge has gone.'

Neil nods. He confesses that during one of the songs he was far too busy wondering what they might have for dinner later.

Pete shows Neil a Polaroid of his red cape spin during 'It's A Sin'.

'That's quite interesting,' he coos. '"Me In A Twirl". It sounds like a Smiths song.'

Chris stands admiringly, just looking at his rack of stage clothes. 'It's *more* than fashion,' he sighs melodramatically. 'These are museum pieces. My Issey Miyake clothes are more than just clothing, they're sculpture.'

Dainton tells them that there are 150 fans outside tonight, waiting.

'We can't sign 150,' says Chris.

'If we wait,' counsels Neil, 'some of those will get bored and go away.'

The fans are mostly girls, old teenagers, with a smattering of serious, fashionably dressed boys and a loud posse of British army girls stationed in Hong Kong. I go out to have a look.

'If I give you 100 dollars will you smuggle me into their boot? Where are they staying? Can I stay in their room?'

'I love Neil Tennant. He is Mr Cool. He is Mr Right.'

'He's cute.'

'He's kind.'

'He's very clean.'

'They're a very clean group. No satanic.'

'The songs are really deep.'

'They're handsome.'

'Can you say "hi" to Craig Logan?'

'They're British. You can dance to their music. I hate American music. Bon Jovi.' (Makes an I'm-going-to-vomit expression.) 'Pet Shops Boys is easy to listen to, a little bit sad.'

'Neil is cool. For fun I'd love go kiss he.'

'The show was brilliant. There was always something going on.'

'I saw Duran Duran and Stevie Wonder and this is the best.'

'I like Chris best. I like his hat. He just stands there and is moody-looking. He seems the strong, silent type.'

This comment prompts debate.

'And they're always the worst.'

Giggles.

'It appeals to a woman.'

'Men who say what they're going to do, don't do it.'

When Neil and Chris come out there is mayhem. The army girls burst into a raucous version of the Righteous Brothers' 'You've Lost That Lovin' Feeling' in imitation of a scene in the film *Top Gun* where Tom Cruise serenades Kelly McGillis in a bar. Chris raises an embarrassed eyebrow in their direction as if to say, 'Who let *them* in?'

The answer to Neil's on-stage contemplation is that we are to eat at the Bostonian, a restaurant in our hotel where the menu is of American food, droll broken-English witticisms and astronomic prices. There they dredge through the 'It's Alright' row. They have just had some good news. The British charts are announced on a Sunday, based purely on sales from Monday to Saturday of that week. Gallup, the company that compiles the chart, gives subscribing record companies provisional midweek charts, based on the sales so far, on Thursday and again on Friday. We have just heard that the Thursday midweek for 'It's Alright' is that it will enter the charts at number two. They are delighted.

EMI, it turns out, had mixed feelings about releasing the record at all. Though the people who work closest with the Pet Shop Boys in the company's Parlophone subsidiary were keen, the wider (and, the implication was, wiser) feeling was that it was a bad idea. Tom and Rob, their management, sided with the latter view. Neil and Chris weren't simply insulted that people didn't like their new record – they also got a distinct impression that people feared their career was slipping. 'There was definitely an "EMI-have-got-the-jitters-about-the-Pet-Shop-Boys feeling,"' says Neil. 'It was "They've been popular for too long. How long's it going to last?"' Much of the record business, perpetually bemused by public taste, is as confused by success as by failure. One marketing executive at EMI has, it is whispered, regally pronounced that he could 'market this record into the Top 20 but not into the Top 10'.

It was Chris who held firm, simply because he was thrilled by the record they had made. He couldn't stop playing it, he had played it to his family and they'd loved it and he wanted it released. He said he didn't care whether it even got in the Top 50: it should come out. Neil is usually the face of the Pet Shop Boys that the record company see, but this time Chris phoned up everyone involved to insist it be released.

Nevertheless now it is EMI who are making the bullish statements – that the record might go straight into the charts at number one – and it is the Pet Shop Boys who are sensibly tempering the excitement. They know that any group like them who have lots of keen fans, who will buy the record early in its first week of release, will find their chart position falling back by Sunday. In fact it's a syndrome – 'the Paul Weller syndrome' as they tartly refer to it – that they are worried about. The problem is this: you can enter the charts so high, thanks to your keen fans, that there simply isn't time for more fairweather fans to get to like the record before it is going down the charts, its life over. Now we must wait and see.

After dinner we go clubbing. We try a disco called 1997 but

they tell us there is no room so we walk down the narrow streets, a large posse flanking the swanky car holding Neil and Chris, to a disco called California. Once they realize they have famous guests they clear some table space. Champagne appears. Neil chats for a couple of hours, then leaves. Chris dances, at first shyly, off the dance-floor by the toilets, then on the dance-floor. At 3.00am we return to 1997 and it's 5.20 when we eventually take a taxi back to the Ramada Renaissance. It's already light and we all have that tired but ecstatic feeling you get when you've stayed up all night having fun.

'This is my favourite part of the day,' sighs Chris. 'Morning has broken.' He sniggers. '*That*'s a good line. I must tell Neil. No one's used it, have they?'

He roars with laughter.

'Morning Has Broken' was a Top 10 hit for Cat Stevens in 1972. One of his other famous songs was 'Wild World'. When the Pet Shop Boys single 'It's A Sin' went to number one Jonathan King wrote about it in his column in the *Sun*, suggesting that they had committed an act of theft from Cat Stevens and that they should be punished for it. (Cat Stevens, who is now a Muslim called Yusef Islam and who was soon to become embroiled in the Salman Rushdie affair, was contacted by another newspaper but said he wasn't bothered.) After Jonathan King repeated the accusation the Pet Shop Boys instigated defamation proceedings.

As the case neared court, Jonathan King even made a record in support of himself, a version of 'Wild World' using the arrangement of 'It's A Sin', so that it went 'It's a/it's a/oh baby baby it's a wild world' (Chris bought a copy because he liked it). If anything it weakened his case, but sneakily the B-side was made up of a medley of the Chiffons' 'He's So Fine' and the song that was adjudged to have been cribbed from it by George Harrison, 'My Sweet Lord'.

Eventually Jonathan King settled out of court, made a donation to the Jefferiss Research Foundation (a charity specified by the Pet Shop Boys) and apologized.

This wasn't the first time, oddly, that Neil had crossed Jonathan King's trail. In the early seventies when Neil was at college in London, he answered an advert that Jonathan King had placed, searching for talent for his record company. Neil dressed up in his best trousers – baggy, Navy-surplus trousers – and went down to a rehearsal studio.

'I played him two songs,' Neil remembers, 'and he said they were too introspective. And of course he was absolutely right. But he said he liked my trousers.'

Saturday, *1 July*

Before dinner, I meet Neil and Chris in Neil's room to interview them formally for the *Smash Hits* piece I am writing. It's hard, having spent the last few days with them talking about anything and everything, to get them to discuss my questions. Again and again the conversation drifts off. Indeed, as I switch the tape-recorder on, Neil carries on talking about the situation here in Hong Kong. The papers are full of a report by a parliamentary committee set up by the British government which has ruled out offering residency to Hong Kong Chinese after 1997.

'They're being slippery,' he concludes. 'They should be taking it up with the Chinese. I think we're crazy to trust the Chinese one single inch. The Chinese will do what they want.'

'And after all the good work that Wham! had done,' sighs Chris.

I make the mistake of asking them how they'd felt before they went on-stage for the first concert. If there's any kind of question that Chris hates it's 'How does it *feel*?' questions, questions that dig for big, deep reasons for things. He likes to give the impression that in his world there are no big reasons.

'What did I say these questions would be like?' he asks Neil, laughing contemptuously.

'I know,' says Neil, tutting. Nevertheless Neil answers the question at some length – 'not very scared' is the gist of the answer. His speech wanders on and on until he starts pontificating at some length about the on-stage monitoring. It is hardly going to make it to my article. I say to Neil that I'll be fast-forwarding through this bit when I transcribe the tape. He tells me that American journalists are forever noting the number on the tape counter next to the corresponding topic 'with a bit where they talk about their sex lives underlined', he laughs. Then he continues his original train of thought. On-stage, he says, he's always scared that he'll forget the words of 'Nothing Has Been Proved'.

'I always think what's the line after "in the house a resignation . . ."'

The correct line is 'in the house a resignation/guilty faces every one'.

'In the house a resignation/guilty feet ain't got no rhythm,' suggests Chris merrily.

Tea and coffee arrive, provoking a small disagreement. Neil has separately asked both Chris and me whether we would like some tea – no choice – and then, rather bizarrely, ordered himself coffee. Chris feigns outrage.

'But *no one* drinks coffee at this time,' Neil defends, illogically. 'I thought it was a tea-drinking time.'

'*We* weren't given the choice,' mutters Chris.

We talk about the costumes and Neil says, 'The whole show is held together by velcro.' It is this quote that will appear a few weeks later in the *NME* in their Big Mouth Strikes Again quotes of the week section.

I ask them about a plan they had told me weeks before the tour: that all the dancers would have to appear naked at one stage. Apparently it was put in the contracts but they had forgotten about it. They tell me that Danny Cummings was ordered to lose two stone (and more or less has). Neil says that during last night's show he noticed two boys at the front staring towards his midriff during 'Later Tonight'. His flies were undone. 'I thought, how do you cope with *this* in front of 7,000 people?' He moved his hand over for the rest of the song, then at the end adjusted the velcro in the darkness.

They talk about Andrew Bull. Ivan and the tour accountant Mike have given him so much grief over the Levi's gaff that he has agreed to cover another 10,000 Hong Kong dollars of their expenses. Then they talk about earthquakes (they're scared of them) and censorship. Someone phones the room to tell them they're on TV and we tune in just in time to see a snippet of the 'What Have I Done To Deserve This?' video. It has subtitles.

'. . . In This World, That We Live . . .' it reads.

'Uhghhh,' moans Neil tetchily. 'Let's get the words right, shall we?'

It finishes and they return to the theme of how boring it is to repeat oneself. 'Perhaps we should have three shows,' suggests Neil, 'that we run in repertoire, like *Richard II*, *Edward II* and *Richard III*. Opera companies do that as well.' They have a keen sense of how differently they do things and, in interviews, a keen sense of advertising it. We discuss Neil's dressing-gown in 'Left To My Own Devices': 'I wonder whether anyone else has ever written a song with the word "dressing-gown".' One immediately pops into his mind, the Beatles' 'She's Leaving Home': '"Father snores as his wife gets into her dressing-gown,"' he quotes. 'It sounds a very Pet Shop Boys word somehow.'

They reminisce about the press conference and Chris's 'We're not a live band really' showstopper.

'I was in a bit of a droll, sarky kind of a frame of mind,' he explains.

'I thought you were doing a brilliant impersonation of a pop star at a press conference,' congratulates Neil. 'It was real John Lennon stuff.'

Neil says that last night he nearly dedicated 'It's Alright' to the Chinese students. Chris stopped him. 'I said to Chris before we went back on and he said, "What you've always said about pop stars is that they don't know any more about it than anybody else – probably less." So I didn't, and he was right. It's cheap. You're just playing to the crowd, aren't you? What you're saying is, "Aren't I a wonderful person . . .?" It's what so many flamin' pop groups do and it kind of nauseates me, so I didn't do it.'

Each time the show comes up they are quick to be excited about any aspect of it – the lighting, the dancers, the film – any aspect apart from their own role in it. It's not modesty in any simple sense – in a simple sense they're not modest – more that they seem to imagine the idea of them on-stage as something of an embarrassment.

They discuss their favourite moments: 'King's Cross', the film for 'Domino Dancing'.

'That's brilliant,' says Neil, 'because it's all quite serious and not just a lot of jolly fun.'

This seems to be a fear: that anyone might see the show as nothing more than 'jolly fun'. 'I don't like the idea of mindless entertainment,' says Neil forcefully.

Eventually I tease a little unqualified enthusiasm out of them.

'Not only have we done a show,' says Neil, 'which sounds good and everything but also it's one of the most spectacular shows, I think, that's ever been done in terms of pop music.' It's this phrase – edited to 'one of the most spectacular shows in pop music ever' – that *Smash Hits* use as the headline to my piece. Afterwards I discover that it was their second attempt. The first headline, born of their amazement at seeing the on-stage photos, was 'Flamin' Nora, Take A Look At Those Threads!'

The photos for the *Smash Hits* cover were taken in the foyer of the Brixton Academy, in rehearsal before they left England. Neil is in his 'Domino Dancing' shirt, Chris in a yellow hooded top and dark glasses. They both look cheerful. Usually – as a rule – *Smash Hits* insists on commissioning all its own photos, but in this case the Pet Shop Boys chose the photographer, Paul Rider, and EMI paid for the photos and supplied them. There has been a long history of *Smash Hits* rejecting Pet Shop Boys photos as uncommercial; this time *Smash Hits* were pleased.

Neil: The first photo-session we ever did as the Pet Shop Boys was with Eric (*Watson*) before we went to New York to see Bobby O. It was on the first 'West End Girls' cover. We had the idea of it just being our eyes.

Chris: Eric bought us white t-shirts and we ripped them.

Neil: Then for the second photo-session we both wore Nike tops – they were the first thing we bought in New York when we went to record and at the time were totally 'black'. You couldn't buy them in England. We wanted to look New York. My hair was swept back and Chris had a perm, because he wanted to look like Bobby O. I suppose we were both image conscious in a way.

Chris: Now it's basically the same – we just take along the clothes we like to a photo-session.

Most people would assume that you're more calculating than that about how you look.

Neil: What do they think?

I think there's an idea that you've taken scrupulous care both in putting together each new image and in how each image has been projected.

Neil: They're very rarely thought out to the degree you're suggesting there: that we have a specific idea and buy the clothes to get it together. People always think we're more clever after the event.

Yes, but people always want to believe that pop stars are incredibly sophisticated and conniving, don't they?

Neil: What you do – and I'm sure any group that thinks about how it presents itself; though to be quite honest I don't think that there are many who do – is make use of what you've got. We'll decide something each to wear beforehand but we don't necessarily think about whether it's going to work together, because we think it will work together somehow anyway.

Chris: Most pop photographs – not so much now but they were – are of the band looking happy and jolly, like a snapshot. We always wanted to be different from them. We did some pictures where we specifically wanted to . . .

Neil: . . . look horrible.

Chris: . . . so you can see our skins. Most pop groups they try and look really nice.

Neil: Also, most groups try to look like all other groups. Their idea of what they should look like is other photographs of such-and-such. Whereas what we were trying to do – and a lot of this is down to Eric – is to not look glamorous. At the beginning the person who had an influence on the way we looked – or the way I looked – is Eric. Eric thought of the long coat. He was the only person with whom we used to have a meaningful discussion about our image and we all agreed that we didn't want to look 'cosmetic', to use Eric's word. Eric was bored of taking cosmetic pictures for *Smash Hits* and I was bored with looking at them. We wanted to look different. We wanted to stand out from pop stars like Duran Duran and Culture Club. We didn't want to look pretty. We wanted to look a bit . . . spooky.

Weren't you worried that you'd just look boring?

Neil: No, not really. We've never considered ourselves to be boring.

Chris: I don't think the pictures are boring. They have a lot to them.

Neil: We had the idea they should look like stills from films: 'something just happened' or 'something is about to happen'. Some of the early ones were unbelievably pretentious. Having said that, then the photo that was used most, the one outside the studio where we both look unbelievably good-looking due to some freak of the light because it's from a distance and there's no skin detail, was a cosmetic picture.

Chris: But it was taken outdoors. It was just the way the light happened to be.

When did you realize that the Pet Shop Boys had an image?

Neil: Quite early on, because the thing people always said to us was 'Why don't you smile?' They still say that to us. In actual fact we'd totally refuse to smile in pictures in those days, totally refuse.

Chris: A smile in a photograph is a false thing. Why would you smile during a photograph, which is a terribly boring and tedious situation?

Neil (to Chris): Because the photographer says something to you.

Chris: But that would be false . . . contrived.

But there will always be some smiling shots in a photo-session. The point surely is that you'd never approve them, that you'd censor them. So it isn't really just the logic of the situation, it isn't just being very uncontrived. You have to make a conscious decision to veto them.

Chris: It goes back to what we were saying about stills from a film. If you're smiling it changes the whole story.

So you are trying to present a particular attitude, a particular story that includes 'how the Pet Shop Boys are'?

Neil: Yes, and there's also the attitude 'we are not begging for anything'. We are not pleading for you to like us. We weren't saying, 'Come on! Buy us! Aren't we just too adorable for words?', like most groups do. They want to look cute. One of the reasons we like the cover of 'Please' was that the photo was so small you could hardly see us, and when you did we were staring out looking a bit spooky again.

And was it also that you would have found it too embarrassing to pose for shameless pop pictures?

Neil: We've always had that, although recently we've given in in a way that doesn't altogether make me happy. For instance the *Smash Hits* cover doesn't make me happy. What annoys me is that over the last two or three years the jolliness of pop music has taken over, overpoweringly, so that you can't really do anything, in *Smash Hits* terms, that you could have done. Five years ago you could have presented something as being weird. Think of the Depeche Mode cover where three of them are out of focus, and in the foreground, with a kind of red filter over it, is Martin Gore wearing a dress. It was very exciting at the time; the first time Depeche Mode were openly 'pervy' in the teen market. Compare that with the Pet Shop Boys advertising their tour, sitting on a box smiling in an 'aren't we pleased with ourselves?' way (*a description of the* Smash Hits *cover in question*).

So what do you think that says about pop music?

Neil: I think the idea of having any content or influence or subversion – I always think 'subversion' basically means 'titillation' in pop music, but anyway – of turning things upside down, of 'it means more than it seems to mean' . . . all of that has left pop music in the main. In terms of chart music it has become totally careerist. So, if you ask a pop group now, 'What would you do to become famous?' and they say, 'Absolutely anything'. To them the idea is to become famous. We never set out to be famous. When I was seventeen years old I wanted to be famous, but when I was thirty-one . . .

Do you make compromises now, like the Smash Hits *cover, because you know it works and because, though you might not have wanted to become famous, you now want to stay famous?*

Neil (sidestepping the question): There's always been the notion that people get too bored with you if you're too available.

But you've given in often.

Neil: Yes, we have given in and I'll tell you why we've given in: exhaustion. Exhaustion over fighting battles. (*To Chris*) Do you agree?

Chris: Yeah. It takes a lot of effort to get what we want. *Smash Hits* reject pictures, *The Face* reject pictures. (*The tour logo, a black and white photo of Neil and Chris representing Batman and Robin, is a rejected cover of* The Face.) For that specific cover of *Smash Hits* we had a whole tour to put together so to start faffing around with a photo-session . . . that was done in a brief fifteen minutes taken out of rehearsal time.

Neil: Ever since the first time we were on the cover of *Smash Hits*, we've had problems. (*For their first cover Eric Watson took a photo of them in hooded Paninaro-style jackets coming out of complete blackness; it was rejected.*) Steve Bush (Smash Hits *editor, 1985–7*) used to be criticized because he'd never use a photograph of anyone smiling on the cover of *Smash Hits*. For three years no one smiled; he used to like gloomy covers and I thought he was right, because he had a rather aspirational idea of the cover, that it should be slightly pretentious. Also he'd identified that that had been what the audiences in the New Romantic era had wanted, something rather aspirational. The Pet Shop Boys are almost the only pop group that operate in an aspirational way now. We're sort of saying, 'There could be more . . . there could be more than just selling entertainment.' If you look at all the big groups now: Bros are selling entertainment, Kylie Minogue is selling entertainment, obviously Stock Aitken Waterman are selling entertainment. They're saying, 'Let's face it – there's nothing more to it than that.'

Tonight's food, Mr Bull's treat, is Vietnamese. Courses come and go – there are about ten. Neil asks for some white wine. He is brought two to choose from and it is plain from his face that he is less than impressed by the selection. 'I'll have the one with the cat on it,' he decides.

Chris suggests a novel solution to the Hong Kong refugee problem: they could be moved to Liverpool. 'The architecture is right,' he proclaims. That was where he was a student and starts off a chain of reminiscences: how he used to watch *Dallas* with his friends in their lodgings, drinking cans of Skol lager and eating Yorkie bars; how he went to see second-rate punk band the Vibrators and, drunk, spat at them, 'because everyone else did'; about his year's practical experience working at Michael Aukett Associates in London, where he helped build a staircase in Milton Keynes; how for the last three months of that year he was so bored by the working life that he'd sleep on his drawing board all day and party at the Camden Palace all night. 'I was quite pleased when the Pet Shop Boys became successful,' he says.

The final course – a half-pineapple stuffed with rice, doused in a colourless spirit and then set alight – is served and a little is eaten by the few diners who have the endurance. Neil leans back and laughs contentedly. He has had some of every course and has only been put into the shadows by Dominic. Dominic, though slender, is already famous on tour for his appetite. Tonight he has had seconds of many of the courses while waiting impatiently for the next. 'Well,' says Neil, 'on behalf of myself and Dominic I'd like to say . . . is that *all*?' Everyone laughs. A few minutes later he is clutching his stomach and cheerfully confessing, 'I'll probably be sick in a moment, but that's rock'n'roll.'

In fact he does feel ill throughout the night. At one point he wakes up and thinks he is hallucinating. He panics a little. He is in a strange hotel room and – unless he is going mad – there is a sinister, low-pitched rumbling noise above his head. Confused, he eventually drifts back into a troubled sleep. It is only in the morning he discovers that Ivan, who has the room directly above his, has been enjoying a late-night jacuzzi.

Chapter Five

After the meal we are expected at Andrew Bull's club, Canton's, for a party in our honour.

'We might not get in if we're lucky,' says Chris hopefully.

Just as we are about to leave the restaurant Steve Beaver walks over. He announces, apropos of nothing, that two weeks ago he met Bobby O.

Ears perk up. Though they have had years of expensive legal wrangles with him, Neil and Chris still have a sneaking admiration for Bobby O, and also a bewildered fascination about what has happened to him. When they worked with him he was a quite well-known, almost respected, cult disco producer, a fanatic businessman and a fitness maniac. Since then he has made a few decent records, has found God and has written a book refuting Darwinian evolution. To this day he still phones them up occasionally – the last call, a few months ago, was to tell Neil that their latest LP, 'Introspective', wasn't much good. He suggested that the two of them play him all the songs for their LP before they recorded them.

They met in 1983. Neil, working at *Smash Hits*, was asked to go to New York to see the Police play live and to interview Sting. He decided that he'd see Bobby O as well, so he tracked down his phone number and arranged to take him out to lunch. (In the end Bobby O insisted on paying.) At lunch, over a cheeseburger and piece of carrot cake at a place called the Applejack, Neil chatted and told Bobby O how much he admired his records. The plan, hatched before the trip, was to ask Bobby O to make a record with them, but, Neil said later, 'We thought I wouldn't dare.' In his pocket, just in case, was a tape of three songs they'd demoed – 'Opportunities', 'It's A Sin' and 'It's Not A Crime'. Eventually Neil said, 'Have you ever worked with any English groups?' and Bobby O replied, 'No, no one's ever asked me' and Neil said, 'Oh, well I'm in a group; there's just two of us actually' and Bobby O famously exclaimed, 'We'll make a record! It'll be fabulous!'

Neil pointed out that Bobby O hadn't heard any of their music, so they went back to Bobby O's office and listened to 'Opportunities' on Bobby O's ghetto blaster. 'He said "I could do this!",' Neil later joked, 'and I thought, "Well, you should be able to, because it's completely ripped off from you."'

Neil: Everyone we knew, literally *everyone*, knew that we were obsessed with Bobby O's records, so when I came back to the *Smash Hits* office and said 'We're making a record with Bobby O' there was a general celebration. Everyone at *Smash Hits* had been listening to Bobby O all day long; he'd had two Singles of the Fortnight.

Chris: He was releasing so many brilliant records. Weekly there'd be more.

Neil: In those days imports cost five pounds but I used to claim for them on my expenses at *Smash Hits*. Anyway when we came back from recording with Bobby O everyone at *Smash Hits* had to stand round and listen and comment. The track everyone liked best was 'Pet Shop Boys' because it was weird. Dave Hepworth (*the editor at the time*) heard 'Opportunities' and said, 'This could be a hit.' I didn't play them 'West End Girls' because I was too embarrassed.

It must have crossed your mind at this point that this might be serious.

Neil: Yes it did, but Chris still had another year to go at university and at this point we were never thinking in terms of Top of the Pops, we were thinking of being an incredibly hip, underground dance group. All we wanted was to make a record with Bobby O that you could buy on import at the Record

Shack. That to us just seemed phenomenal. Fundamentally we wanted to be part of The Bobby O Story. That was our big aim.

Chris: It was so exciting, music, then.

Neil: There were all these incredibly thrilling records . . . Arthur Baker . . . Afrika Bambaataa . . . the Freez record 'IOU' . . . 'Blue Monday' and 'Confusion' by New Order . . . Sharon Redd's 'Never Gonna Give You Up' . . .

Chris: It was new as well. When something new comes along you can just forget about anything else because it's old and *this* is completely new. Completely fresh.

Neil: In fact we felt we were rather lagging behind. We actually thought we'd missed the boat, particularly when 'Blue Monday' came out.

After much delay 'West End Girls' was actually first released not in America but in Britain on Epic records after Eric Watson had played it to CBS A&R man Gordon Charlton at a Fiction Factory photo-session. The *NME*'s Charles Shaar Murray reviewed it as 'a blend of glamour and excitement that is almost perfect' and David Jensen played it on Radio One seven times in a fortnight. It reached number 121.

Neil: The problem with Bobby O wasn't the contract, it was just that it was an unworkable relationship. We were getting very frustrated. When we first recorded with him it was in a twenty-four-track studio, then suddenly we were recording in his office on an eight-track. We seemed to be going backwards.

Was he just being eccentric?

Neil (nods): Also he was saving money. We began to doubt whether Bobby O had any faith in us.

Chris: Also the records he was making himself ceased to be as good.

Neil: Everyone thought we should give him up. We never

received any money from him. We never got a single penny for the original version of 'West End Girls', which has supposedly sold a million copies now. Actually when we settled we gave him all those earnings – which we weren't very happy about – and a royalty on our first three EMI albums. That was when we thought of putting a ceiling of a million dollars on what we would pay him, never dreaming that we would be successful and that he would actually earn that. But, to be honest, I've always felt that Bobby O kind of deserved the million he got. He took an amazing chance, because of the character he was, on us. Most people wouldn't have done anything.

Our idea for breaking with him was that I'd phone him up and say, 'It's not happening – we should split. How shall we go about it?' but we were persuaded that the thing to do was to send Bobby O a letter saying that the contract hadn't gone before a court, and all that rubbish.

Anyway, after it was sorted out, when we were in New York mixing 'Opportunities', we went to see him. His partner couldn't believe we were in an office having spent a year in a legal battle with him. We were sitting around laughing about our lawyers. He gave us a piece of advice: 'Whenever you're in a lawsuit with someone, behave like an animal – that's the only way you'll win.' And actually that's quite a sensible piece of advice, though it sounds a bit horrible.

Chris: Didn't he say it was like finishing with a girlfriend?

Neil: Oh, he went into a *major* speech: 'The Pet Shop Boys aren't like a friend, it's like you're my girlfriend, that's how much I care about you.' It was very sad. He was very, very hurt.

Steve Beaver tells them that Bobby O has changed some more. The man who was famous for his dedication to physical perfection now weighs 300 pounds and says he wants ten children. He is recording an LP of versions of 'West End Girls' with trumpet player Tom Browne. Neil and Chris exchange looks that can only mean 'Oh dear . . .'

We all troop off to Mr Bull's club, Canton's, but don't stay long.

Sunday, *2 July*

Panic. We have known for the last few days that Geoffrey Howe, the British foreign secretary, is arriving today. Now a demonstration of around 200,000 people is expected to 'greet' him at the airport. Last night this had seemed funny – Neil and Chris had been considering staging photos with the crowds behind them so that it looked like a spontaneous outbreak of Pet Shop Boys mania – but now it is a problem. People tell Ivan that the airport will be inaccessible and most of the tour party are booked on an afternoon flight. Ivan investigates whether everyone can be smuggled through the freight terminal, but even that is impossible. He considers getting everyone to the airport before the demonstration, but they'd have to wait for hours. Luggage goes up and down the lifts. Eventually he tracks down a Pet Shop Boys fan in the airline and mysteriously thirty previously booked seats become available on the following day's flight.

Nevertheless some of us are already booked on an earlier flight today, beating the crowds. This advance party is of those who don't have working visas for Japan – the Japanese promoter Mr Udo had advised that if we are caught entering the country it might jeopardize the band's entry. So we carry out a dumb charade, unlabelling our baggage and standing in different queues in Japanese immigration, pretending not to know each other.

Monday, *3 July*

A while after the others arrive at the Tokyo hotel, Neil calls me to his room to discuss the book once more. There is still no agreement about what I'm actually doing on the tour. He is wearing a kimono. He says he is a little annoyed. Tom Watkins, their manager, has just arrived, popped in and immediately asked Neil why he needs a piano in his room.

'I don't think he thinks I can play it,' huffs Neil.

Chris arrives.

'We don't want to concentrate too much on the story – the "how they became famous" story,' insists Neil, 'because, like most stories, it's not very interesting.'

It is quite interesting, I say, but not really what this book is about.

'What *is* this book about?' asks Chris.

Silence.

'It'd be good if you could just pick what it was that we're about,' he continues, 'then look at everything in terms of that. Like, supposing we were the Deconstructionists of Pop. You could then apply that theory to whatever we've done.'

But, I object, are they really just any one thing, like the Deconstructionists of Pop?

'No,' he admits glumly. He sighs. 'We're *nothing*.'

This – 'we're nothing' – is a notion that Neil keenly jumps upon. 'You could apply *that* to the whole. We're *nothing*, so we have *something* around us.'

They laugh.

'It's the same with everything we do,' exclaims Chris, as if we've really hit on something here. 'We're not there!'

'Whatever we do,' Neil chortles, 'we're not normally the main part of it.' He considers. 'In a sense we've stood against everything in pop or rock music that anyone else likes, haven't we? We started this tour by saying, "All rock shows are boring." That is a sort of theme to what we do.'

It was the theme of their film, doing nothing while things happened around you, I remind them.

'Yes,' Neil agrees, changing the point, 'though actually by doing a film we fell into a rock cliché.'

Yes, I nod, but you can't oppose everything at once. You have to do a lot of things the same to form the background against which the things you do differently show up. Of course you do normal things: make records, go on tour etc., etc. Those are all rock clichés. It would be nonsense to try to avoid that. But you have an *attitude* based on an impulse to invert or oppose whatever you can within that. Anyway your most obvious driving force – in opposition to everything you're both saying – is simply that you both obsessively love pop music.

No one quite knows where this leaves us.

'It should be like that Derek Jarman book,' says Chris. He means *The Last of England*. 'It's about the film but it's also his autobiography at the same time,' he declares. Then he turns to Neil. 'Is that right? Is it like that? I've never actually read it.'

'It's a kind of a rant, as well, that book,' answers Neil.

'Oh,' says Chris, 'a *rant*! That'd be good.'

'It's not a bad title actually,' considers Neil, '*A Rant.*' He rethinks. 'It's a bit Paul Morley actually.'

What about the other problem? I ask them. The book is from my perspective but it is their tale.

'It's got to be your perspective,' confirms Neil.

So, I say, if I say something that you fundamentally and totally disagree with, you won't try to take it out?

'Well . . .' says Neil, laughing.

'Of *course* we will,' guffaws Chris.

We are joined by Tom Watkins. Tom Watkins likes to describe

himself as a 'rich fat bastard – and incredibly lucky'. Today he is wearing a peaked leather cap.

'Tom!' exclaims Chris. 'I need a hat like that.'

'That hat!' says Neil. 'It's in the show!'

'Call it $100 a performance, shall we?' smiles Tom.

Earlier Tom has given Neil and Chris expensive watches to celebrate 'five Massive years', the five years that they will have been together in October. (It was the choice of this that Pete's charade in Hong Kong was about.) Their management contract is for five years and at present has not been renewed.

'There's no instructions in it,' Chris now complains of his watch. 'How do you do it?'

'Don't ask me, love,' says Tom. 'I can't even plug my hair rollers in.'

As Neil chats to Tom, Chris and I talk some more about the book. I try to explain the structure I have in mind.

'You know, my favourite books are things like *In Cold Blood*,' he says, 'where a chapter is two pages long. It's just so easy to read. My least favourite books are where there's big chunks of type and there's nowhere to stop before you go to bed. I'm reading Joe Orton's diaries at the moment. I just like all the conversation and quotes from people like Kenneth Williams and Kenneth Halliwell and people on the bus. Those are the interesting bits. When he's going on about his script for *Up Against It* . . .' Chris rolls his eyes to indicate the tedium of it all.

All that is going to be said now has been said. Our decision has been to decide nothing. Instead we go to dinner.

Can you remember the actual conversation that led you to the name Pet Shop Boys?

Neil: It was actually, as everyone knows, when Chris used to stay in this flat in Ealing. It was just before we went over to do the record with Bobby O. He used to know three boys who worked in a pet shop and we used to tell them – in fact I remember telling them as we were driving in a car through Ealing – that they should start a group. One of them was musical; he used to have this enormous Wurlitzer.

So you merely suggested that they should start a group because you thought that everybody should?

Neil: They already had a group but they didn't have a name.

Chris: And we said you should do 'How Much Is That Doggie In The Window' and call yourselves the Pet Shop Boys.

Neil: We thought it was funny because it sounded like an American hip hop group like, say, the Peech Boys.

Chris: Before we went to America we spent quite a lot of time trying to think of a name. We used to do it over dinner for ages.

Neil: We were always slightly embarrassed by the name, because we thought it sounded a bit twee and camp.

Chris: I couldn't tell anyone what the group was called.

Neil: Chris was always embarrassed by the name. Not because of hamsters.

Chris: Just because it sounded so stupid.

Neil: It was just silly, more than anything else.

On the way to dinner Ivan tells me about his previous visits here, driving round Tokyo with Bros. Last time Matt put his head out of the window wearing a Michael Jackson mask and sang along to a tape of Michael Jackson songs. The Japanese were hoodwinked. 'People were walking into walls.'

In the restaurant we perch on stools at a counter surrounding a raised platform just below the height of the counter, where cooks prepare the food before passing it to us on large wooden paddles. Huge prawns are grilled on their backs. With alarm we realize that they are moving, their legs frantically paddling the air as they cook to death. We are disgusted but eat them anyway.

In Japan everything is unbelievably expensive. The cheapest thing available on our hotel room service is a toasted ham-and-cheese sandwich, yours for £8. Tonight's meal, it is later muttered, cost about £100 a head. There are about ten of us.

As we eat, Chris canvasses opinion about whether he should bleach his hair. 'You have to be blond once in your life,' he explains earnestly.

Somebody suggests that it might make him look like Jimmy Somerville. This goes down badly.

Neil reminisces about his own blond period when he was at college in London. 'In 1973 everyone was blond in Tottenham,' he says. When he went back to Newcastle for the holidays he dyed it back brown, expecting his parents not to notice, but of course they did. 'We used to buy women's shoes,' he recalls, 'because you couldn't get good men's platform shoes. They were always two sizes too small though.'

We wander out into the night. It is impossible to get taxis here in the late evening and so we have to trudge the two or so miles back to the hotel.

'*Typical*,' huffs Chris. 'I bet this doesn't happen to Bros . . .'

In the hotel bar (beer £4.50) we carry on drinking. Kaz, who is from Virgin 10 Publishing, the music publishers who administer the Pet Shop Boys songs, asks them if they'd like to meet Ryuichi Sakamoto. As founder of the Yellow Magic Orchestra, actor (most famously in *Merry Christmas Mr Lawrence*), collaborator with David Sylvian and a solo composer, he is one of Japan's most famous artists. He has expressed a desire to meet Neil and Chris.

'Oh gawd,' says Neil. They don't much like things like this.

Chris shakes his head. They discuss whether they *like* Ryuichi Sakamoto.

'What has he done?' asks Chris.

'He did "Forbidden Colours",' says Neil. This was a single with David Sylvian some years ago, a beautiful song.

'That was brilliant,' Chris agrees.

They decide that he may come and meet them back-stage if he likes.

'I can tell him how much I like "Forbidden Colours",' says Chris.

I ask whether simply saying this would be very tactful. How does he feel, four years on, if people saunter up and – ignoring anything he's done since – say they like 'West End Girls'?

Chris shrugs. 'I went up to the Bee Gees and said, "I love 'Saturday Night Fever'".'

We are interrupted by the lighting designer, Patrick, who does a fantastic spiel as one of the rock'n'roll aristocracy. He chats in a warm, fatherly way about how the Pet Shop Boys might do a stadium show as he recently did in Brazil with Tina Turner – 'Tina' – his tone suggesting that he, Patrick, can make their passage into the world of rock'n'roll grown-ups a smooth one. The Pet Shop Boys are but juniors – albeit accomplished ones – in his world.

Patrick tells us how a large trunk accompanies 'Mick' wherever he goes. In it are the learned tomes a gentleman might need to have with him. 'Indonesian poetry and things,' says Patrick, as if for him, too, life without the greatest muses of the South Pacific at hand is unbearably barren.

Chris and I discuss the book a little more but it is too late and we are too tired.

'Couldn't it be a fictional thing?' he asks forlornly – a desperate stab, this – 'about two people who *might* be the Pet Shop Boys?'

A story has shadowed you about the meaning of your name. Often people suggest that it's 'something to do with hamsters'; the full rumour is that 'Pet Shop Boys' are gay American men who derive pleasure from putting doctored hamsters up their bottoms. When were you first aware of this story?

Neil: That wasn't until 'West End Girls' came out. I remember sitting in Epic records doing an interview with Betty Page (*a music journalist*) on the telephone and she said, 'Well, we *all* know what the name means.' I said, 'Well? what *does* it mean?' She told me and I was absolutely *horrified*. We discussed changing the name but then we thought, 'Oh well . . .'

So is it a documented term?

Neil: I don't believe that it is. I've asked people in New York who might know and they've never heard of it. I personally think it's a completely apocryphal story. I once met Fiona Russell Powell (*another journalist, also briefly in ABC*) and she told me she knew about it. I actually just don't believe it, to be honest. But, I mean, it's there, it's part of our history and we've learned to live with it. When 'West End Girls' was a hit Simon Bates was going to tell the story out on Radio One. We were in Italy at the time so Tom phoned him up and asked him not to.

Chris: He announced, 'I've got some really big news about the Pet Shop Boys, so tune in tomorrow,' then when you listened in the next day he did give a story and it was something really trivial that Tom had given him.

But it keeps coming up, doesn't it? If you remember, Stephen Fry introduced you at Before the Act (in June 1988) by saying that he'd just been told what the next group's name meant and that he was flabbergasted.

Neil: Yes, it's endlessly referred to, *endlessly* referred to.

I suppose people think you've been very clever.

Neil: This is a classic Pet Shop Boys situation. People assume that 'it's an incredibly clever in-joke that Tennant and Lowe thought of'. In fact 'Tennant and Lowe' didn't think the name was the remotest bit clever. We just thought, as we've said a million times before, that it sounded a bit like a hip hop group.

Chapter Six

Tuesday, *4 July*

The next day Janet Street-Porter arrives. She is either the most hated woman in broadcasting or the visionary who has revolutionized British youth television, depending upon whom you speak to. She is here on business as the BBC's Head of Youth Programmes, to investigate the possibility of making a TV show later in the year with the Pet Shop Boys. But she is also very good friends with both Tom Watkins and the Pet Shop Boys. One reason they like her is her tremendous, almost preposterous enthusiasm: 'Nothing is ever boring when Janet's around.' And here she comes, up the back stairs of the Tokyo Budokan, spotting Tom Watkins at the top . . .

'Where have you *been*? I've phoned your room thirty-five times. I had to go shopping on my own.'

'How did it go?'

'I've spent £100.'

It is impossible to tell whether this is good or bad, too much or not enough.

The first Japanese show is quietly triumphant. Back-stage Janet raves.

'I *love* the lights! I could *tell* it was done by someone who'd never done a rock show.'

Patrick, they tell her – he of last night's tales of 'Mick' and 'Tina' – does little else but rock shows and is soon off to do the Rolling Stones.

She barely pauses for a second: who cares?

Stevie Hayes, the person from EMI in Britain who has accompanied Janet over here, comes in and explains that he also has with him people from children's Saturday morning TV show *Motormouth*. They are over in Japan, he explains, filming Jason Donovan. It is this final piece of information that is jumped upon with interest.

'Jason Donovan?' Neil exclaims. 'Is he coming to see us?'

Chris chats amiably to two blokes with flat-top haircuts. Stevie Hayes walks over and belatedly introduces them as the presenters from *Motormouth*.

'*This* is *Motormouth*?' says Chris, feigning alarm. He has accidentally been friendly to the media.

'I thought they looked familiar,' says Neil. 'Dainton – throw them out.'

They look alarmed but it's a joke. Janet puts herself centre-stage again with an entertaining account of Bobby Brown's London concerts. 'Disappointing,' she judges, once she has taken us through every piece of trouser-dropping innuendo in his repertoire. She dismisses the after-show party as 'so exclusive that no one was there at all'.

Rob interrupts to ask Neil and Chris whether they will go next door and say hello to some important folk from EMI Japan.

'No,' says Chris.

'They can come in here,' says Neil diplomatically.

'One at a time,' stipulates Chris. 'And they can say "hello".'

And that, more or less, is what happens.

Now Chris, as he often does, begins to enjoy complaining. In Japan gifts are customary, but as yet they have been given nothing by the promoter. 'Where are our presents from Mr Udo?' he inquires of no one in particular. He moves on to the situation of his on-stage lighting. Back in London he had complained whenever lights were put on him to show him doing nothing but playing the keyboard. Now he is furious at frequently being left in darkness. 'Why,' he sulks, 'are there two lights on Neil and none on me?'

The *Motormouth* people explain they must be up early tomorrow to surf with Jason Donovan, and leave. Once they're out of earshot Chris explains that he's met one of them, Tony, before in a club. Tony had come up to Chris and asked when the Pet Shop Boys would do an interview on *Motormouth*. Chris had – out of genuine ignorance – simply said 'Who are you?' and then the friend Chris had been talking to had a go at Tony for his lack of manners and he had slunk off. Tonight Chris had apparently alluded to this previous meeting and Tony had sheepishly muttered, 'I was pissed.'

'I want to go surfing with Jason Donovan,' announces Neil. 'Just think. Tomorrow Jason will probably be *in this room*.' Stevie Hayes has told us Jason plans to come to tomorrow night's show.

Pete makes Chris some hot buttered toast. He happily munches it with a glass of the champagne they drink after each concert in his other hand. This post-show toast and champagne will from now on become a routine.

'Can we go and eat?' asks Chris.

'I want to go back to the hotel and shower first,' insists Neil.

Chris starts complaining about this.

'That can be a chapter in the book!' Neil suddenly exclaims. 'A chapter of Chris's complaints.'

A few seconds later Chris asks Pete, 'Where's my second slice of toast?'

'Write it down! Complaint!' shouts Neil.

Neil and Chris had been quite looking forward to signing a few autographs but we have lingered in the dressing-room far too long and the over-efficient Japanese stewards have cleared all the fans away. As we coast down the long park driveway in the minibus provided by Mr Udo a few straggling girls spot us and we draw up at a junction so that Neil and Chris can sign through a window. As we sit there more and more fans gather until Neil decides the situation is getting out of hand.

'We'll go now,' he says to the driver.

Nothing happens.

'Off! Off!' he shouts in his best 'are you deaf, you silly man?' voice.

Nothing happens. Nothing happens not because the driver is deaf, nor because he is stupid, but because the traffic light in front of us is on red. Neil looks a little embarrassed.

'That's another chapter,' he sighs. 'Me being bossy.'

There are three great themes that recur when people write about you, particularly when they're being complimentary. The first is irony.

Neil (scoffing at the idea of this): Yes. I'm supposed to be the irony merchant . . . my ironic detachment . . .

The whole of what the Pet Shop Boys do is often presented as an exercise in irony, isn't it?

Neil (wearily): Yes. Of course elements of it have been – 'Opportunities' . . . 'Shopping' . . .

But those are simply ironic songs that you've done, which is very different from suggesting that the whole point of the Pet Shop Boys is to be ironic. The picture that is often painted is that the Pet Shop Boys pastiche and in some sense criticize pop music from the inside by being pop music's resident full-time ironists.

Neil: Yes. And there's not a lot of truth in that. Someone once said about us that we made 'pop records about pop records'. I don't think we do and, in fact, I don't really like that kind of thing. Most of what we do is meant totally sincerely. When we started out we got into hi-energy and hip hop music and we liked the power and the rawness and the excitement of it, like a natural force. And we've always tried to make records, in the main, that had the same delirium and excitement, or a very strong feeling about them. Chris really likes 'up' records, more than I do, but my voice cannot sound 'up' when I sing. I literally cannot do it.

Hence your famous 'deadpan vocal style'?

Neil: Yes. (*Laughs.*)

And would it be right to presume that you'd actually prefer people to think not only that you're not as a rule ironic but, on the contrary, you're more serious and more sincere than most pop musicians?

Neil: Yes, I think we are. There are loads of people who do things because they're cynical and I don't think we do those things. People always tend to assume that if a thing's done in such an over-the-top way – like 'It's A Sin', for instance – it's meant to be funny, and of course we just *like* over-the-top things; they're not normally funny at all.

Also we normally do things that we think the people we don't like wouldn't like. Hence '. . . Let's Make Lots Of Money' – that was the entire motivation behind that really. And sometimes the inspiration behind a song is something funny, though often the song itself isn't remotely funny. Like 'I Want A Dog' – I thought 'what a funny title for a song', but the song itself is meant to be rather touching and true. When I was at *Smash Hits* the one everyone liked like that was one called 'I've Got Plans Involving You'. So we try to be funny sometimes, but I think of 90 per cent of our songs as being totally romantic. I love lush romanticism and I think Chris likes it sometimes too.

As we travel back to the hotel they discuss what they'd like from Mr Udo.

'I haven't decided yet,' says Neil.

'I want a Walkman,' says Chris.

Neil looks at Chris as if he's gone off his trolley. 'You can get a Walkman from *anyone*,' he points out.

'Oh.' Chris reconsiders. 'A Mitsubishi jeep then.'

'I want a Mitsubishi jeep,' agrees Neil, 'and I can't even drive. I'll give it to my mum.'

They reflect on our visit from *Motormouth*. I mention that I have read an interview with Tony Gregory in which he repeatedly mentioned how much he liked the Pet Shop Boys.

'Oh, I wish you'd told me that before,' says Neil. He considers how he behaved. 'Actually,' he concludes with relief, 'I was quite nauseatingly nice.'

Then he returns to a theme that is becoming increasingly familiar. 'Jason Donovan is coming! This time tomorrow he will be *in this bus*.'

'This bus' is actually little to be proud of. Plainly it is used to ferry all of Mr Udo's touring acts to the Budokan. It is covered in graffiti:

'Metallica walked all over you . . .'

'Europe invaded Japan.'

'I'm still alive! Dion.'

'Thank you Japan – Aerosmith.'

'Keep Satan warm.'

'Poison 8–6–89 Tokyo kicked ass.'

'Rock My World G N'R'

'Was (Not Was) 89.'

'Thanks for not dying.'

'Guns N'Roses rock the world. Thank you.'

'Thank God for the bomb. Ozzy.'

'We came, we saw, we couldn't play.'

'We should write a song called "Camp David",' says Neil for no obvious reason.

At the hotel a few fans are waiting. One, called Ekko, always follows them whenever they are in Japan. She is twenty-four and works for an important company whose over-intimate relationship with top politicians is in the process of bringing the Japanese government down. She was in England when 'West End Girls' was first a hit and when she heard the follow up, 'Love Comes Quickly', she says 'my heart broke' because she liked the song so much and she thought that the Pet Shop Boys were beautiful.

When they made their first promotional visit to Japan in June 1986 she scoured the passenger lists for incoming flights (apparently possible in Japan) until she spotted their names. She was the only fan to meet the plane. 'I thought they were pop stars but they just looked ordinary,' she explains, meaning it as a compliment. She also confesses that she was surprised to discover that Neil's hair was thinning, but immediately looks very embarrassed, as if she wishes she hadn't mentioned it.

When she later visited England she went round to Neil's flat – she claims, mysteriously, that 'a friend' knew the address – something she now says she regrets. In Japan you only get a few days' holiday a year and she is spending most of hers following them on this tour. It will cost her about £500, including hotel rooms for the days they are out of her home town, Tokyo. She hasn't told anyone at work the reason she has taken the time off. She says she especially likes the words, though she thinks they are 'difficult' and doubts that she has understood all the meanings. She thinks that Neil is 'kind and gentle' and that Chris is 'cute'.

'They are nice people but I know they are pop star,' she concludes with sad resignation. 'Between them and me, long distance.'

She is familiar to all those around the Pet Shop Boys. This afternoon Tom spotted her in the hotel foyer. 'That bleedin' Ekko,' he grunted.

'All the giant egos and tiny minds,' pronounces Janet, inspecting the bus graffiti on our way to dinner. She spots Jon Bon Jovi's name. 'I think he's bald and wears a wig,' she declares. 'It all makes sense. He's got no eyebrows and his dad's a hairdresser.'

Dainton tells her that they have met before. She burst past him into a fight involving some punks on the King's Road in 1976, gathering a story, he says, for the *News of the World*. She laughs.

We arrive at a shabu shabu restaurant, where the speciality is very thinly sliced raw beef that you cook yourself in boiling pots on the table. We are all fitted with kiddie-style peach aprons. Janet tells us unrepeatable media gossip and then talks business. Her proposal is for a TV show at Christmas in which famous folk sing Pet Shop Boys songs. They'd have the Pet Shop Boys' previous collaborators – Liza Minnelli, Dusty Springfield – and others. She suggests George Michael.

'Do you think he'd do it?' asks Neil, doubtfully.

'If you put it the right way,' says Janet. She doesn't explain what the right way might be.

Janet mentions, with theatrical shame, that her current project is a live broadcast of Pink Floyd from Venice.

'When I first met Chris,' says Neil, 'I went back to his flat and he had all these Pink Floyd cassettes. I was *shocked*.'

'I still like them,' protests Chris somewhat surprisingly. 'There were only two: "Dark Side Of The Moon" and "Wish You Were Here".'

'No,' corrects Neil. 'You had "The Wall". On *cassette*,' he adds, as if this somehow compounds the offence.

'Oh yes,' concedes Chris, 'but that's not very good.'

The second great theme that is often associated with the Pet Shop Boys is that of being camp.

Neil: Well, I don't think those people understand what camp is. People misuse the word totally. Being camp is us doing a film with Barbara Windsor – that's *totally* camp, there's no two ways about that. The video for 'Heart' is camp. The word 'camp' means 'overtly theatrical', doesn't it? People always go on about 'camp icons' – and Dusty Springfield and Liza Minnelli are, I suppose, camp icons (*Chris laughs at the 'I suppose'*) – but I don't think we use them in that way. If we did some huge finger-waving ballad with Dusty where she's in a glittery dress on-stage *that* would be camp.

Chris (*mischievously*): Like the video for 'What Have I Done To Deserve This?'? (*Laughs heartily*.)

Why have you been laughing throughout this conversation, Chris?

Chris: I just think it's funny, arguing that Liza Minnelli and Dusty Springfield *aren't* camp.

Neil: No, they are, they are camp. But I don't think we've used them in a camp way.

Anyway, generally you think the idea that the Pet Shop Boys are camp is inaccurate?

Neil: Part of my general theory about the Pet Shop Boys is that we're misunderstood in a rather embarrassing way. We do things and people think they're meant to be funny, or meant to be camp, or meant to be ironic, and they've always been meant to be *totally* serious, with one or two exceptions.

Chris (spluttering): One or *two* exceptions!!? (*He roars with laughter.*)

Neil (ignoring Chris): People see our entire career as an essay in irony and camp. And that, I suppose, is the one really genuinely camp thing about us; it is that, like genuine camp, it is meant *totally* sincerely. There hasn't been an element of irony or camp in 90 per cent of it. I suppose it's a bit sad from our point of view that it's interpreted as being camp, because it certainly wasn't meant to be.

Chris: But there aren't loads of letters in the fan mail saying, 'I thought that was brilliant – it's so camp!'

Neil: No, it's never the fans.

Chris: It's *critics.* (*He shrugs as if to add, 'Well, there you go, we don't have to worry about that then.'*)

Does that misinterpretation frustrate you?

Neil: No, it's embarrassing more than anything.

Why embarrassing?

Neil: Because I realize that I've misunderstood people's reactions to us. Also I'm embarrassed that our intentions are so misunderstood. It makes me feel a bit pathetic. It makes me feel a bit pathetic that we've done something that we think is really good and sincere, and some people think it's 'a birrova laugh'.

Chris (shrugs): I don't really think about this.

Neil: He never reads the reviews. I'll tell you why it's so embarrassing – it's like that opera singer that used to perform at Carnegie Hall . . .

Chris (*protesting*): It's *nothing* like that!

Neil: . . . and everyone used to go because she was terrible, to laugh at her, and she thought they went because she was a really good singer. I feel a bit like her.

Back in the restaurant Chris prepares another complaint. The set menu here costs 13,700 yen (just under £70) and here we are, dipping pieces of meat into a concoction of boiling water and an unidentified oil. He is not impressed.

'You come to a restaurant,' he mutters darkly, 'and you have to cook it yourself. It's a bit like being on camp.' He muses whether or not you expend more calories cooking it than you get from eating it. 'There is one kind of food that is actually like that,' he proclaims. I ask what but he doesn't know.

We discuss accents. Pete, whose accent is deep North London and sprayed with a vocabulary and grammar that is so strange yet effective that Neil frequently compares it to nineteenth-century English, says that Chris gets told off when he goes home. He may be a pop star but his voice is a disgrace. 'She says,' Pete laughs, imitating Chris's mum, '"Timothy's voice has got a *lot* better, but Chris's is worse," then she looks at me.' He mentions, clearly thinking it's of relevance, that Chris went to a public school.

'Direct-grant school,' corrects Chris defensively.

'The same thing, isn't it?' says Pete.

'It's *completely* different!' Chris huffs.

At the other end of the table Neil talks to Kaz, from their publishers. Neil is berating him over his imminent move to Los Angeles.

'You can't *possibly* like it,' Neil insists. 'It's like Swindon.'

'No it's not!' shouts Chris up the table, for this contradicts a theory he has been expounding earlier. Years ago, when the Pet Shop Boys first went to New York, hip hop music bellowed from every window, on every corner there was breakdancing and New York was the most fabulous and exciting place on earth: Los Angeles was dull as sin. Now, he suggests, it is changing round.

'Last orders for drinks,' says Kaz, prompted by an anxious waiter.

'More of *everything*,' announces Neil.

'What happened to Ryuichi Sakamoto today?' complains Chris.

'He's coming tomorrow,' Kaz answers.

'Should we ask Issey Miyake to come?' ponders Neil. Issey Miyake is probably the Pet Shop Boys' favourite designer. Many of Chris's most famous outfits (the striped sunglasses on the 'Suburbia' sleeve, the 'fisherman's' affair for the 1988 BPI awards and 'Heart' sleeve, the inflatable rubber suit in which he performed 'Rent' on Live at the Palladium) are by Issey Miyake. Chris is particularly impressed because Miyake used to be an architect and Chris attributes his brilliance to the fact he has taken the design rigour of architecture and applied it to clothing.

'You should ask him,' pipes up Janet. 'He's lovely.'

'Let's face it, Chris,' says Neil, 'he was *nothing* till you wore those glasses.' Neil chuckles at this preposterous arrogance. 'Anyway I would like to meet him.'

'I would like him to design our second tour,' says Chris. 'It'd be fantastic . . . sculptural . . .'

And the conversation drifts elsewhere. To the best of my knowledge he is never invited.

Neil looks forward to the back-stage introductions tomorrow night. 'It'll be "Ryuichi – *Jason*". . . "Jason – *Ryuichi*".'

Janet expounds at some length about the late-night sexual activities that go on in the park outside her house. She explains how she hates the taxi drivers, voyeurs who just drive round and round, watching, without joining in. She says she phones up the police to complain about them.

Someone mentions Hong Kong and everyone laughs about the mishaps that befell everyone who had a cheap suit made. Neil opines in his haughtiest schoolmaster tones that 'You don't get a cheap suit without getting a cheap suit.'

Neil recommends to Tom that he should get a sumo outfit, looking as like a sumo wrestler as he does.

'They'll think you're a God,' says Janet.

'Many people do,' says Tom.

We depart, leaving a table littered with undrunk alcohol.

The third quality that is harped on about is the Pet Shop Boys' 'Britishness'.

Neil: Oh, that's true. For one thing, we never understood why people sing in an American accent. Hence 'West End Girls', as I've said a million times before, was meant to be a rap in a British accent.

The 'deadpan voice' and the Britishness are linked, aren't they?

Neil: Yes. And I've found it's very difficult to be deadpan on the stage. I don't like the way I do the spoken bits – my voice sounds hectoring and rather harsh. But also I think we are British in our taste. (*He gestures towards Chris.*) You want tea! 'We're English!'

But it's hardly pride in Britain, is it? On the most superficial level you're both forever saying things like 'the only cars to buy are German'.

Neil: Oh, we're not *patriotic*. (*He spits out this last word as if he can only just bear to say it.*)

Chris (by way of agreement): Eurghhhh!

Neil: The Britishness is that we live in Britain and our experience of life is of Britain and that's what we're about. The occasional song – like 'One More Chance' – is set in America, but for a lot of them, like 'West End Girls' or 'King's Cross', the starting point is British life in a very direct sense. It's kind of a 'gimmick' for the Pet Shop Boys.

But do you think there is also anything peculiarly British about the whole Pet Shop Boys' way of doing things?

Neil: There is a kind of *caricature* of Britishness that goes on . . . of British reserve. We kind of play up to it. (*Chris challenges Neil with an inquiring stare and Neil voices Chris's unspoken question.*) 'Do you Neil?' I think we do actually.

Chris: It's because we *are* British.

Neil: You sounded just like your mother when you said that.

Again, there are no taxis to be had late evening in Tokyo so we wander the streets. Neil returns to a familiar topic.

'. . . and I'll say, "Jason, *leave* Stock Aitken Waterman – *we'll* do your next album. It doesn't *matter* that you can't sing. Neither can I! Who can? . . ."'

Chris complains that the hairdresser who trimmed his hair earlier arrived, despite express instructions, without clippers and so couldn't finish the job.

'Another complaint,' notes Neil.

'I don't want to come across as a whinger,' moans Chris.

'That's the title of Chris's complaint chapter,' Neil announces. '"I don't want to come across as a whinger".'

At the hotel there are more fans with more presents. In Japan you don't get given cuddly toys or cheap boxes of chocolates. The Japanese fans – the ones who hang around hotel foyers anyway – are rich and generous. And clever fans always get to know what pop stars like. Spandau Ballet, for instance, can rely upon their fans' generosity for a bottle of their favourite tipple, Jack Daniels. Likewise, the Japanese fans know the Pet Shop Boys' weakness for fine clothing. Tonight's offering comes, promisingly, in an Armani bag.

'I hope it's some briefs,' mutters Chris as he frantically unwraps the package. 'I'd like some briefs.'

'Shut up about underpants,' says Neil, who is politely thanking and kissing the fan while Chris paws away.

'It's swimming trunks!' exclaims Chris. 'And,' he adds, one presumes sarcastically, 'they're my size. Extra large!'

'You can always borrow a marrow,' says Tom.

'It's the best present from a fan we've ever had,' says Chris.

'Give her a kiss, for God's sake,' instructs Neil.

'I need more for a kiss,' Chris insists, but of course kisses her anyway. 'We just throw them away when we get upstairs,' he lies.

Janet is amazed. In the lift she says, 'You know how much that fan's spent?'

'They have pots of money,' says Neil matter-of-factly. 'She's staying in the hotel.'

'She's into matrimony,' surmises Chris.

Neil opens the letter that came with the present. 'I had one yesterday that said, "I love your secret smile".'

In his room Neil opens a bottle of champagne sent by Bros and phones London. He speaks to the head of Parlophone Records, Tony Wadsworth, and tells him that the tour is going 'extremely well, believe it or not. We're talking standing ovations.'

I ask if he's been using the keyboard at the other end of the room. He says he's been writing a song that they may possibly record with Dusty Springfield when they get back to London. 'It's called "She's In Love With The Man She Married". Another one that sounds as if it's from a musical,' he adds apologetically.

He mentions that he's annoyed at the bickering that has been going on. There has been fuss over rooming arrangements, particularly between two of the cast who are sharing a room. The rooms here are about £300 a night. But one of them gets up early, the other late. And one of them thinks the other smells.

'I thought that Americans liked sharing,' says Neil. 'They have pyjama parties.'

There is also unrest because Rob and Mark Farrow have been

ordered to go home tomorrow by Tom and are both annoyed. Neil is upset because, having been invited out and paid for by the Pet Shop Boys, they are now going home convinced they are victims of an injustice.

The Simon Frith article in the tour programme mentions not only your Britishness but highlights a common factor between the two of you and Morrissey: you're all Northerners and you've all been attracted to London and the high life it represents but you are still able to look upon it as outsiders.

Neil: I don't know how true that is. (*He thinks.*) Actually I don't think of myself as a Londoner.

You both frequently refer with some pride to your Northern roots.

Neil: Yes.

Chris: It's definitely different. You can't pretend that England is one.

So do you take that outsider's viewpoint and use it in your songs?

Neil: Yes, I think it's true that we do. I've always felt an outsider. When I was at school I used to hate going to school and the reason was because I was an outsider. I was never one of the gang. Basically because I wasn't very good at football: that defined my feeling about school. It was a very sporty school and football is very important in the north-east.

You quite like being an outsider though, don't you?

Neil: I made a virtue of it, to be quite honest, because really I'd quite like to have been one of the gang. I think most people would. But you get so used to it you just make a virtue out of it. Then, by going to the youth theatre, I got to know other people who were outsiders at their schools and we had our own little group of outsiders and we all hung round together. I still know them. We used to skive off school together.

I also felt like an outsider when I went to college for the first two years. I always thought of students as being a bit dreary, and of course they were. Then, as I got older, I got more and more tolerant. At one time I wouldn't speak to people because of the way they looked. We were horrible snobs.

Chris: I think snobbishness isn't a bad quality.

Neil: No, I don't think it's a totally bad quality: it's an aspirational quality but in some ways it's a bad aspiration. There's a lot of pathetic snobbery.

Chris: A lot of people think of snobbishness as being rich people being snobby about poor people but the kind of snobbishness I prefer is your working-class, street-cred snobbishness.

Neil: Oh, well I'll tell you what I *don't* like: I don't really admire pride in class. I don't admire people who say, 'I'm working-class and proud of it.' And of course the middle class are never supposed to be proud of being middle-class. I know I'm middle-class . . .

Chris: They're the ones who usually pretend to be working-class heroes. Was Joe Orton middle-class?

Neil: No, he *was* working-class. But I kind of think it's a fantasy, saying the working class are all terribly . . . I think it's like saying black people have got a fantastic sense of rhythm, to say working-class people are all . . .

'In tune with life', maybe?

Neil: Yes, and sexier and more vigorous and earthier and less pretentious. Anyway, I think, as it says in 'Left To My Own Devices' – the 'if you want to belong . . .' bit – I've made a virtue out of being an outsider. I just developed a snooty attitude as a protection.

One could almost say that the Pet Shop Boys are the snooty outsiders of pop.

Neil: Oh, I think we are. My attitude to the rest of pop music is exactly the same as my attitude to other people at school. It's actually *identical.* In that they are quite nice if you get to know them but you wouldn't really want to. Because I just get the impression that they do things I don't do, and they make me feel a bit uncomfortable and I don't like to be confronted by them.

And are you scared that if you got to know them . . .?

Neil: . . . I might become one of them? Yes. I used to feel like that at school. They all used to drive to school when they were seventeen – well, a couple of them did anyway – and I always felt like a little worm in the foundation of it all. I didn't really want to be part of their thing. And I also used to look round and think, 'I'll be a star and you're not going to be.' That was my defence.

And you feel in the same way that if you're very pally with the rest of pop music then you'll start appearing at Prince's Trust concerts?

Neil: Yes. Deep down I think we're morally superior to all of them, but I would never really say that.

You just did, I'm afraid.

Neil: Mmmmm. But actually (*he looks over to Chris*) you're the same.

Chris: I know (*smiles*). But I don't talk about it.

Chapter Seven

Wednesday, *5 July*

Rumours that the tour is to be extended have been rife over the last few days. It's going to Europe. It's going to the rest of South-East Asia. Thailand is certain. Australia is probable. The Iron Curtain is being investigated. Brazil is under negotiation.

This afternoon Ivan makes an announcement as everyone – but not Neil and Chris – gets on the tour bus. Neither Europe, nor Asia, nor Thailand, nor Australia, nor the Iron Curtain, nor Brazil are mentioned (nor will they ever be). But, if everyone is available and willing, New York (at Radio City Music Hall) and Los Angeles (at the Universal Amphitheatre) look likely, expanding the tour by nearly two more weeks. 'We can't ignore the biggest market in the world,' says Ivan, 'and the boys like the show so much . . .'

At the back of the coach sits Mark Farrow. The only flight today went via Anchorage in Alaska and took nineteen hours, landing in London in the midst of a London-side transport strike. Rob and he have decided to stay until tomorrow.

At the venue I find Neil and Chris unwrapping presents in the dressing-room. Chris uncovers a doll with a striped top and a hood – a Chris Lowe mannequin. 'It's you!' exclaims Pete. '*That's* going back to England.'

Next is a large oil painting. It is not very good. In fact it is only really the fact that it has been delivered here that suggests that the two people represented are the Pet Shop Boys. Furthermore it seems to have been painted by someone who only had orange and purple paint at their disposal.

'It's horrible,' states Chris, unnecessarily. Nevertheless it is clearly a labour of love. 'Will it fit in the bin?' he asks.

'Alan!' shouts Neil to head of wardrobe. 'I want my make-up now! Pete! I want a cup of tea!'

Chris sniggers, amazed at this outburst. 'You just come in with orders. That's for your bossy chapter.'

Neil reports that it won't be as big as Chris's complaints chapter.

'I don't complain a lot,' protests Chris.

'You *do*,' says Neil in a manner that suggests the subject isn't open to further debate.

They go downstairs and do a surreal telephone interview live with Radio One's morning DJ Simon Bates. They are in Japan, Simon Bates is talking from a boat in the Pacific as part of a round-the-world trip and it is being transmitted in Britain and conversation is hampered by an echo on the line. Perhaps surprisingly, they like Simon Bates. 'I think he's funny,' explains Chris. Afterwards they say that the interview was boring: 'It's hard to be spontaneous with that delay.'

The show is a success and without incident, except that when Chris comes on-stage at the end there is no spotlight on him. He is furious.

I watch the encores with Tom Watkins. During 'It's Alright' he says he thinks they should project the video for the 'It's Alright' single: them and dozens of babies. I say I prefer it like it is.

'Let's sell more product,' he implores.

The credits roll up at the end and Tom's name appears. He feigns a lack of interest.

'I only want the money. I don't want the recognition.'

Back-stage Chris is still furious about the lights.

'I'm going to bring my own light tomorrow, like Top Cat's standard lamp,' he grumps.

Someone comments on the ghastly oil painting of them, still not in the bin. Chris admits there are others.

'Where's that one of you as a woman, Neil?' he asks.

'It's us as a married couple,' Neil explains. It has conveniently disappeared. There are more: Japanese fans are keen to represent the two of them interacting in strange ways. They were once given one of Chris crying and Neil comforting him. Another depicted them kissing.

'That *really* turns them on,' laughs Neil.

'Is Jase here?' asks Tom.

'I don't think he's making an appearance, rather tragically,' says Neil. The surfing has taken all day, we later discover, and he has a migraine. Maybe he'll come tomorrow night.

A grey-haired bloke and his wife, local EMI bigwigs, appear at the door. He congratulates Neil, who chats amiably. Mr Collins, for that is his name, tells Neil that when he came to Hong Kong three years ago audiences never even used to stand up. He says hello to Chris who grunts back a half-hearted welcome through a mouthful of toast.

The room fills up. Already in here are Neil, Chris, Mr and Mrs Collins, Lucy from EMI in Britain, Tom and his friend John, Janet Street-Porter, their British booking agent Pete Nash, Alan (working, tidying up clothes), Pete, Mike Lynch the tour accountant, Lawrence the photographer. Patrick is filming us all on Super-8.

Janet Street-Porter tells Neil that the audience is 'full' of middle-aged Japanese businessmen in suits, dancing. (I haven't seen any.) Excited by this, Neil asks her to film tomorrow night's show on Super-8; they can use the footage in the live video.

Neil: We deliberately made a decision early on, after we did an interview with the *Sun*, that we wouldn't talk to the tabloid press. We were persuaded to do it and we got that ridiculous

'Rudest Men In Rock' thing. To be fair to the *Sun*, David Hancock said, 'Don't worry, don't look so miserable, I'm not going to ask you about your sex life,' and he didn't. But anyway, we realized early on that there was no point us being involved in the tabloid press because we weren't going to run our lives as a totally public soap opera, which you have to do. We didn't think we'd be good value on those terms and also we didn't want that kind of press attention because we didn't think it was going to be helpful to us. In fact we have occasionally spoken to them. When 'It's A Sin' came out we did a piece with Linda Duff, who we knew anyway (*she was one of Neil's contemporaries on* Smash Hits) for the *Daily Mirror*, for the centre-spread, and we had copy approval. It's difficult to think of a good angle on the Pet Shop Boys. She did the 'Odd Couple' piece.

Then we did one with David Wigg for the *Daily Express*, but he did this not-very-good interview and he didn't run it at the time. But there's no point getting involved because people who work for tabloid newspapers genuinely have that attitude that all publicity is good for you.

The person who pioneered the tabloid approach to pop music was Adam Ant, who correctly credited a lot of his success to the tabloids in that famous quote. (*The quote was: 'The success of the Ants has been due to television, to the national press and to colour magazines like* Smash Hits *and* Flexipop, *and that represents, I think, a revolution in the music industry because we've been absolutely hated by the official music press . . .'*) And of course Duran Duran did a lot of that and Boy George was the extreme example.

Lots of groups have pictures of themselves arriving at Heathrow airport. Chris and I have *never* been pictured arriving at Heathrow airport, though we spend our lives arriving there. I don't think the photographers recognize us, to be quite honest. Maybe they have to be tipped off. I don't know. But we've never really operated as family household name personalities like Bros do. Bros's entire career has been a tabloid controversy: are they crap or not?

Do you avoid it purely on career terms or because you don't want to bear the invasion of privacy?

Neil: It's on all terms. I don't like the intrusion of privacy that you would get as a result. We're never going to deliver the kind of thing they want in a million years.

What do you think they would want?

Neil: They want sex and romance. Interestingly David Bowie just did one. He obviously felt he needed tabloid support for his Tin Machine . . . 'project'. It said: '"My ex-wife is a bitch," says David.' I'm surprised he lowers himself. It did nothing for his record.

Chris: That's the other thing . . .

Neil: . . . *it doesn't* sell your records.

It just makes you 'famous', doesn't it?

Neil: It makes you famous, but in my opinion being famous makes you despised by a lot of people. I remember my mother's attitude towards someone on television would be 'D'y'know, it's *pathetic* really, isn't it? To have to flaunt themselves like that . . .' And I have the same kind of attitude, that it's pathetic for people to flaunt themselves across the pages of the press all the time, just because they've got a record to sell.

Do you worry that at your level of success there's a market for dishing-the-dirt stories about you?

Neil: Yes I do.

You've escaped to perhaps a surprising degree. Do you think you've been lucky, or is it the way you've handled the whole business?

Neil: To be honest, I don't think there's a lot of dirt on us.

It doesn't take much to make a story.

Chris: I'm glad they haven't. I couldn't stand it. I find it very unnerving to be exposed. Even if there's a small piece about us in Jonathan King's page, I feel terribly exposed.

Neil: Ironically, because we were always accused at the start of being a hype, of being pop strategists and all the rest of it, I think we've done it totally on the quality of our records. I don't think we've given a lot of aid to it otherwise. I think there are few groups over the last ten years that have got as far as we've got without doing the tabloid business. I think we've proved you haven't got to do it.

Tonight, however, they have agreed to talk by telephone with Gill Pringle, the *Daily Mirror*'s main pop writer.

Back-stage Tom suggests to Neil, half-jokingly, that perhaps Neil could tell Gill Pringle that Tom had persuaded them to do the interview. He wouldn't mind the kudos; Gill Pringle can – or at least he believes she can – be very important for his other acts.

Janet Street-Porter tells me about the time she attacked Gill Pringle with a handbag at a dinner in honour of Michael Jackson because Gill Pringle had suggested in the newspaper that Janet was having an affair with someone she worked with. 'I was on the A table and she was on the Z, Janet remembers. 'I hit her with my Chanel handbag. I said, "This is a Chanel handbag – that's the closest *you'll* ever get to class . . ."'

We all hoot.

'I could have sued her about the story,' she says. She adds that it wasn't the inaccuracy that hurt so much. 'He wasn't even *attractive . . .*'

They all consider what should be said in the interview. Neil says he'll say, 'Mr Udo says it's the best show he's ever seen. We only did three shows but we could have sold out twenty-five.'

'Are you talking to Gill?' Tom asks Chris.

'I don't talk to the press,' announces Chris.

'Don't you think we should do this *Daily Mirror* thing?' asks Neil with genuine concern.

'I want *you* to do it,' says Chris.

I ask Neil to tape his side of the interview and hand him my tape-recorder; in doing so I absent-mindedly call it not 'the Gill

Pringle interview' but 'the Janet Street-Porter' interview. Janet hears this and, perhaps understandably, is offended by the implied comparison. She launches herself towards me and rains blows – fairly hard ones – on to me. 'I *have* a shit list, you know,' she scowls.

In the hotel elevator Chris asks me if I'm going to sit in on the interview. 'I don't think so,' I say, before Neil, who looks horrified at the suggestion, can say it for me. 'I am,' says Chris, 'I'm going for the laugh.'

They have agreed to do the interview because they have been promised a colour centre-spread: two pages. The piece eventually appears, after several delays, the following week. It is about one-third of a page in size and includes two colour photos. It may be interesting to compare the quotes given in the piece with what Neil actually said.

> SPREE AT THE SHOP
>
> Pets Splash Out On A Show To Remember
>
> As the Pet Shop Boys' lavish stage show finally explodes in front of British fans, pop's top duo aim to outdazzle anybody you've ever seen on tour before.
>
> 'We've spent £300,000 making it unforgettable,' says the band's elusive Neil Tennant in an exclusive interview. 'Our show is far more elaborate than Michael Jackson's, George Michael's or any other recent tours.
>
> 'Michael Jackson's was dreadful in comparison. I couldn't even see him on the video screen, let alone make out the tiny dot on the stage.'

The relevant quotes, as actually spoken, are as follows.

Following a question about why they weren't making much money off the tour: 'Well, because we spent so much more money on the show than we were meant to. I mean, the production cost something like £300,000 – I don't know if you know, but normally a group will spend £20,000 on their stage show. We've had forty-five minutes of film made ... that cost £150,000, and then the costumes cost £60,000 or £70,000 ...'

Nothing, you note, about 'making it unforgettable ...'. Then:

'... when I saw Michael Jackson's show I couldn't see anything. I don't know how you felt about it but ... I think the mistake that people have made in the past is doing theatrical shows in stadiums, well, it's a contradiction in terms, that. You can't see a theatrical show in a stadium. You can barely see the video screen. I mean, I remember seeing the David Bowie "Glass Spider" tour and I couldn't see the video screen, never mind David Bowie.'

George Michael, you notice, isn't mentioned.

The *Daily Mirror* piece continued:

> You certainly won't miss the Pet Shop Boys. There's a 45 minute movie by top director Derek Jarman, a host of dancers and mime artists, plus twelve costume changes.
>
> Nervous about playing live for the first time, the band launched their mini-world tour last month in Hong Kong. Tonight's performance at Birmingham is followed by sell-out shows in London and Glasgow.
>
> 'We both had a few butterflies to start with, but we've decided we like touring now and can't wait to do it again,' says Neil.

'Well, you know ... I had a few butterflies in my stomach.'

Then later:

'Well, the idea is of course that at some point we'll do

another tour . . . um . . . you know, if you think about it from our point of view we've come this far and we've never done a tour and we decided originally to do this tour as a sort of . . . to see if we liked touring or not . . . to see what it was all . . . and as it happened we do quite like it.'

There is no 'can't wait to do it again'.

For the record, their Glasgow concert was not sold out at the time of speaking, at the time the piece was printed, nor, indeed, ever.

> Since 35-year-old Neil Tennant quit his job on teen magazine Smash Hits and 29-year-old Chris Lowe handed in his notice as an architect's assistant, the pair have enjoyed extraordinary success.
>
> As well as their own hits, they've written songs for Dusty Springfield, Patsy Kensit and now Liza Minelli. Says Neil: 'We couldn't believe it when Liza asked us to write a whole album for her.
>
> 'We had a few incredible nights out with her in London. One evening we went to the club Heaven, which is a kind of bizarre place to take someone like Liza.'
>
> Heaven, the notorious gay club at Charing Cross, regularly features bondage evenings.
>
> 'We made up a foursome with Matt Goss from Bros. Afterwards she took us to Tramp nightclub and we had bangers and mash and champagne.
>
> 'I could listen to Liza's stories for hours. She knew eeee-veryone. Marlene Dietrich, Noel Coward, Andy Warhol, Marc Bolan. I hope one day we'll feature in her tales too.'

That is how the *Daily Mirror* piece ends.

Minnelli is spent with two 'n's.

Neil actually said:

'Well, Liza Minnelli was the one that came out of the blue. We always work with people who've . . . well, she's such a star to start with, and big stars kind of fascinate us . . .'

Then later:

'She'd never sung this kind of music really, so it was an incredible challenge to work with someone like that.'

No 'we couldn't believe it . . .' etc. Then:

'Oh we did, we went out to dinner a few times. Then, one night we went nightclubbing. She wanted to go to Ronnie Scott's . . . we took her to Ronnie Scott's and actually Matt Goss from Bros came with us, so there was Matt, Liza, Chris and me, then we went to Heaven. Ironically it was called the Land of Oz Night . . .'

Which, incidentally, is nothing whatsoever to do with bondage.

'. . . it was an Acid House evening, which she was intrigued by. Then we ended up in Tramps at 3 o'clock in the morning having bangers and mash. Actually that was the first time I'd ever been to Tramps and it was totally empty. I was expecting to see Rod Stewart or somebody in there, but it was totally empty.'

Finally:

'Oh yes, she's very . . . she tells you . . . you know she always stays at the Savoy Hotel and she reminisces about her mother, Judy Garland, and she was once staying there and Marlene Dietrich was in the suite next door, Noël Coward was on the other side. She knows loads of people. Liza's amazing because she knows so many people. She knows everyone. You know she was a good friend of Andy Warhol, for instance . . . anyway you'll have to interview Liza when she comes over and get all the stories out of her first-hand.'

If Liza Minnelli did know Marc Bolan, Neil didn't mention it. Where he *did* mention Marc Bolan was in talking about the early seventies, when his friends were obsessed by David Bowie and Marc Bolan and also loved *Cabaret*, starring Liza Minnelli, a film which was assimilated into the same glam rock 'divine decadence' culture.

And he did not, of course, anywhere say the wonderfully unconversational, trite line 'I hope one day we'll feature in her tales too'.

Why did you talk to the Daily Mirror*?*

Neil: Because the tour was going so successfully. It was so exciting that I thought it would be great to have it recorded in the tabloid press: it was interesting, it was doing well and there'd be really good pictures.

Would you have done it if all the British shows had already been sold out?

Neil: Yes. The *Daily Mirror* isn't sold in Scotland, you know (*that is where the early ticket sales are weakest*). I just thought it would be exciting. It's very difficult in the Pet Shop Boys to have a moment that would be interesting for the tabloids. I was proud, really. To be quite honest I was proud and I wanted to show off. But it wasn't really worth it.

Chris, were you never interested in the idea?

Chris: I can't remember what my official line was.

Neil: You were in a going-along-with-it attitude. Because I was saying 'Chris, if you don't think we should do it we won't do it,' and you were going 'No, no . . .'

Chris: I was more narked that we didn't get the centre-spread. They promised, but I knew that they'd go against it. And they did.

Chapter Eight

The Japanese girls hanging round the lobby make a beeline for us. We're off out to dinner. Before they can ask, Chris barks, 'I don't know *where* we're going.'

Mr Udo's dinner is at a place called the Cavern. 'You always wanted to play the Cavern, didn't you?' says Tom as we draw up outside. Funnily enough its name isn't a coincidence – though there is no attempt to re-create a Liverpool cellar-club, here is where you go in Tokyo if you want to eat while listening to the Beatles all evening.

Mr Udo is a short, stocky middle-aged man who favours slick suits and loud ties. He is the most successful promoter of foreign acts in Japan. The best story we are told about him goes like this:

Mick Jagger is flying into Tokyo's Narita airport to play some Japanese dates in 1988. Mr Udo is the promoter. In the airport, just through customs, is the place where photographers will snap Mick Jagger arriving. These are the photos that will appear in the Japanese press. Unfortunately Mick Jagger will be standing about ten yards further into the airport than it is possible for anyone – even Mr Udo – to get while greeting an arriving passenger. So, it seems, Mr Udo will not be in the photos. Mr Udo isn't happy about this because he wants to be in the photos. So he buys a ticket to America, flies there, waits an hour or two in the airport without leaving customs, gets on the plane with Mick Jagger, and flies back to Tokyo. Nearly twenty-four hours in the air and one round-trip ticket all for the sake of ten yards and one photo.

*

The Pet Shop Boys have met Mr Udo before. When they were last in Tokyo he took them out to dinner, in an attempt to woo them into playing live. They went to Maxim's, expensive even by Japanese standards. To wash the food down they had a bottle of wine which cost £150 and which Neil and Chris liked so much they cheerfully ordered a second bottle. At the end of the meal Neil announced to the crestfallen, and somewhat poorer, Mr Udo, 'Of course, we'll never play live . . .'

That hospitality has heightened expectations. Everyone has been assuming that tonight's meal will be very special. Members of the crew who have been to Japan on Mr Udo-promoted tours before have talked glowingly of huge banquets. Recently some of them came with Stevie Winwood. He did poor business but was treated royally by Mr Udo.

So we are a little surprised at what we see. The Cavern is the sort of restaurant people call 'intimate' when they're paying. Mr Udo owns it. In the middle are a couple of tables laid out with a selection of Chinese dishes in metal catering trays, the sort of trays from which British school food is served and which the back-stage food has turned up in all week. In fact it seems to be the very same food. It's nice, but . . .

Neil and Chris frown darkly.

'Is it just me,' asks Neil after we've stood around for a while, 'or haven't we got a drink?'

He asks for champagne. There is none.

'The beef's cold,' moans Chris. (It is chicken, but no one points this out.) 'I want a sit-down meal.'

He discusses the film they are making of the tour. 'It's not going to be like any film that's ever been made,' he claims, getting carried away. 'We're going to look at film from first principles.' This statement draws quizzical stares.

'This is very nice, Chris,' says Neil, munching away. 'Why are you complaining?'

'I want to go to a really dodgy disco,' says Janet.

'The last time we went to a really dodgy disco with you – in Los Angeles,' John reminds her, 'we got thrown out.'

Janet tells Neil and Chris that she really likes their version of 'Always On My Mind' in the show. It's a song first made famous by Elvis Presley.

'I think you should put it on a B-side,' she says.

They gawp.

'Do you think so?' asks Neil, stringing her along, setting her up.

'Yes,' Janet replies, her enthusiasm growing, pleased that they seem interested in her idea.

Neil points out that it has actually been an A-side of a single already and that in fact it was number one for four weeks the Christmas before last.

For once Janet is speechless.

You decided to reprint that article by Simon Frith in the tour programme, but when Mark Farrow and I were putting the programme together Chris came in and muttered about 'Neil and that bloody Simon Frith article'. Why do you have that attitude to it? Do you think it's silly to take something that earnestly?

Chris: Well . . . you know . . . I don't know really. That Simon Frith article lost me. You see, most of the architecture books I used to have to read are so Pseuds' Corner, such intellectualism for the sake of it, that I just kind of rejected it all. If you can't *feel* something, then it's not worth it.

But whatever language it's put in, those sort of questions – what do you do? why do you do it? – are quite important and fundamental. Is it silly to think about them?

Chris: It's like 'what is the meaning of life?' You can go on and on about it.

Neil (to Chris): But why shouldn't you think about the meaning of life?

Chris: I'm not interested.

*

The Beatles' 'Abbey Road' LP is playing. 'Something' comes on.

'Frank Sinatra sang this at his concert,' observes Neil. He laughs. '"Frank," as he is to us.'

Someone mentions Cliff Richard.

'I don't know *why* he's called the Peter Pan of Pop,' says Chris. 'He looks so old.'

Neil observes that 'Abbey Road' was, until last week, EMI's biggest-selling ever LP in Brazil. It is now the Pet Shop Boys 'Introspective'. Chris reminds him that in interviews on the album's release he did indeed call it 'The Sergeant Pepper of disco'.

'We're more popular than the Beatles!' crows Neil.

'That's what Pete Waterman says about Stock, Aitken and Waterman,' comments Janet.

Patrick sidles up to our table. He is forever 'impressing' the entourage with his magic tricks.

'You're not going to do a trick, are you?' moans Chris, eyeing him uneasily. Chris hates magic tricks.

He is. He gets some salt, pours it into the top of a lightly clenched fist, then opens the hand. The salt is gone. He takes his other hand from behind Janet's head. As one would expect it contains the salt. Patrick explains, for no fathomable reason, that he was thrown out of Marlborough public school. This triggers an earnest debate on education.

'How many children have you got, Patrick?' asks Tom.

'Just one. My wife sent me a fax the other day suggesting we have another one.'

'How hygienic,' says Tom.

'We haven't had any gifts from Udo,' complains Chris, then talks about his visit to the hairdresser's earlier. They played Fairground Attraction's LP and David Bowie's 'Tin Machine' LP. 'It's not so bad after five listens,' he says of the latter, 'but it's still crap.'

He complains about Mr Udo to Patrick. 'There's been no champers.'

'Maybe he's just being original,' suggests Patrick. He has taken up a role as Mr Udo's apologist and one suspects that deep down he sees the roles here rather differently from anyone else: of some slightly stroppy fly-by-night newcomers (the Pet Shop Boys) getting uppity with a venerable promoter friend-of-Mick (Mr Udo).

'He's been cheap and cheerless,' says Chris.

'I want a son who looks like Lord Snooty,' says Janet, returning to the education debate. She explains that she has no qualms whatsoever about private education. *Power*, that's what she wants her children, should she ever bear any, to have.

•

'Chris! Chris! Chris! Chris!' shouts Mr Udo.

Chris deliberately ignores him.

Patrick – trying to smooth over the fractured atmosphere – proposes a toast.

'Oh good,' says Chris, pretending to perk up at the mention of some *proper* food. 'Toast!'

'A toast for Mr Udo for his hospitality . . .'

Chris grimaces.

'. . . and to everyone for their imagination and experience . . .'

'And ourselves the Pet Shop Boys,' prompts Neil.

'. . . and to the courage and imagination of the Pet Shop Boys,' says Patrick.

'*Thank* you,' says Neil.

'. . . for this wonderful holiday in Hong Kong and Japan.'

Mr Udo follows the toast with a traditional round of rhythmic clapping – '3–3–1 3–3–1' – in honour of Neil and Chris.

In a corner, as these formalities take place, Tom and Ivan

huddle deep in discussion. The gist of the conversation is that Tom doesn't think the Pet Shop Boys should play in America at the moment and is furious that everyone has got worked up about the idea.

'Whoever has got them excited about it, they shouldn't have.' It is clear that implicitly the blame is Rob's.

'I'm very concerned that the excitement gets curbed fast. Let's get them the facts. With this tour we have already achieved what we set out to achieve – that is, the boys' *confidence*.'

He suggests that maybe they'll warm up in Europe or behind the Iron Curtain before releasing an LP late next spring and then tour America in the early summer, perhaps playing 'long multiples' at theatres. Perhaps they could do a three-way headline rotation tour with New Order and Depeche Mode, or maybe with the Cure.

Neil and Chris don't hear this, thankfully. The Cure are, just now, their particular pet hate. One suspects that they would react badly to the suggestion of touring with anyone – it makes as much sense as them appearing on a compilation album, something they loathe – but with *the Cure* . . .

Neil: I sort of think of us as belonging to a different tradition – a broader cultural tradition, to be completely pompous about it. In the same way that groups like the Beatles are part of a broader cultural tradition. They're not just part of pop music. I see us in the cultural tradition of, say, Joe Orton and Noël Coward, in that I think we're serious and comic and lighthearted and sentimental and brittle. Like middle-class playwrights we're *of* the middle class and totally *against* it. It's funny that the middle class are the only people who go to the theatre; they go to be slagged off for being middle-class, think 'How wonderful' and go home. Ibsen will tell them 'the middle classes are totally awful' and they'll go 'Mmm, where shall we go for dinner then?' And I think we kind of belong to that tradition. We slag off suburbia but we both come from suburbia and more or less live in it.

And so does that devalue the sincerity of what you do?

Neil: No. 'Suburbia' is true *anyway*. One of the things about being middle-class is to know that you're thoroughly imperfect. Therefore you don't think your football team is the best in the world, you don't want to command an army. It's to be obsessed by your own conscience. If Janet had a child and I had a child she would be the one to send it to Eton, not me. She would do it because she wants the child to be powerful. Which I quite admire, in a way.

Chris (laughs): She'd make such an impression at the school. Could you imagine the child's first day? She'd collar the headmaster.

Chris, do you agree with what Neil has said about your middle-classness and its consequences?

Chris: Yes, I think we are middle-class and, as opposed to someone like Spandau Ballet, the Pet Shop Boys give across a load of insecurities and doubts. With Spandau you get the confidence and the arrogance of Gary Kemp. We've got arrogance as well, but it's a different kind of arrogance.

Do you deep down think that doubts and insecurities are the most interesting things?

Neil: Well they *are*! Doubts and insecurities – it's a middle-class obsession. It's very *Hotel Du Lac* by Anita Brookner: a slim volume about doubts and insecurities.

So are the Pet Shop Boys the Anita Brookner of the music world?

Neil: No, because there's also something undeniably, essentially superficial about us. Just as Noël Coward towards the end of his life wrote that he'd realized he'd always been an essentially superficial person. (*They both collapse in hysterics.*) I think that's quite like us. But I think one of our strengths is that we're both highly perceptive. I think we often write songs that make people say, 'Oh yes, I agree with that. I know just what you mean.' That's different from 'I Should Be So Lucky' or 'Put

Your Hand On My Heart' – people don't think, 'Wow! I know what you mean' about those. A woman came and told me she'd got back together with her husband because of 'Why Don't We Live Together?'; that's obviously a rather banal example, but I've always tried to write about *adult* concerns in pop music. In a *Village Voice* review it said that here's someone who writes pop songs about making the most of what you've got – you 'make do' with a relationship – and that's the Anita Brookner-ish bit. It's a middle-class analytical way of looking at things, an unrebellious, unsexy way of writing, if you like. There has also always been a stream of grim reality. When I was a boy I used to like *The L-Shaped Room* and *The Loneliness of the Long Distance Runner* and all those sixties realist things, and that's why we've always had a mixture of lush and grim. 'King's Cross' is a grim song. I think there's a similarity between us and Madness there, that song about the home for . . .

Chris: I love that.

Neil: . . . the one about Arlington House ('One Better Day'). Suggs used to write very perceptive lyrics that were slightly corny. 'Mother's got her hairdo to be done/she says they're too old for toys' (from 'Suburbia') could come straight out of a Madness song. They're real, whereas a lot of people, like Wet Wet Wet . . . I tend to feel they're quite talented but they're apeing other songs. 'Sweet Little Mystery' is an American phrase, it sounds as if it's out of a 1950s song. They're not really writing about their own real lives. They did though, in that one, the one about unemployment.

'Wishing I Was Lucky'.

Neil: Yes. It seems to me that 'Wishing I Was Lucky', which sounds like a Scottish phrase, has a real meaning in the way that that song 'Temptation' doesn't have. Our songs give a fairly true idea of the kind of people we are.

We stroll into the night, a long ramshackle convoy looking for a club. We are heading for a notorious place called the Lexington

Queen, a Westerners' hangout also known as 'the model's graveyard'.

Janet announces that she feels an affinity with the Pet Shop Boys because she shares their working method. She explains how everybody thought that *Network* 7, an innovative, Sunday-lunchtime, youth TV programme full of wonky camera angles and on-screen information, was thrown together when in fact it was a careful analytical exercise. 'Everything that Neil and Chris do is the same and that's why I like them so much. They make it look easy.'

Patrick takes it upon himself to defend his poshness, an odd endeavour as no one has thought to attack it. He gets stuck in the middle of a sentence.

'. . . astut . . . astute . . . astitution?' he splutters. 'Is that a word?'

'I don't think it is, actually,' pronounces Neil. 'Astute*ness*.'

Again without being prompted Patrick discusses his contribution to the show. 'It was a symbiotic thing,' he says.

'That sounds a bit hippie to me,' says Janet dubiously.

The two of them vie to put their finger on the fundamental impulse behind the Pet Shop Boys. Patrick tries out a vague notion. 'It's more negative,' says Janet.

Neil, catching up, hears this and agrees. 'Me and Chris have a lot of negative energy. We know what we *don't* want.'

Patrick accuses Janet of arrogance. What would you do, he says, if someone came to you with a great idea . . .?

She cuts him off. 'I'd tell them to stick it up their arse,' she says, 'because *I've* just won an Academy award . . .'

As we enter the Lexington Queen, the waiters confront Chris, who has been swigging a beer as he walked down the road and still has half of it left. It is forbidden to bring drinks in, so they confiscate it. Then, because he is a pop star, they give him a free drink of their own.

We are greeted by the sound of the Cure's 'The Caterpillar'.

'You don't go out to hear the Cure,' frowns Chris. 'We'll get Ivan to sort out the disco.'

The next two records are 'Ask' by the Smiths and 'Boys Don't Cry', again by the Cure.

'Do you like the Cure?' Neil asks Tony from *Motormouth*, who has met us here. He nods enthusiastically. Neil, who doesn't, gives him a 'well, you *would*' expression.

'Some skunkhead has stolen my bag,' announces a blonde girl, drunk at the very least, staggering into our seats. She stares at us, unfocused but accusingly, then stumbles off and takes her shouting elsewhere. Two minutes later I see her find her bag, on the floor where she had been sitting.

'What music do you like?' Tony asks Neil.

'I like New Order,' he says. 'At home I listen to classical music.'

I mention Jason Donovan's LP to Tony. He looks at me as if I'm mad. 'I've got researchers to do that,' he says.

The first open chord of the Beatles' 'A Hard Day's Night' sounds out. We decide that the Lexington Queen is useless and leave.

You quoted Noël Coward admiringly, but you also said you didn't think what he did was as superficial as he made out, in the end. Do you likewise think you're not, in the end, so superficial?

Neil: Well, no, I think I *am* quite a superficial person.

So what would it be to be less superficial?

Neil: To be more involved. Actually I think the word he used was frivolous. A lot of my concerns are quite frivolous really.

Are you just demeaning yourself here? You usually seem quite serious and thoughtful.

Neil: Yes, but I'm always aware how I don't really match up to the things I'd like to be. I mean (*laughs*) part of me would like to be an intellectual. But I would never be an intellectual because I'm just simply too frivolous and I can never apply myself. I lack the intellectual discipline to be an intellectual. But really I would quite like to be an academic – that's what I'd be really happy being. But I've never had the intellectual dedication or discipline to do it. I went to see a friend of Jon Savage's (*a journalist friend*) who is a professor at Cambridge University and he had these rooms and books and I thought that I'd have been completely comfortable if I'd been clever enough to do that sort of thing. I'd be quite happy with life. My frivolous concerns would have been the college gossip, I would have been intellectually stimulated talking about history and ideas and, of course, you've got an ever-changing group of people going through that you fancy. I always think that's one of the major attractions of the academic life.

Chris: Well, you can still do it. You're not too old.

Neil: Yes . . . I could also still be a priest. That could be a late vocation.

Chris: Yes. (*He sniggers.*) You've still got plenty of time to become the Pope.

Do you really think you'd like the academic life though: not much money, only ever addressing a very limited audience?

Chris: Lots of the lecturers at universities just live in a complete fantasy world. I just find it depressing. They're sadder than children. I suppose you get those letters after your name but . . .

Neil: Yes, maybe you're right.

So Chris, are you frivolous?

Chris: Yes, I'm not a deep person at all. I rejected depth at an early age. (*He hoots with laughter.*)

You're determined, aren't you, that no one should think of you as 'deep'?

Chris: Yeah, but despite that fact I'm really *not* deep.

Neil: Behind the façade of superficiality lurks a superficial person. (*They both laugh.*)

Chris: That's the gag.

Chris, do you think you're an immature person?

(*Chris shrugs and doesn't answer.*)

Neil, do you think he is?

Neil: I'm asking if *he* thinks he is. I want Chris to talk about himself. Otherwise I'll give one of my *extremely* fascinating theories about Chris.

Please do.

Chris (after a lengthy pause): It can be a bit of a pointless task learning a lot, because there's always someone who's going to know that bit more. So, if ever you've got an opinion, there's probably someone around who's got a different opinion based upon a greater bit of knowledge. So this pursuit of knowledge can be a complete and utter waste of time.

But isn't that just a classic I'm-not-going-to-play-the-game-if-I-can't-win attitude?

Chris: Oh, I'm *very* much like that. If I can't win, I'm *sorry*, there's *no* way I'm going to play that game.

Neil (laughs): You just summed Chris up.

'I want to go somewhere that plays disco music,' says Chris. 'I *love* disco music.'

We try a club up the road but the man on the door wants nothing to do with the rabble who are fighting and joking on the street in front of his club, Pet Shop Boys or not Pet Shop Boys.

'We don't want to go here anyway,' mutters Neil to the bouncer.

'We're talking Rough Guide to Nowhere,' says Mark Farrow.

For some reason Janet attacks Neil, screaming obscenities.

'Call the police, there's a madman around,' says Neil, indulging in an occasional habit of quoting his own lyrics.

Janet sees me noting down this exchange and attacks me once more.

Down the street we find a lift, glass-sided so that you can be seen in it from the street. On the seventh floor, we are told, is a good disco. Its name is Bingo Bango Bongo. Neil tells someone to go up and check we'll get in – he doesn't fancy being turned away twice in one night. The word comes down in due course that they'd be delighted to have us.

We cram into a lift. Whenever asked in interviews what scares him Neil's stock response is 'lifts' and right now he looks very uneasy. He screams for only a few people to come into the lift, but the desire to get partying is too great and they assume he is joking. As many as will fit cram in, then a few more. The lift ascends, the door opens. It is a disco and we are being ushered in. Prince's 'Batdance' video plays above our heads. But, someone points out, this is not the seventh floor. We carry on up. Again the door opens, again there is a disco and again it is not the seventh floor. There are discos, we discover, on five floors.

Bingo Bango Bongo is, we quickly decide, fabulous. There are few other people there, there is a long thin dance floor about forty feet from end to end (perfect for promenading and prancing up and down catwalk style as the night draws on), there are large cold bottles of beer thrust at us without mention of payment and there is fine music.

'We are,' summarizes Chris, beaming, 'club happy.'

'Keep an eye on Chris,' says Neil to Dainton. 'He's in one of his moods.'

Bobby Brown's 'Every Little Step' blares out. Mark Farrow and Chris start doing 'the Bobby Brown dance'. Neil, bottle in hand, joins them both on the dance-floor and they teach him. The DJ puts on the twelve-inch version of the Pet Shop Boys' 'Opportunities'. 'I *never* liked this record,' says Neil, but by the time the song breaks down into the dub section he is waltzing to it, beer bottle still in hand, with Janet Street-Porter.

Chris decides that one of the *Motormouth* people looks like the *Coronation Street* character Brian Tilsley. He walks over and says, 'You look like Brian Tilsley.' Neil joins them and Chris says, 'Brian Tilsley – meet Neil Tennant. Neil Tennant – meet Brian Tilsley.'

Tony from *Motormouth* suggests to Neil that the Pet Shop Boys do a single with Bananarama.

'It's been mentioned before,' says Neil wearily. 'We haven't time. I would like to some time.'

Royal House's 'Can You Party' comes on and Chris starts raving about it.

A few minutes later Neil is merrily dancing to Milli Vanilli's 'Baby, Don't Forget My Number'.

Neil dances once more with Janet. They talk as they dance. She tells him about her Anthony Price clothes. 'I call it my results wear,' she says. ''Cause when I wear them I always get results . . .'

'Results!' he shouts. 'That's it! That's the Liza Minnelli LP title!!' He rushes over to Chris and Chris agrees: it's perfect.

Very late, but with most people still 'club happy', Neil decides he must go to bed. I get in a car with him and Janet. Either they are very drunk or I am very insignificant for they both separately ask me the next day what time I got home from the club.

On the way back we pass a restaurant with the sign The Jack and Betty Club – We Love Food.

'I love broken English,' says Neil.

'We still haven't found a club with cages like I did last time I was here,' says Janet.

'Janet, that was probably last year's thing,' says Neil in a seen-it-all voice.

In the hotel lift Neil's thoughts turn back to Mr Udo. 'The EMI dinner better be better than that. I'll check, and if it's not I'm not going.'

Chapter Nine

Thursday, *6 July*

The next morning I go to Tom Watkins' room. The entrance is stacked with bags of shopping, probably presents. There is little he likes more, say Neil and Chris, than giving presents.

He tells me the Tom Watkins Story. He went to a Church of England school in the East End, full of Jewish pupils – 'a complete contradiction really'. After school he wanted to study architecture but he didn't have the qualifications so he got a job in the Metropolitan Region Hospital Board's architectural office. After a while he realized that he didn't want to do architecture anyway – he preferred interior design and for that you needed fewer qualifications. Those he got and in 1969 or 1970 – he can't remember which – he began working for Allied Breweries, designing pub interiors. He got the sack for insulting the architect: 'I told him he couldn't design.' He got a job with Terence Conran; soon afterwards the business split and he went with Rodney Fitch and worked on interiors for the Top Shop and Peter Robinson. His design jobs changed and improved; meanwhile he became interested in his sister's boyfriend's band, the unpromisingly named Love Country Music: 'a dreadful cabaret band'. By his account he changed their name to Ice Cream simply because he already had a three-dimensional badge of an ice cream. Ice Cream signed to Phonogram Records and supported both Gary Glitter and Barry Blue: he was a manager. They soon parted company. 'I wanted much more pop music and they wanted to be the new Blood Sweat And Tears.'

He began putting together packages for the university circuit, mixtures of radio DJs and bands, 'my dodgy acts, as Neil would call them'. The most notable of these were one called Grand Hotel, signed to CBS, and another called Giggles, signed to EMI. One idea for Giggles was to use comic-book imagery to promote them, so he phoned the British office of Marvel Comics and spoke to the editor there, a graduate called Neil Tennant.

Neil had left college just before his twenty-first birthday. He was considering postgraduate work and had chosen his subject, a branch of Imperial and Commonwealth History, but a journalist friend pointed out a job in the *UK Press Gazette*. He applied even though he didn't really want it – 'I felt like I'd doss around for a while' – but they liked him and a couple of weeks later he started. He got paid £25 a week, raised to £30 six weeks later. His job was to change American spellings, decide which cleavages should be covered (Marvel Comics were marketed to a younger age group in Britain than in America) and oversee the production of *Spiderman*, *The Mighty World of Marvel*, *Dracula Lives*, *Conan the Barbarian*, *Planet of the Apes*, *The Titans and Captain Britain*. He also introduced the odd interview with pop stars interested in comics: he talked to Alex Harvey and – to his joy – Marc Bolan.

In those days he'd compose songs at home on a guitar he'd been given for his twenty-first birthday. He'd write out the words and remember the tune because he didn't have a tape-recorder. Before, living in Tottenham, they had had a piano and he'd play his songs to friends. It was then that he'd discovered the basic chord – 'an octave E bass with G major 7 at the top' – that was to be the starting point of 'West End Girls'. 'It was meant to sound like Barry White.' He used to answer adverts for songwriters in the back of *Melody Maker*. When he was eighteen he had turned up at a publishing company, April Music, 'mega-glammed up in enormous flared trousers and huge shoes with enormous platforms'. There and then he sat at their piano and played them a song called 'Telephone Blues' from a play called *The Baby* that he'd written in his youth theatre days. They liked it, and they liked the next song, 'Summer Rain', even more.

'They liked it but they didn't know what to do. They thought I was too young; they thought I might fizzle out. I visited them again but then the people left.'

He even demoed three songs for another company, Ambassador Music, and also went to the Jonathan King audition, but nothing happened.

By the time he'd left college and had started at Marvel Comics he'd decided 'it was never going to happen'. He'd write songs and just play them to his friends. Then 'it got to the stage where I didn't even play them to anyone.'

He remembers Tom Watkins perpetually hustling him at Marvel Comics to borrow their Spiderman costume. (Marvel Comics would use it for Spiderman 'personal appearances' in places like Brighton, where an actor would wear it and some bright, annoying youngster would insist that it wasn't the real Spiderman and demand to know why he didn't use his 'amazing arachnoid abilities' to walk up walls.)

'Tom still has a copy of a really snooty letter from me to him because he used to borrow the Spiderman suit and he wouldn't give it us back, or it'd be returned in disgusting condition.' (Tom confirms he has the letter: 'I'm saving it for *my* book.')

Neil was interested enough to go and see Giggles a couple of times (at one concert he told Tom EMI shouldn't sign Giggles, they should sign a group he'd just seen at the Nashville pub called the Sex Pistols). They lost touch, but Neil remembered one thing about Tom that impressed him: 'He was such a hustler.'

'He was a real prick – absolutely *unbelievable*,' says Tom of the younger Neil. 'He had glasses and he was terribly officious and toed the company line like you wouldn't believe. He was really geeky-looking and not at all helpful. He gave me such a hard time. He was deeply into bands like the Clash who I loathed. I thought he was a little oik. He saw Giggles a couple of times but he didn't like pop music. He was a big fan of all this punk rock music.'

Tom suggests that Neil was naïve, that Neil thought punk was purely a sincere musical movement. 'Let's face it, it was also an incredibly high-fashion thing.'

Giggles, most of whom went on to become Sheena Easton's backing band during her early flush of success, did all right but never had a British hit. Tom also worked with a band called Portraits (later to have a little success as the Fixx).

'The philosophy was always the same,' he says. 'I've always believed, the same as I did with Bros really . . . manipulation's a strong word, *marketing*'s, the word that I use. They've got to be talented and they've got to be good-looking because you're selling sex as well as anything else; I've always said that.'

He used to believe that if you got all this right success would roll along. Simple as that.

'Because I came from an aesthetic background and not being musical particularly myself I felt that possibly you could make anyone a star.'

He now admits that there was one thing missing. He talks a while about 'a unique chemical element', not wanting to come to the point. Which is? He sighs, as if admitting defeat. 'I think it's basically *talent*.'

At the same time Tom continued designing – concert posters and record sleeves as well as interiors. With a friend he formed XL Design who did work for Nik Kershaw, Duran Duran, Kim Wilde and – most famously – for Frankie Goes To Hollywood. They also designed the sleeve for a one-off release on Epic Records, 'West End Girls' by the Pet Shop Boys. Neil was also brought into their office because he was editing the Frankie Goes To Hollywood book *And Suddenly There Came a Bang!*, another XL Design project.

'The first time I saw him again I probably thought, "Oh, it's that vicious little git from Marvel Comics," but we started chatting and I just liked him. I don't know if we'd both matured or if he was just being nice.'

Everyone in Tom's office loved the demo tape that Neil gave Tom (it included two future number ones, 'It's A Sin' and 'West End Girls', as well as 'Rent' and 'Opportunities') but his co-directors were already unhappy that Tom had moved XL into management in his spare time, forming a company called Massive Management. (He looked after a trio called Spelt Like This who were to be one of EMI's most hyped launches, and most embarrassing failures.) Nevertheless, when Neil asked him to take on Pet Shop Boys he agreed.

He remembers being intrigued by Chris. 'He was such a moody bastard it absolutely fascinated me. He came into the office and just sat there and was exactly the same as he is now. He had this persona of being disinterested in the entire world – "that's it, take it or leave it" – in a fun, playful way that amused me.'

These days Neil and Chris will refer, only half-jokingly, to their management organization as 'being surrounded by "no" men'. It didn't take long for their relationship to settle into one of opposition.

'They were very exact and very precise about what they wanted and what they didn't want,' Tom remembers. Early on Chris and Tom had a huge row about Memphis Design that still reverberates quietly to this day. They also had a row drawing up the initial contract.

'I was being really queenie and saying "take it or leave it" and doing an entire number,' admits Tom, 'and they nearly didn't sign it, it turned out later, because they were pissed off by that degree of arrogance.' A year later XL went bankrupt,

Tom bought Massive Management, and the Pet Shop Boys renegotiated the contract anyway. A month after that, 'West End Girls' reached number one.

Tom admits – perhaps even over-exaggerates for effect – how little they agreed over presentation.

'I always wanted all the glam and the glitz and the rest of it, and they wanted the complete opposite. It was chalk and cheese. I wanted them to have an enormous glitzy band all around them, and I wanted Neil to have dancing lessons and I wanted five black drummers – real sort of mad ideas. And they quietly said, "Yes, *thank you*, Tom and now *we'll* do this. We'll go on-stage as the two of us and be dull and boring" . . . which they always maintained they were.'

When Neil said recently in an interview that Tom had tried to get them into ripped jeans – Bros's earliest fashion emblem – Tom had denied it to him. I ask him now and he says 'I probably did' and laughs.

'It's always driven me mad, ripped jeans. I'm sure I did. I'd have had them in cancan outfits at one time. I'd be very excited about something and then Neil would say, "Shut up, you fat bastard" and they would do whatever they wanted to do.'

Why did you ask Tom to be your manager?

Neil: I thought we should have a manager because I realized you couldn't do the whole thing yourself. If we were going to get a proper record deal we were going to have to have a manager who was going to do it for us. At this point I was just assuming that Tom would just deal with Bobby O. Of course Tom wasn't interested in signing us with Bobby O involved because too many rights were tied up. The way Tom functions as a manager is to get a 20 per cent advance for the publishing and the recording so that he gets good money immediately.

But what was his appeal?

Neil: He was a big fat man with a loud voice, and we needed someone who could spiel, basically. I knew that Tom was a major spieler. He came to our attention also because Gordon Charlton (*A&R at CBS*) told us that he managed Adele Bertei – which he did for a while before – and we loved her record 'Build Me A Bridge' and we thought, 'Wow! he *must* be good! He manages *Adele Bertei*!!!'

What did you make of him at first, Chris?

Chris: He's quite impressive the first time you meet him, mainly because of his size. But I've never liked people who are very dominant. He's got a lot of bravado, particularly before you know him very well, before you can get through to his insecurities. Do you know what I mean? He's very . . . *big*.

Did that rub you up the wrong way?

Chris: Not really, but walking down the street with him I used to feel like I was a little schoolboy with his dad.

Neil: Tom's bulk has always been quite important in our relationship with him. You can literally *hide* behind him.

Chris: He's got more front than Woolworth's and I felt like this small – physically small – person.

Neil: And he used to make us laugh.

Chris: Although now I see him as completely different. We've been through a lot so I can speak to him on my terms now.

What are your terms?

Chris: I can treat him like I treat anyone. Whereas before I was a bit in awe of him. I was still a nobody student and he was big and impressive . . . he always exuded wealth. He still does.

Neil: He has an attitude, which is a part of his appeal to us, that he likes taking the piss out of the whole thing, the music business. We have a similar attitude. Though now I think Tom's got too serious about the music business. But actually he still likes to take the piss – we plot how we can get something outrageous out of the business. He gives the impression of being someone who is outrageous and who has no morals about what he does, which is kind of true and not true at the same time. You know he says, 'I'm a rich fat lucky bastard'; I find that quite embarrassing because he's actually worked quite hard for it all. It's hard to pin down his good and bad points – his good ones in particular (*laughs*) – but he has them. Let's face it, he's made himself the only well-known manager in Britain.

You don't like that much, do you? You're always narked when there's a magazine article about Tom Watkins, the extraordinary pop manager genius.

Neil: Yes, I would rather have a low-profile manager. Of course sometimes I do like it, but what we don't like is, we've felt in the past that Tom has tried to give the impression that everything good about the Pet Shop Boys is his idea. For instance, about this show he'll say, 'What *we've* done is . . .' Well, a lot of it he didn't really approve of us doing. There's the famous time when he said to someone 'all that minimalism – it's all me', when Tom spent three months designing our first album cover and it was so complicated (*eight interlocking stripes one and a half inches wide in either direction*) that the reason we had the cover we had was to be the exact opposite to him. Maybe it was all him; it was certainly a reaction to him. At the start when he was really trying to package us in ripped denim again we did the opposite. To be quite honest a lot of what the Pet Shop Boys have done has been reacting to Tom.

Chris: Yes, reacting against being a manufactured group, which we never wanted to be.

Neil: In some ways I think one of the things that has kept the Pet Shop Boys strong – even now, with no one wanting us to use Derek Jarman or release 'It's Alright' – is always having to fight against people, including our own people. We've never been surrounded by 'yes' men ever. If anything we've been surrounded by 'no' men. We use up a lot of energy fighting, but maybe it's a good thing. I can't decide really.

What do you think Tom saw in you?

Neil: I think he just liked our records.

Do you think he saw that you'd be successful?

Neil: I don't think Tom necessarily knew. I think he signed us because he loves hi-energy music and he liked something about us. We represent something that Tom wishes he was. Tom would like to be – I personally think – a sensitive intellectual and he sees Chris and me as being . . . unusual people. He thinks we're sort of clever and intellectual and so he gets a lot out of us mentally. Also, Tom has always been able, from day one, to reduce Chris and me to hysterics. My earliest fond memory of Tom is when we went to someone's Christmas party. Tom always says how mean this man is and we arrived, behind Tom like the seven dwarves, and he shouts out, 'Three cheap red wines, please' and then says, 'Oooh! she's *really* splashed out on the peanuts this year – don't eat too many of them, boys.'

Chris: And actually there *wasn't* much food.

Neil: And Tom hates that. Tom is a lavish person. He likes to entertain lavishly. If you go to Tom's house for Sunday brunch there's tons of food, loads of salads, about fifteen desserts and you all drink champagne. Chris and I never entertain.

'I don't know if Tom thought we'd be successful. He had a lot of faith in us. He loved our demo tape. I'm still not sure if it isn't the favourite thing we've made so far as far as Tom is concerned. He'll still say, 'Are you going to record "In The Club Or In The Queue"?'

Tom says he had all sorts of mad ideas you threw back at him – costumes, dancing lessons, big black drummers . . .

Neil: I don't really know what you mean. He might have wanted to send me for dancing lessons. All I can remember is the ripped denim.

'Chris?' Tom considers. 'I think he continually pursues youth. I think he's somebody that missed out to a certain extent on a lot of his youth through academic studies, because he's very bright academically. I think he's enjoying being young. He's discovered himself in all sorts of ways and now he's got time to play and enjoy himself. He likes to think that he's moody and bored but that's all part of his act really – deep down I think he's very kind and very considerate. I think he's selfish about many things . . . he only wants to do what he wants to do, and I'm not saying that's a bad thing, because I think we're all selfish. Sometimes I've seen Neil get hurt by him; sometimes he's hurt me. Both Neil and I are incredibly fond of him and I only want to do things in his best interests and he has a strange way of saying thank you, or repaying you. It's odd. But that's maybe what everyone gravitates towards. I don't know. I just like him. I didn't like him in the first instance – I found him very sulky, very difficult and I think he needed to lighten up, but he was discovering all sorts of things and I think it was important for him to go through all of that.'

I ask Tom if he thinks Chris is the way he is for self-protection.

'I don't know. Listen – I'm no more a psychiatrist . . . I don't know. I'm glad he does it and I don't want to analyse it any more than that: he is what he is and thank God he is because he gives the act that edge.'

I wonder what Tom thinks Chris gets from being a pop star.

'Money, I should think.'

Just that?

'Nah,' says Tom. 'He loves music. It's entirely music for him. I suppose he's learning to enjoy what the financial rewards bring, but I know essentially it has to be music.'

So what does Tom think is Chris's main contribution to the Pet Shop Boys?

'I just think he understands this dance thing. Neil has a huge understanding of the classics, and the fullness of the sound, and I think Chris understands the basic dance thing. He's a very good dancer as well. He enjoys that side of it. I think that's it really. The rough and the smooth.'

Chris, Tom has this theory that you missed out on your childhood and you're having it now.

Chris: The search for the youth I never had! (*Thinks.*) It may well be, actually. I did spend a lot of time studying. It's funny. There are some people who mature very early. In the sixth form some people were very mature and then they went to work in banks and I always used to think they were like thirty-year-olds. I was a swot but I never had that *look.* When I went to university I went back a step, and becoming a pop star (*laughs*) allows you to go even further back, if you wish to.

And you do wish to?

Chris: It's nice to be able to be irresponsible. That's one thing I didn't really like about working in an office – you've got to be so *serious* all the time. I don't think my basic nature is that.

How much do you think you rely on Neil being sensible?

Chris: I'm glad Neil can do that.

Isn't it true though that you can be the most irresponsible person on earth when you've someone compensating for you but that, as soon as you need to be, you become very sensible? It's a device really.

Chris: Having the foil? Yeah. Neil was amazed the first time he came in a car with me driving because he knew what I was like, but of course I'm incredibly sensible. He was quite surprised.

So why do you do it – pretend to be irresponsible?

Chris: I don't know.

'Neil? Oh I adore him, absolutely adore him. I don't know really. He probably wouldn't see it this way but I just feel almost that I've known him in another life really. I think we both irritate each other to the *n*th degree. I have a great respect for the man's talents, I have a great respect for his conceptual abilities, for the way he sees things as a whole and sees them through. I get frustrated with him in terms of nit-picking about details; when I always think there's a broader whole he'll go on about one particular detail. It did irritate me but now I recognize they are important also. Every now and again he can be very pedantic about certain things, even now. He'll home in on something and he'll nadger away until it's sort of got resolved. That annoys me no end, but now everybody just knows it's Neil. He's just a prissy old thing and we know that we've got to do what he says otherwise he drives us bleedin' mad.

'The joke is, because I'm a wheeler-dealer, they give me such a bad time about being a shark. I don't think they've ever trusted me really. I'm sure they think that secretly, even though I don't handle their money, I'm ripping them off. They're always telling me I'm ripping them off. Yeah! I rip 'em off the whole time!

'As a person I think Neil's very lonely. He talks about circles of friends but . . . I don't really know. I think that possibly I'd like to think I would be his friend outside of this relationship but it's very difficult to call someone your friend if you manage them, if you have a business relationship with them.

'I don't know. I'm in awe of the man. I have the greatest respect for him. I'd like to be in business with him. I'm in a business now with another man and I think he would add something that none of us have, another dimension. I think he certainly needs the gregariousness and extrovert qualities that I have coupled with his sort of more sober . . . (*Trails off.*)

'He reads an awful lot. He's very *concerned*. He always seems to be politically very well opinioned. I don't share his political views necessarily. I just enjoy the kind of people who are in very sharp contrast to me. Because I don't have the ability – not the ability, I don't have the *time* – to indulge myself in the way they would. I'm more orientated to business than to enjoyment and literature and all that, so I'm somewhat envious of that.'

I wonder what he thinks makes Neil tick.

'Good food, good wine . . . I think he likes *quality* things. He went without them for a long time. He comes from a middle-class background so it wasn't as if there was a total absence of these things in his life but, when he was working as a journalist, he had a pretty meagre existence.

'I've always told people that he suffers fools badly. He doesn't like bullshit, to be honest. If I start to waffle he'll quickly correct me. I think I learnt in the first couple of years that I was wasting my time. Neil will turn round and say, "Don't talk bullshit." He has that very direct way.'

So what, I ask, does he get out of being in the Pet Shop Boys?

'He's always been fascinated by the pop industry and pop stars and all the rest of it and I think he's doing it a new way and I think what he likes is the idea that he has created this huge success his way. Like me – though the word is unfortunate I can't think of another word to describe it – he is a manipulator. He understands exactly what you have to do to have success in this business, which is an incredibly unprofessional, tedious and nasty business to be in. I think he gives it a degree of credibility.'

That makes it sound as though he's very calculating.

'Yes, I think that's entirely what he's doing. The pair of them.'

I ask Tom why he thinks Neil and Chris work together.

'I would imagine that there is a fascination on both sides; an admiration of what the other's about. I think that the academic and intellectual side of the other's being – though their characters are completely different – fascinates each other. It's like dissimilar poles attracting. There's a lot of common ground and a lot of dissimilar characteristics. It's the combination.

'I made the mistake once in the very early days of saying to

Neil, "You don't really need him," but Neil was very quick to pick up on that and say, "I do" and I knew very quickly that that was a mistake, because there is most definitely that balance, that stabilizing effect on both sides. It's like a catalyst thing that they each trigger in each other; it's vital to the chemistry and the success of the duo.'

Tom says that he once tried to split you up.

Neil: Tom was always – and probably still is, for all I know – obsessed with thinking that Chris and I were lovers, and quite simply couldn't believe that we weren't. He said to me, '*Everybody* knows . . .'

Chris (amused): That's classic Tom.

Neil: And I'd say, 'Everyone may know, Tom, but in actual fact it's not true.' And he'd say, 'Everyone will know why he's in the group – this is going to do you no good at all' and he suggested it would be better if I went it alone. I said that I couldn't go it alone, there are *two* of us. Tom didn't believe that Chris did anything in the group. I said, 'Tom, we've just written a song called "Suburbia", for instance, where Chris wrote all the music.' He didn't believe me. I said, 'He *did*!' and he *still* wouldn't believe me: 'Everyone knows Chris doesn't do anything – and don't tell me you don't know what I'm talking about.' Eventually I got bored with it. He admitted to me about six months later that he was wrong.

Did you tell Chris about this at the time?

Neil: I probably didn't tell him at the time. (*To Chris*) I think I told you about two years later. I didn't tell you at the time because I knew you'd get in such a rage and probably kill Tom.

Were you furious when you found out?

Chris: I can't remember. Was I, Neil?

Neil: No, I think you thought it was funny. It *is* funny. You can't really hold that against Tom.

Chris: It's quite reasonable behaviour for a pop manager.

Who, I ask Tom, does he think is the boss in the Pet Shop Boys?

'The obvious thing is to assume that Neil's in control. He's the obvious group leader. He's the one who we see most as a management team, talk to the whole time, because he's more readily contactable than Chris is. I'm sure Chris is there but never answers the phone.

'But I'm sure it is very well balanced. I know musically it is very well balanced and I'm sure, really and truly, that, although he says a lot less than Neil does, Chris's input is just as great. But I can see how other people don't see that. Every now and again I get a bit narked when people don't see it that way, but then any lead singer always gets more attention than any of the band.'

'They're very proud of what they do and very passionate about it,' says Tom.

'Chris particularly, he hates every kind of music except for the kind he plays, and that's fantastic . . . You can see there are two incredibly consuming passions at work and the result is huge . . . like a huge volcano.'

Have they changed? I ask.

'I don't think they have at all. They have more money. They have changed but only in the way everybody changes, everybody matures, but basically their ideas and aims are fundamentally the same.'

I ask Tom if, in any sense, Bros were a relief to him because he could exercise the control that he had never been allowed with the Pet Shop Boys. He deflects the question over and over. At other times – both in private and in interviews – he has boasted of his role, of his skill and vision, in shaping Bros, but now is perhaps not a good time. If they have been on a leash then they are rather messily wriggling free. Right now, in the summer of 1989, they have 'that difficult second album' out soon, they have discovered a mind of their own. And, well, it's simply not a good time to talk about them in terms of being moulded. Nowadays his spiel, for both Bros and the Pet Shop Boys, is one of hammed-up modesty:

'I am a *tool,* and I am a tool to be *used*, in the hands of the right craftsmen I am a perfect tool. Remember – I work for them. They don't work for me. That's what management is.'

Whether or not it has influenced what he has said today, this conversation is given a certain edge by the current situation. The management contract between the Pet Shop Boys and Tom Watkins is a five-year one and it expires at the end of this October, just a few months away. A decision by the Pet Shop Boys on whether they will sign with him once more is imminent. It is by no means certain that they will.

'I hope they're going to stay with me,' he says. If so, he concedes, there will need to be a renegotiation in their favour. He says he would be happy to continue without a contract. And if they leave him? At first he simply says that he'd be disappointed because he doesn't think that anyone could service them as well, could be 'more loyal and have more belief in them'. Anyway, he says, it'd be stupid of them not to, as they have to keep paying him a percentage of various things for some years ahead anyway.

He carries on talking about this, unprompted, and gets more emotional. 'They can call the shots on that one – I *can't* call the shots . . . I would probably shed a tear . . . I think it's only the beginning to be honest . . . I've got exciting plans . . . but life's too short to be bitter and twisted . . . without talking about clichés I *love* them . . . I'd be *very* upset if they left . . .'

When I turn off my tape recorder he quizzes me on what I think they will do. I have no real inkling, except to know that, to the best of my knowledge, they're undecided; I try not to say anything that can be interpreted in any way at all.

At the end he returns to a theme he'd mentioned three or four times that, whatever else happens, 'I am their biggest fan.'

Several days later, over dinner, Neil and Chris ask how my chat with Tom had gone.

'Very interesting,' I say. I mention that he was almost embarrassingly unwilling to wrest the credit from them for anything.

They ask whether he thinks they'll leave him.

'I don't think he knows,' I say.

Chris laughs affectionately. 'Did he say he's our biggest fan then?'

Chapter Ten

In the last twenty-four hours, someone has added Pet Shop Boys graffiti to the bus. It says:

'Pet Shop Boys. We came. We saw. We left. We kicked some yellow ass. Rock out man. Alright. Woah. Aaaaaahaagh. Yeuuch.'

Neil and Chris are absolutely *appalled*. This is worse than any number of unapproved Levi sponsorships. But what to do? They must clearly cover it up but it would take an age to black out. It is Pete who comes up with the solution. He takes a black pen (which apparently he carries for Neil and Chris to sign autographs with – and for him to write 'Arsenal' everywhere) and blocks over the words Pet Shop Boys. In their place he writes 'Bros'.

When we arrive at the venue there is another crisis, less easily solved. When Courtney Pine was approached to play on this tour he had asked Ivan to deal directly with him, not via his agent. This Ivan did. Because he has no manager then, for some obscure reason, he has signed no contract. Now his agent, understandably miffed at being left out of this current deal, has been deliberately perverse. In the days to come, on the nights of British dates, Courtney has been booked to appear at three venues, reputedy Folkestone Town Hall, Wigan Working Men's Club and at a wine bar in Bristol. Ivan says he will sort it out.

Neil talks through the Liza Minnelli album title brainwave. He was so excited by it that when he got to his hotel room he telephoned Liza straight away in New York; she loved it. Now, he says, they should record an extra song called 'Results' when they return to Britain: 'a power woman song'.

'Results,' considers Chris. 'It's a bit like getting your pregnancy test. It has all those connotations. It should come out in August when everyone gets their exam results.'

The end-of-tour party has been a cause of contention for some days. A public party somewhere like Clapham Common has been considered, run by the Sunrise people, with a private tent for guests – they might even make money out of it – but, perhaps thanks to the media attention for the last Sunrise 'do', that idea has been forgotten.

'I had this idea of having it in a football ground. I'd love to have it in Arsenal,' says Neil.

They agree not to decide yet.

In the hospitality room in the venue the talk is of Mr Udo. Lee, the production manager, is perplexed. He has dealt with Mr Udo many times before. This isn't the royal treatment he has been used to. Even Mr Udo's people in the production office, usually friendly, are being cold and uncommunicative, as if this is a job they can't wait to be finished with.

The discussion fades into more conventional back-stage banter. Someone tells a story they've heard about an American rock star. It's about a sort of incentive scheme. The crew would be given extra back-stage passes with their initials on, to hand out to particularly pretty girls. Whosoever's initials were on the pass that ended up in the rock star's room would get a 50-dollar bonus from the tour accountant.

In the Pet Shop Boys' dressing-room Neil and Chris receive their invitation to tonight's EMI dinner. They are not happy: it says 'snacks will be provided'.

A minute before they go on, as they march downstairs, Pete is surprised with a cake. It is his twenty-sixth birthday.

'*Who* is responsible for this?' he frets, secretly pleased, as everyone sings 'Happy Birthday'.

I watch the show from back-stage, to see the frantic costume-changing. They slip in and out of their clothes – velcro frenzy –

in small dressing-tents on either side of the stage. Passing one, I see the wardrobe people and Neil all spill out – the tent has gone dark, the power gone, and Neil must speedily change for a number that is just about to start. Alan holds up a portable light and the change is carried off all right, if with a certain amount of panic. It's only as I watch that my mind connects this scrabbling with the way I had half-tripped over in the near-darkness a few seconds before. I had knocked the plug out. Someone soon works out what has happened, but not who is responsible. Embarrassed, I say nothing.

During 'Domino Dancing' Chris stops playing and walks off. As he doesn't return, Dominic cancels the instrumental coda and goes into the next song, during which Chris eventually, grumpily, reappears. Once again, he is furious because he had no spotlight on him. Only with some persuasion from Neil does he agree to carry on at all.

Back-stage the champagne flows, the toast is browning and Neil and Chris are discussing Japanese uniforms.

'The roadworkers look *fantastic*,' says Chris. 'I don't know who styles them.'

'The traffic wardens are brilliant,' adds Neil.

'I saw all the dancers stark bollock naked tonight,' says Chris. He means the girl dancers. 'Well, stark bollock naked without the bollocks.'

They discuss a liaison between two members of the touring party.

'Good for him, that's what I say,' says Neil.

'I'd be very surprised if they hadn't,' says Chris wisely.

Mr Udo is in the corridor outside. Chris insists that he won't leave the dressing-room until Mr Udo is removed from his path. 'I'm not walking past him.'

Eventually there is no choice.

'Goodnight, Chris. Very good show,' says Mr Udo as Chris passes.

Chris says precisely nothing.

Chris: My basic reason for a sleeve design, or something like that, is that it's to please myself. I don't care about anyone else. It's purely for me.

Neil: Chris does most things that way, ultimately.

Chris: I think that's the only way you can.

Do you think you're selfish?

(*Chris doesn't answer. Neil explodes with laughter.*)

Why are you laughing?

Neil: I'm laughing at his discomfort.

Chris: I'm not naturally a generous person. I don't like giving stuff away.

Neil: Selfishness isn't really about not being generous.

Chris: Then it depends. Something like a sleeve design you just end up terribly upset and unhappy if you back down on it. So if that's being selfish then I am.

Neil: I don't think that's being selfish, I think that's having integrity.

Chris: Sometimes we back down. On the tour, for instance, we backed down on a few points rather than completely overpower someone else's will and it's been to our detriment.

Neil: Normally if Chris and I agree on something, in my opinion we're right, to be honest. People will probably think we're arrogant for thinking that.

Well you are, aren't you?

Neil: Well, there's a difference between arrogance and confidence, I think. We gave in to things we weren't happy with so as not to be selfish.

Though you hardly baulk from mentioning them.

Neil: No, because as Chris said it irritates you if you're stuck with some useless person because you weren't being selfish. I think of other people quite a lot; at the same time I don't want to do something that I think is a stupid idea because that's not going to help anyone. Chris has, in some ways, got more integrity than I have. I will do something to please people because I don't want to be selfish. Chris will not do something if he thinks it's not right, regardless of the effect it will have on people. And in a way he's right to act like that. He has very good instincts. I always want to know what he thinks because he has very good instincts and is less confused by other issues. I tend to get confused by 'you can't be so horrible to so-and-so . . . you've got to do this because they play our records'. Whereas Chris's attitude is 'aren't they lucky they've got our records to play?'

Which is arrogant.

Neil: Which is arrogant, but at the same time kind of true.

'How is he so ridiculously well off?' Chris asks. He's talking about another famous pop star.

'He's totally hopeless,' says Neil.

'He's such a nice person,' Janet disagrees.

'We have given a million dollars to Bobby O,' Neil points out.

'But that still doesn't add up to his money,' says Chris.

'He started investing in property to start off with,' says Janet.

They still look unconvinced.

Neil: Since Live Aid, pop music has tended to become very chummy. All groups know each other and a large part of pop music has become rather worthy. Not just charity records themselves – you have things like the Prince's Trust, and it's just pop stars trying to get OBEs. I'm sure they will do, but it makes it all a bit pompous when Phil Collins phones up Prince Charles and says, 'Perhaps you'd better not come to the première of

Buster.' It's like they're all pals together. I think the Prince's Trust is fundamentally right-wing. The royal family know people are impressed by them. Prince Charles uses it to give himself a role in life, and he knows that one of the powers he's got is that people are impressed by the royal family, so he uses that.

We don't like the royal family. We'd like to abolish it. If they had a concert to abolish the royal family we might play. It's all too establishment – you get those pictures of all those pop stars together: Phil Collins and Eric Clapton, Howard Jones, Rick Astley and Status Quo all in the same photo. It reduces it all. And at the same time they become world figures. You have these semi-important people like Jim Kerr or U2. They're only pop stars. I don't think that U2 have *anything* interesting to say. I quite like some of their records, but they're just pop records.

Have you anything to say?

Neil: Actually of course I think we do. People always ask in interviews, 'Does your music have a message?' and of course it doesn't have a *message* as such, but I think our records are good at individual comment or commenting on or describing feelings, and they're very individual. And we deliberately don't set ourselves up as something. All those rock stars are embarrassing.

To be fair to U2 I'm not sure that they've *tried* to say anything interesting about anything. They write incredibly traditional pop songs. But it's their style and their presentation that's so pompous. Like, you get Big Country who go to Moscow and say to people, 'Do you get the message?' Well, *what* is the message? The message is that they're promoting a new album (*'Peace In Our Time'*). But you're not supposed to say that, or you're accused of being cynical. The fact is that they've used an enormous media event to launch their new album. As it happens, unsuccessfully. But you're supposed to think that the total aim of what they do is to make a sincere statement about world peace. There are some far more sincere things you can do about world peace. The problem is really that pop stars always do these things publicly to get maximum publicity value out of it. And of course the idea is that they get publicity for the cause. I think it would be better if they worked individually – in other words not as pop stars but as people.

But they would counter that it's precisely by using their pop star status that they can have a beneficial effect.

Neil: Yes, but I don't know what effect they have really. At the moment pop music is just a branch of ecology, the public face of ecology. But I think that a good documentary about ecological issues on television does a lot more than all the pop stars put together. What I don't like is when pop stars behave like 'Hey! Listen kids! We know something you don't know! The ozone layer's really screwed up! It's, like, terrible! You shouldn't use aerosol deodorants!' *Everyone* in the *world* knows that. It's like when pop stars are against war: 'Listen! We're all against war! It's a really bad thing!', as if people think, 'Oh, we think war's fantastic actually but I've now changed my mind because John Lennon's told me peace is a good thing.'

Chris: He's enough to make you want to *go* to war, John Lennon . . .

Don't you think that quite often these records, and the general worthiness, is partly these people apologizing for pop music because they're embarrassed that pop music is 'only' pop music and they're slightly ashamed to be involved in it? That's what drives them to do their worthy things. Except that in doing so they put pop music down and try to devalue the rest of it.

Neil: A lot of these people are just very self-important. Also, one of the points of pop music is that it kind of defines a generation. I don't think that it does that so much any more but that, in a way, defines the generation now. Lots of seventeen-year-olds went to see Cliff Richard at Wembley Stadium. Why? I don't get it really. What has also happened to the pop market is that people who loved pop music in the sixties still love it. Journalists are often in their late thirties or even early forties, and you can see their perspective everywhere. It would be interesting to analyse the reviews of U2's 'Rattle And Hum'. Rock critics liked 'Rattle And Hum' because they want a return to the traditional rock values. What they basically want is for it to be like 1969 again. It's this thing where British – or in U2's case Irish – groups discover the roots of American music. U2 have discovered this and they're just doing pastiches (*his voice rises*) and it's reviewed as a serious thing because 'Dylan plays organ' on some song and B.B. King plays on some throwaway pop song 'When Love Comes To Town' that could have been written by Andrew Lloyd Webber. It could be in *Starlight Express* if you ask me.

People fall for that because they want to believe those myths. The myths of rock music were totally battered by punk but now people want them back. Now, once again in 1989, you can talk frankly about how you used to like Genesis or Yes. U2, together with all these people writing in the papers, have helped create that.

The fact of the matter is that the Pet Shop Boys stand against all of this, so it's quite right that people like that should slag us off. Because we hate everything that they are and stand for. We hate it because it's totally stultifying, it says nothing, it is big and pompous and ugly. We hate it for exactly the same reasons Johnny Rotten said he hated dinosaur groups in 1976. To me U2 are a total dinosaur group. They're saying nothing but they're pretending to be something. I think they're *fake*.

As only 'snacks will be provided', Neil and Chris decide a spot of proper dinner is necessary before the EMI party. Chris is fed up with oriental food and we go to a French restaurant; French cuisine in Japan is, we are told, the second best in the world.

In the hotel reception a fan, trembling with excitement, asks Chris, 'Will you take a picture of me?' She means, 'Can I have my picture taken with you?'

'Yes,' he says, taking her literally, and, to her bewilderment, snatches her camera and points it in her direction.

In the car Chris examines the present she has given to him. 'I always look at the card first,' he says virtuously, for my benefit. The card includes a stamped addressed envelope and says, 'It would make me very happy if you thought of me for just one second . . .' He shrugs as he reads it, as if to say, 'That's that taken care of then.'

He opens the package. Inside is an Armani t-shirt. He is literally thrilled. 'You know,' he says, 'little things like this make it all right.' He methodically examines the t-shirt. 'It's fantastic. It's got a good neck on it. It's *crucial*,' he says, talking directly to me in an advisorial manner, 'to have a tight neck.' He decides he likes it so much that he wants to wear it immediately and so, though he is crammed between Pete and me in the back of a taxi, he rips off the t-shirt he is wearing and puts on his gift.

'You can say he's got a hairy chest,' says Pete to me.

'No,' counsels Chris. 'They don't like that. Say it's smooth.'

'She makes you feel inspired,' says Chris as we arrive, talking about Janet. 'Last night I was really tired and the food was bad but Janet's just not going to be sad, is she?'

In the restaurant, where it is immediately evident that, once more, Janet is in no immediate danger of being overtaken by sadness, there is the evening's second chorus of 'Happy Birthday' for Pete. A Polaroid is taken of us sitting there. As usual, Neil turns up his nose at the result: 'One of my Mrs Thatcher looks.'

Mr Udo is discussed once more. No one is quite sure why Mr Udo has taken such wholesale umbrage if, indeed, he has. Neil asks Kaz, who is Japanese, to find out. Meanwhile, there is a fresh grievance. At all their concerts – at *Pet Shop Boys* concerts – there have been leaflets on the seats advertising future appearances by Charlie Sexton, Simply Red and Richard Marx. It is the latter that rankles the most.

Chris examines the menu. He is drawn towards tuna – one of his favourites – but confesses he is worried about stories he's heard that dolphins are caught in the tuna nets.

'You can't eat tuna any more,' he explains with regret, 'because it's got dolphin in it.'

There is silence as the enormity of this sinks in. It is Pete who finally talks.

'You can eat dolphin, can't you?' he chirps. The logic of this immediately appeals to Chris.

'Yeah,' he says, cheering up. 'What's *wrong* with eating dolphins?'

Tom gives Pete an art deco footballer for his birthday.

'Pity about the scratches,' says Pete.

'It's only fifty-nine years old,' says Tom.

Tom casually mentions that he is going to sack Rob next Monday because he didn't go home when Tom told him to.

'You've got to get a silence clause out of him first,' says Chris.

The calmness with which this news is greeted suggests that all present think that this is just one of those things Tom says; that 'I'm going to sack Rob' actually means 'Rob is going to get a fairly huge bollocking when I get back'.

Neil mentions a man he saw on a scooter earlier. He was wearing a riding hat. He says that he has noted the idea for future use.

Tom's food arrives. It is sushi. We are in a French restaurant. Chris is dumbfounded.

'Raw fish,' he gasps, 'when you don't *have* to have it?'

Janet mentions that some TV idea or other has gone 'on the backburner'.

'I'm going to write a song called "Backburner",' announces Neil, adding, 'Janet's worth her weight in gold for song titles. Like Pete and "Domino Dancing".'

'I didn't say it,' Pete reminds him.

'No,' agrees Neil, 'but you did say, "I want a dog, a

chihuahua. I've only got a small flat"' – the words from their song 'I Want A Dog' – 'and I wrote it down and said, "It's a song!" and it was, days later.'

Neil mentions how Liza screamed when he told her the LP title. Chris reflects that Liza lets them have control in nearly everything.

'Liza bought them boxes of underwear,' Pete tells me.

'She told us she was going to buy us presents and said, "What do you want?"' says Chris. 'I thought "Calvin Klein underwear!" So she flew over two boxes of Calvin Klein underwear in every colour. It was fantastic. I *love* getting underpants. You can't have enough underpants, can you?'

Tom tells us, with some pride, of how some 'private' photos of himself, taken one morning on the same roll of film as some Bros photos, ended up at CBS Records, copies circulating throughout the building. They weren't even flattering, he sighs. 'It was one of those "Is there anything down there?" mornings.'

He criticizes John for his thriftiness.

'He's *so* mean. He sticks stamps back on if they're not stamped.'

Everyone tuts.

'He saves food in the fridge.'

Puzzled looks.

'That's not *totally* unusual,' points out Neil.

Janet returns to the subject of underwear and tells how when Gianno Sanmarco (TV's Adrian Mole) interviewed Morten Harket, singer of A-ha, on the children's Saturday morning programme *Get Fresh*, he said he never wore the same underwear twice and asked fans to send him some new pairs as he was running out. In colourful detail she describes how packets of underwear poured through the post into their offices. It is told with such defiant, joyous confidence that you wouldn't dream of doubting it. Except . . .

I say nothing but Neil obviously notices my dubious expression. He saw the programme too.

'I know,' he whispers. 'It was socks.'

Neil tells the tale how David Hepworth, the editor of *Smash Hits* when Neil joined, thought it was brilliant when on *Saturday Superstore* in December 1987 Chris was asked what presents he wanted and said, 'Socks and underpants'. 'He said he'd never heard a pop star say that before.'

'I wonder how our party's going?' wonders Chris. 'It's probably over by now.'

The waiter takes orders for coffee.

'An espresso please,' says Neil.

'Cappuccino,' says Pete.

'Cappuccino-oh-uh-oh,' sings Chris, to the tune of 'Paninaro'.

We arrive at the EMI party at 11.15; fashionably late, you might say. It turns out that EMI have actually done them proud. The party is in an impressive castle-like building – the nicest building we've been inside in Japan – the 'snacks' are a huge table of delicacies that have easily outlasted the appetites of the rest of the entourage and the champagne is flowing.

They are applauded as they enter. Neil is introduced to the head of sales. 'Oh,' he says, 'the man that counts.' The head of the company makes a speech into a microphone.

'We are very much honoured to have the world-famous Pet Shop Boys by EMI and Udo company . . .'

A whispered but very obvious boo fills the room at the mention of the promoter.

'. . . so much excited by beautiful concerts by band. Coming to Japan encourages us very much and we get very ready to devote ourselves to promotion. Please get ready and enjoy tonight.'

Chris hides in the corner while Neil makes a short speech.

'Did I miss it?' asks Chris, like a truant schoolboy pretending he didn't know any prep had been set, once Neil has finished. 'I went to the toilet . . .'

Yuri, who handles their press and promotion in Japan, quizzes

Neil about the precise symbolic meaning of the 'It's A Sin' piece. She mentions that the head of EMI 'was surprised to see the big sex thing'.

'Penis, you mean' says Neil helpfully. 'Do you think anyone was offended?'

She shakes her head. 'I don't think so.'

'In Britain,' says Neil, 'people will pretend to be offended . . .'

She says that she feels Derek Jarman's staging was influenced by Fellini's *Satyricon*. Did Neil think that Fellini was a big influence on Derek Jarman?

'Quite possibly,' says Neil in a tone that suggests 'I haven't the foggiest'. 'I've not discussed it with him.'

Chris is enjoying himself. He points at the upturned peak of his cap, usually down over his eyes. 'I wear it up if I'm in a good mood.'

There is more ritual clapping – 3–3–7–1, 3–3–3–1 this time.

'Here we go, here we go, here we go,' shouts Chris by way of British response. 'We should do that 3–3–3–1 at Arsenal next season.'

He talks to Mike the accountant. Mike is Scottish. Chris asks him if he used to come to Blackpool, as many many Scottish people do, on Glasgow fortnight when they all take their summer break. Chris used to work in Blackpool as a glass collector.

'I could never understand a thing you said,' he tells Mike as if Mike represented the whole of Scotland. 'They'd put a pound note on a string and I'd go down to pick it up and they'd pull it away and be wetting themselves laughing. They'd say, "Do you want a fight?" I'd say . . .' – he puts on a timid voice – '. . . "No, I'm just collecting glasses."'

In the corner, sitting down, Neil is talking to Janet.

As they talk Lawrence takes a photo from some distance away. 'Too far away!' shouts Janet. 'It won't come out. It'll just be dim dots.'

'I rather like that,' muses Neil, drunkenly, '. . ."dim dots" . . .'

He is dragged over to meet someone from the TV programme *Hot Studio at Night*, on which the Pet Shop Boys have frequently appeared.

'Did you see the show?' Neil asks him.

'No, next time,' says the TV person.

'There might not *be* a next time,' counters Neil.

'This is our farewell tour,' says Chris.

Chris talks to someone from Nissan. He tries to get a £100,000 car in return for appearing in a TV ad. Neil agrees that Chris can do it alone.

'£100,000 is nothing together,' he explains, pretending that such sums are chicken-feed to him. 'Take off Tom's £20,000 and I get £40,000 – absolutely *nothing*. And I'm associated with some dodgy product.'

'And you lose credibility,' says Janet.

'Not here you don't,' smiles Neil. Here they would do adverts if the money is right. Janet says that she was asked to do an advert recently – for spaghetti letters.

Presumably you think that, in so much as some groups are fake, the Pet Shop Boys aren't?

Neil: Yes, because the Pet Shop Boys are utterly contemporary, which is very important. We do not pay homage to a previous era. I've got nothing against previous eras but I'm bored with people paying homage to them. In many ways the history of pop music is a hangover from the sixties. We've always tried to be of the present.

What about the things from the past that you do look back at, like musicals?

Neil: That's different because that's outside the pop music tradition. It doesn't really belong to it, so you can bring something like that in.

So it's just an outside resource, like being inspired by books or films?

Neil: Yes it is.

Isn't there a danger though that soon the Pet Shop Boys will make records that will be in homage to, say, the golden age of hi-energy?

Neil: No, I don't think we'd ever do that. We always take – just as the Beatles or the Bee Gees did – the contemporary dance feel of the time and write songs within that. That's why Paul McCartney's not very successful at the moment – he doesn't do what he did in the Beatles, or even what he did in Wings. He doesn't take the contemporary dance feel of the moment and write a good pop song that goes with it. That's all we do.

As I get into the car to go back to the hotel with Janet and Neil, we are rushed by Pete and Chris, frenzied with excitement.

'We've got the title for the book!' screams Chris. 'We've got it!'

'What?'

'*You Know the Story. Pet Shop Boys: You Know the Story.*'

We all laugh.

'It's absolutely fabulous!' agrees Neil.

Pete later explains that it's a saying among his friends – if they see someone they fancy they'll nudge the person they're with, indicate the person and say, 'You *know* the story . . .'

'You know . . .' is anyway the most distinctive on-tour saying. If someone looks smart Dainton will say, 'You *know* you're happening'; if a restaurant's pricey, 'You *know* it's expensive' (or, in Japan, 'You *know* it's a lot of yin-yangs'); out late, 'You *know* we're partying.'

But when I next mention the title, a few days later, everyone seems to have gone off it.

★

'What larks, eh?' says Danny as we draw off.

'I always say,' says Neil, 'it's better than working for a living.'

Danny asks about the book.

'It's coming out posthumously,' says Neil, 'when we're all dead.'

He and Janet sketch out plans for an old people's home for, as Janet puts it, 'special, brilliant old people, not vegetable old people'. She means the two of them.

'We'll have our own rooms,' she says.

'*Suites*, actually,' corrects Neil.

'A castle with a moat. A helicopter. And in the evenings we'll watch our best moments on TV.'

'I'll come downstairs and say, "I'm thinking of having a gala performance on the video tonight of *It Couldn't Happen Here* – full evening dress, and no champers unless you say you liked it when it first came out."'

'Posthumously,' he muses. 'That's a great idea for an LP.' The idea being that you record your posthumous LP, 'Posthumously', before you die. 'I think we might do that.'

Chapter Eleven

Friday, 7 *July*

We meet in the hotel lobby at 12.30 to leave for Osaka. We are going on the bullet train, a journey keenly anticipated by members of the entourage who have heard about this glorious twenty-first-century invention that glides at high speed across Japan. Neil and Chris have been on the bullet train before and they successfully dampen all enthusiasm – it's a bit like an Intercity, that's all, they say, but not as good.

Neil has been reading the Japanese fanzine called *Out of Order*. It's a professional affair, well-printed and with each article in both Japanese and English. (The English translations, one suspects, are specifically for the Pet Shop Boys themselves – it is littered with messages like 'We try to make it close to your casual word'.) *Out of Order* is filled with interviews 'borrowed' from British magazines, fan drawings and endless interpretations of and improvisations based upon Pet Shop Boys lyrics.

'I recognized the dawn break, and another borderless day has just begun. My life became like that, because I was left to my own devices,' reckons someone called Keiko. Miyaki prefers combining words and pictures. 'Their future,' Miyaki writes, then there is a picture of Chris with stubble – 'still loose', it says – and a picture of Neil with glasses – 'still nervous'.

'I have a fear,' confides Ikumi, 'of PSB will break up because he have no plan . . . what is worse! . . . after a few years Neil may write a book of how to hit singles, and Chris may hide out in somewhere. Please let me wake up such nightmare!!'

There is a debate – translated back into English – about what a meaningful Japanese translation of the title 'Domino Dancing' might be. 'How about "Domino of Sorrow" for repetition,' offers one reader, Saiko, 'or "Pathos Dancing" . . . or "Domino At Dusk" like popular song of youth.'

The B-side of 'Heart', 'I Get Excited (You Get Excited Too)', draws an even fuller response. 'I think songs of PSB has many aspects,' says Taeko, 'a portlay of person's mind, a social matter, a sad love song. And another one is suggestive song to make us feel like we're thrown in the street. They display street's inorganic feeling, that makes me feel like I'm standing in the street. It's certainly suggestive but I think the PSBs don't express it too much, and make us imagine the blank by their way of singing like "then you'll know what I'd like to say". That is their character, the PSB's good taste.'

The magazine's highlight – the article Neil mentions this morning – is a two-page discussion between two fans about the true meaning of the song 'Rent', an earnest debate round the relationship between love and materialism, ownership and security, food and love. The crucial issue, they conclude, is 'the lost conjunction' between the chorus lines 'I love you' and 'you pay my rent'. They toy with 'but' and 'that' and ask for suggestions.

Neil is amused and fascinated by this. He takes the issue raised seriously enough to reflect on it later, but decides that there is indeed no conjunction and none is implied – if it was anything, he says, it would be 'and' or a semi-colon, 'two separate functions: "I love you" and "you pay my rent".'

Neil: I thought of the couplet 'I love you/You pay my rent' first and then I had to think what it meant. It was like a puzzle, making sense of it. Then I sort of got the idea of the story, a kept man or woman, a mistress. It was always set in America and I always vaguely thought of Edward Kennedy for some reason. This politician, I suppose, who keeps this woman in a smart flat in Manhattan and he's still got his family and they have some sort of relationship and they do love each other but it's all kind of secret and at the same time he pays the rent of the flat and she does love him really. And she's thinking whether it's been a wasted life or not – the emotional currency spent on a not-totally-satisfactory relationship – and at the same time maybe she's quite a lazy person and she's had quite a nice life thanks to him. She hasn't had to go out to work. She's survived, but at the same time it's not satisfactory. There's a sense of excitement but also an enormous sense of resignation. Is this it then? Is that all there is? But then actually it's not that bad. I think in the song there's also a tremendous loyalty on both sides and the money doesn't *really* matter. She doesn't really care about the money 'when you're lying next to me'; the point is he isn't always. The reason there's no conjunction – 'I love you/ You pay my rent' – is that they're two separate functions. If anything it's a semi-colon: 'I love you; you pay my rent'. It's not 'because'. It's not 'but'. It's put very bleakly. It's someone who's totally realistic. The romanticism and excitement has been shattered and only the luxury remains.

Ivan is furious. The hotel bill isn't ready and so Neil and Chris have to wait on the forecourt in their car while it is sorted out. He prides himself that such delays never happen. 'They could be upstairs drinking tea,' he fumes, his frustration obvious.

It's a frustration that spills out as Pete and I travel with him to the train station. 'In their contract with Mr Udo,' he says, 'it says "first-class attention". They're just *skimping* and *saving*. They won't even keep the van waiting outside clubs because it's costing them money. It's a long way and a lot of trouble to come to Japan, and it's Mr Udo's job to make sure they're having a good time.'

As far as he's concerned, whatever Mr Udo's unspoken grievances, he is simply being difficult.

'Let's forget about personalities. Let's talk about *business*. Let's talk about *income* and *expenditure*. Let's talk about *turnover*.

When I say, "Send the bus" I know what I'm saying. I mean, "Send the bus! *Now!*"'

This morning – the final straw – Mr Udo's people complained that Neil and Chris hadn't packed their bags to be collected the previous night (as the rest of the entourage has been required to do).

'As far as they're concerned,' instructs Ivan, fuming, 'Neil and Chris are *Gods*. If Neil and Chris want to stand on their heads naked, they can.'

Pete laughs. 'I said to Chris yesterday about the bags,' he chuckles, 'and Chris said, "I don't have to! It's our tour!" '

'The amount of shit I've had flying at me,' rages Ivan. 'If they'd had it they wouldn't go on tour again. Mad! Mad! We're really lucky that they're so easygoing. If this was Bros then Matt would have marched down the road outside the hotel, saying "I'm not waiting."' Bros, he concedes, aren't exactly patient.

Pete says that as far as Neil and Chris have been concerned there have been no real problems.

'No,' says Ivan, but says that things have been made easier because when there have been complaints they have reached him informally via Pete or Dainton. For him this is a new and refreshingly low-hand approach. 'With Bros it's like the Spanish Inquisition.'

The biggest trouble has been over cars. 'If I was Neil and Chris I'd want to get on the bus,' says Ivan, referring to the large coach in which most of the entourage travel.

'Chris does,' says Pete, adding 'not Neil'. (Neil later comments that the exact opposite is actually true.) He points out that neither of them like travelling in coaches much because of what happened to Bucks Fizz (in December 1984 Bucks Fizz had a serious coach crash on tour).

'I've booked coaches for England,' says Ivan, sounding worried.

★

How do you like having a whole organization based around how important the two of you are?

Neil: I don't. I don't like there to be a hierarchy. At the same time there is. We've got suites and they've all got rooms. But I suppose it's our tour: we're paying for it. But I find the whole situation slightly embarrassing because part of me thinks that I'm totally and utterly talentless and hopeless, and here we are with all these fantastically talented people like Courtney Pine and Danny Cummings and Carol and Juliet and sometimes I sort of feel afraid. But then I think, 'We've written all these songs anyway, and people do seem to like them.' I do keep thinking, 'Do they resent it?' because they're all good singers and, particularly live, I'm not a very good singer. The other thing is, I don't like to see people being told off. I find the fines system acutely embarrassing.

Chris: I find the whole thing completely against everything I . . . I'd rebel against that, and I feel bad because we're outside that system and Ivan made it perfectly clear that we could do what we want, but otherwise it's like being back at school, and I hate that.

Neil: At the same time the sensible side of me sees why they do it. To take fifty people round Britain and the Far East and to have them all there at the right time takes a fantastic amount of discipline. And all the people concerned don't seem remotely bothered.

Chris: I think that's the way it is on tour.

Neil: They're all totally used to it.

Ivan's attitude is that the artists are to be God.

Neil: I don't agree with that philosophy. I've never agreed with it. I don't wish to be treated like God. Also, to be honest, it's often quite an inefficient way to be treated. We both found it odd getting about one million wake-up calls in the morning.

Chris: When you go on tour you're immediately assumed to be a hopeless person. You couldn't *possibly* get yourself ready on time. I can get myself ready in fifteen minutes.

Neil: And I have a routine. I have my breakfast ordered. I get up an hour and a half before we leave.

Is it giving you a glimpse of how easy it might be to get caught up in it all?

Neil: Yeah, but I still think with all those it's easier to do things yourself. Somebody takes your bag off you and then you don't know where it is. Having said that this is the first time we've had security, and we need it.

Chris: But I like having Dainton and Strugger (*part of the security on the British leg*) around as friends, not security.

Neil: I get hassled more than you do. I get people having boring conversations with me.

Chris: You allow yourself to get wound up in boring conversations. I just turn my back.

Neil: I'm not rude.

Chris: That's not rude.

Neil: That's rude. To turn your back when someone's talking to you.

Chris: I turn my back in a *friendly* way.

We arrive at the train station about twenty-five minutes early. Most of the entourage wait on the platform, but Ivan ushers Neil and Chris to a station café where we drink tea and Neil sings 'As Time Goes By' under his breath.

Chris examines his new watch and declares that from now on he will put it on his keyboard so that he'll know how much longer there is to go each night. Neil recounts how Chuck Berry took to setting an alarm clock for the agreed performance time – forty minutes or whatever – and when it rang he would walk off in mid-song, and depart with the money; he insisted on being paid in cash beforehand. 'He was no fool,' says Neil.

Chris tries to go to the toilet but soon returns. 'Hole in the floor,' he explains. 'I didn't want to risk it.'

As we board the train he sees a familiar face boarding the

next carriage along. 'Oh,' he exclaims dryly. 'Ekko's on the train. *What* a surprise . . .'

A dozen or so fans gather outside the window on the platform. Neil and Chris wave.

'You see her with the black-and-white headband?' points Ivan. 'She was following Bros when we were here.'

'You know what?' says Neil. 'They'll all be slipping round after Simply Red next week.'

This bullet train, everyone has to concede, is actually rather marvellous. It is on two levels, extremely spacious, the large comfortable seats can be swung round to face in either direction, there is nice food available either from a canteen or via waitress service, and travel feels almost motionless. Neil and Chris confess that whatever they've been on before has been decidedly inferior to this.

The journey to Osaka is three hours and Ivan is determined that the time should be used to sort out some business about the British tour. First, should they stay in a hotel in Birmingham or commute to London?

'If everyone else wants . . .' begins Neil.

'It's not what everyone else wants,' Ivan reminds him. 'It's what you want.'

Between Birmingham and Glasgow, Ivan suggests, we can drive overnight and have a bus party.

'Oh *hello!*' says Neil.

Yuri passes. Neil has been reading something in which she is quoted as describing Chris as 'impish'.

'Congratulations,' he says to her. 'It's a very good word.'

She demurs. She actually said something in Japanese and 'impish' – a word she says she doesn't know – was the writer's translation. 'What does it mean?' she asks.

'It means being like Chris Lowe,' says Neil.

Ivan mentions the tour video. At one time the plan was to hold a special performance in a London theatre and shoot it there, but pressure has been put on by PMI, the video company, and also by Tom to make it more like a standard live pop video to be shot at the NEC. As yet they don't concede. Ivan tells them that James McKay, Derek Jarman's producer, wants 'points' (i.e. a percentage of profits). Neil and Chris concede that this is a reasonable request but no one has the foggiest what a suitable figure might be.

'Whatever he wants,' instructs Neil, 'give him half.'

They're not that worried about giving away royalties on it anyway.

'I don't think there'll be any. For *It Couldn't Happen Here* we had a 50 per cent royalty and we haven't seen a penny.'

They ask Ivan how the figures for the whole tour are going. A potential profit of £250,000 is mentioned.

'Wardrobe is £20,000 over budget,' he warns.

Then they discuss the end-of-tour party. Ivan suggests a venue called Westway Studios and says each room should have a different theme. He says that his girlfriend's parents can provide a fairground ride.

'We must have food,' says Chris, 'and it *has* to go on all night.'

'So America's not happening?' Neil suddenly asks Ivan.

'No,' he says firmly and it is discussed no more.

Neil: America these days has totally become a fantasy. It's very post-modern in that respect. America is a fantasy of what it's supposed to be about, because no one can cope with the reality.

So do you think that relates to your mixed fortunes there?

Neil: Yes, because the Pet Shop Boys aren't a fantasy, funnily enough. There's elements of disco frenzy fantasy but essentially we're not. We're not a macho fantasy. We're not a heterosexual beach fantasy. Our music isn't macho. It's barely masculine, our music. I think to an American there's something rather creepy about us. We just can't be part of it. We just can't be a part of the notion 'life's just a party'.

So are you suggesting that in relation to America the Pet Shop Boys are the little boy pointing out the Emperor's new clothes for what they are?

Neil: Yes, I think we are to a degree, and people don't like that being pointed out. Bruce Springsteen is a major example of the fantasy. The sensitive man with his 'woman', does a job, comes home in his denim, watches the TV, drinks a 'Bud', goes a bit sensitive . . . gets paranoid sometimes. It's a fantasy. They don't want to know that Bruce Springsteen is the Emperor with no clothes on. (*He pauses.*) Though I don't know that he is *totally* without clothes. He's got maybe a pair of shorts on.

So in what way don't the Pet Shop Boys fit in?

Neil: We give off very confusing signals. To be successful in a mass market you have to have one very simple idea. Bruce Springsteen basically is 'I'm a man – an American man. And I *care.*' That's it, the whole idea. George Michael is 'I wear a black leather jacket. I'm kinda sexy, but I'm sensitive.' Madonna is 'I've got attitude, honey.' Michael Jackson is 'I'm weird but I can dance. And I'm incredibly talented. And (*he laughs*) I'm actually rather boring.' U2 are 'We're Irish, but we like your culture. And we care. And we're passionate about it. We're in the passion business.'

And the Pet Shop Boys? I don't know. The Pet Shop Boys seem to everyone like a complicated joke. We give out different signals. We give out 'we care' signals; we also give out 'we don't give a damn' signals. We also give out 'we hate everybody' signals. We give out 'we like all the kinds of music you don't like because we're mega-snobs and you don't know anything' signals.

And also 'we're thrilled about life' along with 'we're complacent about everything' signals . . .

Neil: Yeah. And it's not a simple idea. We give out kind of a vibe of confusion.

Is that a good thing?

Neil: It's not a good thing at a 'selling out Shea stadium' level. That's why I think we've always appealed to the kids at the back of the class who sort of hate everybody. But then that used to be the audience for rock'n'roll.

In many ways it's the most traditional pop music message of all, isn't it? – 'This is for the other people . . .', the rebels, if you like.

Neil: Yes, but in America in the class they all like U2 and there's maybe one at the back who likes us, and maybe also Depeche Mode.

Chris: People 'quite like' us there.

Neil: It's a 'quite like' place.

Chris: They're not really impassioned, not like the English.

Neil: That's why our biggest success in America has come as a novelty. And because maybe they think we're cheeky. I don't know. I think we give out confusing signals. I think that's why we will never have total, utter, mass-market success, because we will never give out one signal.

Do you regret that?

Neil: No, because actually I don't think we seek it. We could never go through with the bullshit. America requires a level of professionalism that we don't have.

As the train silently speeds to Osaka the Pet Shop Boys munch food while Ivan raves about a disco we 'must visit' tonight. It is called Genesis and 'the floor and ceiling come together like a sandwich'.

Chris asks Ivan to sort out some 'elephant pills' for the flight home.

'You can't sleep on the plane back,' says Ivan, meaningfully.

'Oh,' says Neil, realizing what Ivan is driving at. 'It's my birthday.'

'We'll get that over and done with quickly,' Ivan promises.

'The bumps,' sniggers Pete.

'I'm not having the bumps,' says Neil, forcefully and not without concern. 'At thirty-five I'm too old for the bumps.'

They talk about Mr Udo.

'He has no respect,' says Ivan.

'He's banned from the gig,' says Chris.

'Banned from the gig?' says Ivan, worried that this is a serious instruction. It could be tricky. 'He's the promoter,' Ivan reminds them.

Bros are discussed some more.

'They love touring,' sighs Ivan. 'That's how they like to live: have everything done for them. They don't want their own lives.' If this sounds uncharitable it isn't: it's nothing that Bros themselves wouldn't say, albeit put slightly differently. Only weeks later Matt Goss is telling *Smash Hits* how much more secure he feels when he's on tour: 'You get a sheet of paper put under your door every morning telling you what the agenda is for the day and every day is filled with pressing things to do. Suddenly you're home and there's no bit of paper and your house is so silent that it's too loud.'

For some reason the on-train conversation turns to currency.

'Do we still have half-pennies?' asks Ivan.

'No,' says Neil.

'We don't have pennies any more, do we?' asks Chris.

'Yes,' says Pete.

Ivan wanders down the corridor and, while he's away, Chris rifles through his CD collection, reading out the names . . . 'Tin Machine . . . Kingdom Come . . . Led Zeppelin . . . Simple Minds . . . Phil Collins . . .' Chris frowns. Later he will inform Ivan that this selection is 'depressing beyond belief', an opinion that he will cap with the beautifully gratuitous insult 'you've probably got "Godley & Creme's Greatest Hits" somewhere'.

'It's so much easier by train,' sighs Pete.

'There's no trauma,' agrees Neil.

'There's no trauma of dying in a plane crash,' says Chris, returning to one of his favourite topics. 'You can have plane crashes that last for half an hour.'

'That famous Japanese one took forty minutes,' says Neil, clearly also a man who knows his aviation disasters. 'They knew they were going to die and all wrote farewell letters. Chris *always* mentions this in planes . . .'

'Then you have bombs,' muses Chris cheerfully.

'And the ones where the roof blows off but the pilot still lands the plane,' offers Neil. 'That's why I always wear seat belts.'

Mr Udo's popularity increases momentarily when we are picked up in Osaka by a limousine. But at the door of Osaka's Plaza Hotel there is a sign: 'Due to renovation there will be noise . . .'

'Let's not check in,' grumbles Chris.

However, we do. Half an hour later Neil phones – everyone is checking out. He and Chris will go today – the rest of us will move in the morning. There is no gym – as specified in their contract. There is no keyboard in Neil's room – also in the contract. The manager has also been rude about the fans downstairs. So they're off.

In Chris's room (his room for the next few minutes anyway) Neil puts a tape of the second Tokyo concert on a cassette player he's just bought. 'Paninaro' is playing.

'What a geeky northerner,' says Chris when he hears his own voice. 'It sounds good though. It sounds like the record.'

'There's a reason for that,' laughs Neil.

'Mmmm,' concedes Chris. 'Even the backing vocals are sampled.'

Neil fast forwards to 'Later Tonight'. At the end of each line there are words ending '-tion', which are spat out as '*-shun*'. 'It's the only way I can do it,' he says. He plays a few more bits. 'Well,' he sighs, wishing he hadn't bothered, 'I think it sounds really ropy.'

Having declared how useless the hotel is and having checked out, the plan now is to have dinner here. First we go up to the rooftop bar for drinks. Neil notices the date and realizes he was due to become an uncle for the second time yesterday – the baby is clearly late. He already has a niece: 'If you mention my name she starts to dance,' he says. Two old Newcastle friends, Krysia and Eric, also had a baby recently (Chris holds him, Eugene, in the 'It's Alright' video which Eric directs).

'Krysia maintains that our records are popular with babies,' he confesses. 'Eugene loves "Left To My Own Devices". Eric also has some gold discs and Eugene loves gold discs. He's thrilled by the sight of them.'

Neil and I continue a pointless argument we had started out shopping the previous day when he had mentioned a recent dance record, 'House Arrest' by Krush, and said that it had been number one in Britain. I had said that no, it had reached about number five or six. In the end we bet – 10 yen; about £5 – though cannily he broadened the bet to be whether or not the record had reached the top three. Now we continue the disagreement and try to work out how to resolve it. He says he can think of three ways – he could phone up his sister Susan and ask her to drive round to his flat and look it up in the *Guinness Book of Hit Singles*, we could phone up the British Council in Japan or we could phone up DJ Paul Gambuccini.

Instead we have another drink and he produces a photo he has been given today by a fan. It was taken on their first visit here, three years ago. 'I've aged horrendously,' he declares. 'Chris,' he says – Chris has just joined us – 'you used to be quite good-looking. It's like looking at the first-year-at-school photo. No wonder we became popular in Japan – we looked adorable. Now,' he sighs dramatically, 'we're old . . . haggard . . .'

We descend to the restaurant on the fourth floor.

'I don't know why we're leaving this hotel,' says Neil. 'It's quite nice.'

'That's not the point,' Chris reminds him.

Kaz joins us. He mentions that he has just heard the next Tears For Fears LP (it will eventually be released three months later under the title 'The Seeds Of Love'). Their last LP came out in early 1985, just as the Pet Shop Boys signed their Parlophone record contract.

'When we first had a hit in America,' reflects Neil nostalgically, 'we were "this year's Tears For Fears". And then the next year Swing Out Sister were "this year's Pet Shop Boys".'

The conversation drifts on and he mentions that the ex-Smiths guitarist Johnny Marr, whom they have met while helping New Order's Bernard Summer with his solo LP earlier in the year, declared that their song 'I Want To Wake Up' is his favourite dance record.

'On a par with Chic,' quotes Chris proudly.

'Although,' muses Neil, 'I don't know that it is a dance record.' He is silent for a moment. 'There were a lot of people dancing to the Smiths at the Lexington Queen,' he says.

'That's why we left,' Chris reminds him.

'That was "A Hard Day's Night",' corrects Neil.

'You know,' says Chris, 'I wish the Beatles had never happened.'

Neil disagrees in a long-winded fashion by explaining how 'incredibly sentimental' it had been on a recent episode of the American TV series *Family Ties* when they'd gone on a camping holiday and sung the Beatles' 'In My Life'.

'I love watching *The Waltons*,' says Chris.

'You should have seen Chris and me watching *Arthur 2* on a plane,' says Neil. 'We were in tears. There's this bit where she says she's going back to Brooklyn and we were reaching for the Kleenex.'

She, of course, is 'Liza': Liza Minnelli.

'We told Liza we loved it and she was so surprised. I think she thought we were taking the mickey.'

This notion leads to a consideration of the Pet Shop Boys' Career in Film.

'Instead of making incredibly boring obscure films like the last one – marvellous though it was – we should make a sentimental film with Liza Minnelli,' suggests Neil. 'You should like that,' he says to Chris and recounts how Chris keenly swiped the soundtrack to *Annie* from the reject box when Neil worked at *Smash Hits*.

'The first three tracks are really good,' says Chris, a little defensively. 'I like "Bet Your Bottom Dollar"' (actually called 'Tomorrow'). 'I like that so much.'

Recently they say they went to the cinema to see the full-length version of *Lawrence of Arabia*. As they paid for their tickets, £7.50 each, they asked how long the film was. Nearly five hours. Too long, so they decided to go to dinner instead. They offered their tickets along the line. The first couple stubbornly refused to have anything to do with them and then were outraged when the people behind gratefully accepted them for nothing. 'It was the best fifteen pounds I spent that week,' Chris says, revelling in the double joy of having seen the outraged couple's faces and the freedom of having skived off. Typically Chris thinks that the premise of the new version – to restore lovingly reams of film dispatched to the cutting-room floor – is silly. 'I'd like to see the edited version,' he proudly declares.

Tonight's meal is being cooked on hot plates in front of us. When the cook finishes he takes a bow.

'He's just like Sammy Davis Junior,' says Chris.

'We know all the stars,' murmurs Neil.

Someone mentions that, once again, the midweek prediction for 'It's Alright' is for number two. I say that I suspect the latest Stock Aitken Waterman record, by a girl called Sonia, may be a problem.

'Where's she from then?' asks Chris. Liverpool.

'They've done more for Liverpool,' he says, 'than the government's ever done.'

Yuri pays the bill and we give her a '3–3–1 3–3–1' handclap.

'Hmmm,' Neil muses. 'Could be an album title – "3–3–1".'

Yuri has some news for us. 'Did you know that Jason Donovan was in Tokyo and he really wanted to come to the show but . . .?'

Yes, they say, they know.

Downstairs in reception they find a copy of *Billboard*, the American music business trade magazine. In it they are slightly surprised to find that the record they made with Patsy Kensit, 'I'm Not Scared', has been released in a new mix by Little 'Louie' Vega – it is out to coincide with her and the song's appearance in the film *Lethal Weapon II*. The review is nice: '. . . Vega mixes entice, as do the brilliant original and French versions.' They look pleased. They look even more pleased when Kaz mentions that he thinks they earn more than CBS do for the song appearing in the film. Kaz is from Ten Music, to whom the Pet Shop Boys signed their publishing after 'West End Girls' was a hit. Because of the timing they were able to drive a hard bargain – they have had a good percentage and, whereas many artists never own all of their publishing, after a few years all rights revert to the two of them.

'"I'm Not Scared" should be released again in Britain,' Chris suggests, 'and then we could say we object because it's milking it.' He laughs, then notices the American chart. At number two is Simply Red's version of 'If You Don't Know Me By Now'. Next week it will be number one. He explodes. Neil and Chris are somewhat jealous of Simply Red's success there and Chris mutters that they only have big hits because they do cover versions anyway. I point out that they wrote their other American number one, 'Holding Back The Years', themselves, but he's not interested. The truth isn't the point. It's a little like the day I interviewed them both over lunch in the summer of 1987. After the interview we went to Tom's office where they saw – to their horror – the German sleeve of 'It's A Sin'. The cover photo had been surrounded by a horrible purple border and they were incensed. Neil picked up the phone, dialled straight through to the managing director of EMI Germany, exchanged muted pleasantries and then raged away. From the other end one could hear the desperate managing director objecting that he wasn't aware they'd messed up the single artwork. As they talked Neil's eyes roved in disgust over the offending sleeve, eventually settling on the French credits. 'Sorry,' he snapped, 'it's France. Everything's fine. Bye,' and put the phone down. (When I mention that incident during this tour Neil remembers it and says it didn't matter as it turned out the Germans had made a mess of their sleeve anyway.)

The two of them prepare to leave for their new hotel. The third of the day, I remark.

'Oh *hello*!' pipes Neil. 'It's the three Popes in one year!'

Saturday, *8 July*

While waiting to move into the new hotel most of the band spend the next day shopping. We all wander up and down a long walkway, past shirts bearing slogans like 'Nothing venture, nothing have. Be try it', and discarded 'YG Sports' boxes outside shops bearing the friendly motto 'Have a good day with nice underwear'. Back in the Plaza Hotel lobby the fans circulate anxiously, clutching presents. The Pet Shop Boys haven't appeared all day and they are doubtless imagining all sorts of chicanery involving secret lifts, disguises, decoy cars and back entrances. Bored, they photograph each other, first singly, then in pairs, then in groups.

On the bus between hotels the band talk about musicians who sell stories. Someone mentions the man who got £30,000 for dishing the dirt on Wham! – cash plus a fortnight in Greece and Spain while the story cooled off. (There is no provision, incidentally, in these musicians' contracts to forbid them.) The general consensus is that it's a bad thing.

'Imagine if you worked with him,' says Courtney, meaning the musician who ratted. 'You'd have to think what you were saying.' This is an odd thing for Courtney to say only because he is a man of few words and seems to think extremely carefully before saying anything in the most relaxed of circumstances.

'I saw him afterwards,' says Juliet, 'and he had no remorse. But . . . the *principle* . . .'

As usual it is Carol who takes the most straightforward heartfelt position on this. 'It's like an unwritten rule,' she proclaims as if she was defending the moral integrity of her entire profession. 'You *don't*.'

This is said in such a way as to forbid any further argument.

At the venue the accountant Mike Lynch is striding around with a wry smile on his face, counting seats. Mr Udo's 'estimate' of the venue's capacity as the seats are laid out today is, he says, farcically low. As the Pet Shop Boys have been paid large advances and not all the shows are completely sold out, it will not make any difference to their revenue, but still . . .

One of the dancers, Jill, is still in hospitality when the soundcheck starts. Hearing the music, she gasps in alarm and scarpers. Seeing her go one of the road crew raises his eyes from his meal in despair. There are some funny things going on here and he doesn't like it at all.

'You'd better make sure it sounds all right for you,' he huffs at her, once she is safely out of earshot. He grunts. '*Dancers* turning up for soundchecks.' He is appalled.

They run through a few songs, finishing with 'It's Alright'. As the last notes fade away Neil steps up to the microphone and says in a silly ad-land voice, 'Available in Boots, John Menzies and all good record stores.'

Back-stage someone mentions shopping.

'I'm post-shopping,' Neil reminds everyone.

'That's because you've bought everything there is to buy,' says Chris.

Yuri comes in.

'Can I ask a favour?' she says nervously.

'That,' says Neil, 'depends upon what it is. No interviews.'

'No,' she agrees.

'No radio IDs,' says Chris.

'No.'

'No TV shows,' says Neil.

'No,' she says. 'Can you pick your ten favourite records for a radio show?'

There is a sigh of relief. They say yes, then postpone it 'until later'.

Pete comes in and says that there are three Americans outside the concert hall with only 7,000 yen between them. Can they come in?

'As long as it doesn't get around,' Neil agrees.

'They've only got 7,000 yen?' checks Chris.

Pete nods.

'How are they getting back to America then?'

Earlier I had phoned *Smash Hits* and learned, to my distress, that 'House Arrest' by Krush reached number three. I confess and pay up.

'Oh *hello*,' says Neil.

Pete says that while we're talking of such matters there's a mistake in one of the British chart positions listed in the Pet Shop Boys annual I'd written last year. I strongly deny it. Neil agrees. Pete bets me £5 and offers to bet Neil £50.

'I can't take it off you,' says Neil. 'Just your ego against mine.'

'It's Alright', we now hear, has a Friday prediction of number three.

'It'll go down,' moans Chris.

Pete returns to the subject of the annual. He announces that one of the Polaroids in it of the Pet Shop Boys travelling round the world, though identified by them as a harbour on holiday in Antigua, was actually taken on a promotional trip in Finland.

'Confusing Finland with the Caribbean is easily done,' defends

Neil. (The next day they compound the error by realizing it was actually taken in Oslo: 'They all become a blur, these Scandinavian countries,' says Chris.)

They discuss the logic of signing your name when travelling under a pseudonym. They are booked into hotels as famous boxers. Neil is 'J. Louis'. Chris was 'T. Farr' in Hong Kong but then discovered that Tommy Farr was not only defeated but defeated by Joe Louis and so he insisted his name was changed – he is now 'R. Marciano'. In the spirit of this deception Chris has developed an 'R. Marciano' signature for hotel documents. Neil has a more perplexing tactic.

'I print "J. Louis",' he explains, 'and then sign "N. Tennant".' He is surprised that we find this amusing.

Chris opens some fan mail. He comes across a drawing of himself. 'Look!' he exclaims, delighted at how he is depicted. 'I'm not happy. That's fantastic.'

Alan walks in and Chris tells him that he wants a special leather cap made by Giorgio Armani for the British concerts. Neil looks at Chris despairingly. 'You won't get Giorgio Armani to make you a leather hat by next Wednesday.'

After the show Alan asks Chris to take his jeans off. This is a routine that occurs most nights, where Chris changes from jeans – his stagewear – into jeans, his normal wear. 'I have stage jeans and off-stage jeans,' he explains, 'and they're no different but I feel better in the right ones.' Once they're off Alan examines them and has some crushing news. These are the wrong jeans. Tonight, on-stage, he was wearing off-stage jeans. 'It's a good thing I didn't know, isn't it?' says Chris.

'Are we going to eat?' asks Neil.

'Of *course* we're going to eat,' says Chris.

'Kaz?' says Neil.

'Indian,' suggests Kaz.

'*Indian?*' scoffs Neil. 'Italian.'

'I want a shave 'n' shower first,' says Chris.

'Ten o'clock,' says Neil.

That sorted out, Neil reads some fan mail. He sees me taking notes. 'Every letter to the fan club,' he dictates, 'is personally read and answered by both Neil and Chris.'

He reads out a letter.

'. . . before of I get excited I forget your name . . .'

'It's heartbreak time,' he commentates.

'. . . please write to me . . . I keep on writing . . .'

'It's like Madame Butterfly,' he says.

They discuss the show. Tonight Neil had said to the crowd 'arigato' – 'thank you' in Japanese.

'I thought "how *shameless*",' says Chris. 'I bowed my head in shame and thought, "He's a tart."' Still, there was a consolation. 'Only two "Thank yous" tonight,' he tells Neil. 'I keep count.'

'I keep thinking when I say "Thank you" I should then say "1–2–3–4" and go into "Career Opportunities",' mutters Neil.

'You know,' says Chris, 'I don't like it when everyone has a good time in "It's Alright". I feel uncomfortable.'

'I know,' agrees Neil. 'I *am* singing about starvation.'

'Audiences are naff all over the world,' Chris sighs. He's thinking about London, whether that'll be true there or not.

'You'll have celebrities there,' Pete points out.

'They'll have gone by "It's Alright",' says Chris.

'Anyway,' says Neil, 'we're not worried about what Sinitta and Lionel Blair think.'

'Maybe we should have a picture of starvation and leave them depressed,' suggests Chris.

'Then sing "Feed The World" and have a collection,' says Neil sarcastically.

Pete suddenly lets out some news. 'Rob has been sacked.' It turns out that Tom went straight to the office from his flight home and sacked him. The mood changes dramatically.

'I'm not very happy about that,' says Neil. 'He told us the other day but I didn't believe him really.'

'I thought it was all talk,' agrees Chris.

A long heated debate follows.

At the hotel Ekko is going frantic. She has a fresh cream cake, an early birthday present for Neil, and has been terrified that it might go off before she can present it.

'Did you make it?' Chris asks.

'Yes,' she says, perhaps misunderstanding the question.

'How come it's got a shop's name on the front then?' asks Chris.

Ekko kisses Neil, leaving lipstick on his face. Meanwhile a fan asks Chris to sign a copy of *Newsweek*.

'What's *this*?' he says, gesturing at it. 'There's no picture of us.' He signs anyway.

The fan looks awkward and improvises. 'Do you sometimes read it?' she asks Chris of *Newsweek*.

'No,' he answers.

Before dinner Ivan telephones to tell me I am invited but am not to take notes. Whether it's because it's a smart affair (jacket and tie), because earlier they had looked annoyed as I had noted down their reaction to Rob's sacking, or whether they're simply fed up with being recorded no one ever tells me.

At dinner they talk about 'It's Alright'.

'I really wanted another number one,' says Chris. 'It's so good when you're at the top of the pile.'

They also talk about money. When they were in Antigua a cocktail party was thrown at the hotel where they were staying. The same week a list of Britain's hundred wealthiest people had been published and several were at the party.

'That's when you decided you wanted to be rich,' asserts Pete, 'when you saw that list and realized you wouldn't even be millionth.'

'That's when *you* decided you wanted to be rich,' replies Neil defensively.

'I've *always* said that,' counters Pete, unabashed.

After rushing from the table we reach Ivan's recommended club, Genesis, five minutes before its official midnight closing time. We needn't have worried. It turns out that there is no way an Osaka club is going to shut with such distinguished celebrities inside. The club is seven or eight flights of steps below ground, the walls are irregular, like the inside of a cave and you can sit in cushioned grottoes. The music is Acid House and the dance-floor, which shows no signs of sandwich motion while we are there, is packed. 'This is more like it,' grunts Chris approvingly.

Within a few minutes Chris has quietly climbed upon a small wall next to the dance-floor. He is wearing a white t-shirt with the letters MEAT spelt out in bold black letters and he dances privately but wildly to himself. No one takes much notice. A while later Cooley jumps up and joins him and they dance together. Then the DJ, presumably alerted to the presence of his guests, plays the twelve-inch version of 'It's Alright'. Normally this would signal the end of all fun and, indeed, Chris steps down immediately with a weary 'you hardly think I'm going to dance to my own record, do you?' expression on his face. But Cooley will.

Throughout the tour the dancers display two different dance repertoires when they visit discos. Before, when he was dancing with Chris, Cooley was just dancing, dancing as one does as part of a crowd in a disco. Now he begins *dancing* – showing off, body popping, moonwalking. Someone turns a spotlight on to him. One by one the people on the dance-floor lose interest in their own motion, slow up and turn to face Cooley. Soon there is a semi-circle looking towards him, cheering him on.

He jumps down and Jill takes a turn. Then Casper comes up and calls Cooley back. There isn't enough room for both of them on the wall so they try the floor but – hey – who can see that? So they clear the long bar along one side of the club of glasses and bottles, jump up and dance together. It is the sort of thing that happens in very corny American films or in the TV series *Fame* and, one would have imagined, nowhere real. But here it is.

It brings out the best in them. Casper turns his back to the crowd and makes his back muscles – *just* his back muscles – dance. Cooley rips off his t-shirt – by now the DJ is playing 'Left To My Own Devices' – and shows off his chest muscles.

'They are totally shameless,' says Neil, thrilled. Later Chris will call it 'the best moment of the entire tour'.

Chris: Rock'n'roll . . . guitar-orientated music . . . (*He sighs.*) I just don't like the sound of it. Fundamentally I find the music boring and dreary and uninspired. It doesn't fit in with the environment of my life. It's not part of it. It's not the music that is the soundtrack to my life.

What is different about the music you do like?

Chris: It's music I can be *ecstatic* about.

Do you think that people who like rock'n'roll music get from that what you get out of the music you like?

Chris (*looks dubious*)*:* I don't know. I suppose they must do, but the way rock'n'rollers react is different. It's literally ecstatic, the response to a dance record.

Trouble. A middle-aged, drunk Australian barracks Cooley – 'He's not a dancer, he's a wanker' – and then starts howling graphic homophobic abuse at him. Ivan takes the Australian and ushers him into the corridor; Dainton follows. The Australian protests as only the drunk and guilty can that he has done nothing. Dainton suggests to him that if he'll just calm down and promise to do no more they'll leave it there. Part of his conciliatory pitch is to finish each sentence by referring to the Australian as 'my friend'. Each time he says it the Australian, transparently pleased at his riposte, snaps, 'I'm not your friend.' Eventually Dainton's patience tires and quietly, gently, he leans over and, in acknowledgement of the Australian's insistence that in fact they are not friends, makes a suggestion.

'Why don't we discuss this outside,' he says, 'enemy to enemy.'

Wisely the Australian backs down.

Meanwhile Neil is besieged by a woman from Hawaii. She has a shop called Pet Boy there and has, she says, flown over especially to give the Pet Shop Boys some t-shirts. They like some of them – Neil shows people one with the motto 'socially correct' – but she is endlessly pushy and interrupts him over and over again when he tries to talk to other people. Neil looks fed up and eventually has simply to ignore her. Afterwards Chris, who skilfully avoided her in the first place, teases him.

'She flew all the way over,' he laughs, 'and you were rude to her!'

'I wasn't rude to her,' Neil insists touchily. 'I was *snooty*.'

After a while we go to another club where Cooley and Casper used to dance; Japan, particularly Osaka, is a top employment spot for American dancers. There we drink and dance for several more hours. On the way there Chris berates me when he sees me taking notes; apparently my ban is still in force. Then again, a few minutes later he seems to have forgotten. 'It's great,' he hoots, 'walking around and having someone write down everything you say.'

Chapter Twelve

Sunday, *9 July*

In the morning, on the way to the railway station.

'Well done, Pete,' sighs Neil. There was, I have discovered, a mistake in last year's Pet Shop Boys annual, just as Pete had claimed.

'I kept well out of it,' observes Chris. 'I wasn't going to put *my* integrity on the line. I don't have any.'

Pete flicks triumphantly through my copy of the annual. He stops at the sleeve photo for the 'Please' LP, a photo of Neil and Chris with white towels round their necks, as if they were just rubbing down after a shower, or stepping out towards the ring for a boxing match. 'What *were* you doing in that picture?' he sniggers.

'Trying to look sexy, Pete,' sighs Chris.

Pete turns some more pages and finds a photo of Chris taken in 1984, his hair permed into tight ringlets.

'That was his Bobby O look,' Pete hoots. 'Chris used to have a picture of Bobby O by his bed in Liverpool.'

We board the train. Nagoya is our destination, an hour back down the line towards Tokyo.

Neil is wearing one of the Pet Boy t-shirts they were given last night. It says DOWN BOY and the 'WOOF' inside a speech bubble coming from the direction of his waist. It is only much later in the day that he realizes the innuendo, when Pete points out to him that the bark is supposed to sound from what Pete charmingly refers to as 'your dingly'.

'Ekko's just told me that it's three years to the day since we first arrived in Japan,' says Neil. 'That's a fascinating fact.'

'It must be costing her a lot,' muses Chris. 'I wonder how she'll find out where we're staying in Nagoya.'

'I told her,' says Neil. 'You don't mind, do you?'

Tonight's soundcheck is unreasonably jolly. No one can work out why we're here, why on earth the Pet Shop Boys tour should include Nagoya. It is a depressed industrial town with a huge stadium that fills for no one. The Pet Shop Boys are expected to draw about 3,000 people – under half-capacity. That will fill most of the seating on the floor – the ring of arena balconies will be empty. They would cancel if they hadn't been sternly informed that it would be seen as abominably insulting. We speculate that maybe there is a government incentive to bring acts to this area but we don't really know. Stories spread about how badly Stevie Winwood did here – estimates sinking as low as 600 – and this cheers everyone up a little, but there is an air of unreality. This isn't a proper concert. Normally at soundchecks Neil is the quiet disciplinarian, calmly frowning at any hi-jinks as if to say, 'Once you've *quite* finished mucking about at the back of the class we'll begin.' Tonight he's messing about too and soon he and the backing singers are camping their way through a medley of Supremes songs.

'Let's do something else,' he chirps. 'What would you like to do? "Some Enchanted Evening"?'

Perhaps more appropriately they choose 'It's My Party', which Neil sings in a ludicrous falsetto.

I wander about outside and a teenage girl gives me some fan mail, not for Neil and Chris but for Jay and Pete. I take it back-stage. Neil feigns disgust at this strange turn of events and says, 'I knew it was getting out of hand when Dominic was asked for an autograph this morning.'

The concert starts in forty-five minutes. Outside the fans trickle in, doubtless imagining that back-stage the Pet Shop Boys are psyching themselves up, maybe working out or running through songs or taking lots of drugs. Back-stage Chris lies on the sofa and announces, 'I'm just about to get myself half an hour's kip,' shuts his eyes and goes to sleep.

When he wakes up he chats about who will win the Wimbledon final (many of us have been watching Japanese live broadcasts early each morning when we get back to our hotel rooms). He has divided loyalties between the finalists. 'I can't stand Edberg,' he confesses, 'but I can't stand Becker more.'

Neil says that they've decided to call the concert video *What A Performance!* The sleeve will show the performers' heads at funny angles, like a pantomime poster.

Ivan comes in to tell them they're on-stage in a few minutes.

'You've got to leave time for the *masses* to reach their seats,' jokes Chris dryly.

'Nobody forget – it's Neil's birthday tonight,' laughs Chris.

Neil responds by swearing, embarrassed.

'We've got a few surprises tonight for you,' teases Chris. He knows full well that nothing would be less appreciated than someone playing a trick on Neil on-stage (except, quite probably, someone playing an on-stage trick on Chris).

'You better not,' threatens Neil. He announces he's 'breaking with tradition' and has some red wine.

'Do you think that's wise?' teases Chris some more. 'You *know* I'm superstitious.'

'It's freezing in here,' Neil complains.

'Oh, but soon we'll have a nice warm audience,' guffaws Chris.

They try to work out some ego-protecting reasons why the hall might not be full.

'There's not some big international event tonight, like Live Aid, is there?' inquires Chris hopefully.

'Everyone's staying home to see who's number one in Britain,' says Neil.

Suddenly he realizes something.

'Socks!'

He has forgotten to put them on.

'They were thrown into a blind panic,' commentates Chris. 'This evening's performance will be entirely in the nude.'

'It's called *Oh Nagoya*,' says Neil. 'In tonight's performance the part of Neil Tennant will be played by Mike Henry and the part of Chris Lowe by Dominic Clarke. Well, we *said* it was theatrical . . .'

The red wine must be having an effect, for now there is a second, more serious clothing palaver. Alan points out that Neil has forgotten to put on pyjamas underneath the 'Opportunities' suit.

'Why did you tell him, Alan?' moans Chris, disappointed. 'He could have performed in his underpants.'

'Yes,' says Neil, 'and I could have shown my bottom to the audience. *That* would have got a round of applause.' He sighs once more. 'I wonder if the audience are here yet. Not that there's much difference between them being here and not being here.'

Danny Cummings walks in.

'Oy, hop it,' says Chris. 'What are you doing in *my* dressing-room?'

'Isn't he *one of the band*?' says Neil, feigning snootiness. 'What is he doing here? Have a ten-pound fine.' He returns to commentary. 'Yes, it's quite a relaxed ambience on tour, between the fines, bullying the promoter . . .'

Ivan asks them how they feel about tonight's expected chart position.

'We're not a chart-orientated band,' says Chris. 'It doesn't bother us.'

'I never pay much attention to our chart positions,' says Neil. This pose is of course both a little true and deeply, deeply untrue.

'We did print a table of our chart positions from around the world in our annual,' he hoots.

Pete mentions a fan letter in front of him and Neil starts

singing the old Boxtops hit 'The Letter' under his breath. Then Pete takes a Polaroid of the two of them which they watch develop.

'What a pair of divs,' says Neil.

The show, predictably, is more relaxed than usual and goes well. The Japanese dates are over.

'Are we off then?' asks Chris, getting his things together. 'I want to go to bed. I don't want to hear the chart position. We'll still be at number five.'

This is taken as an example of Chris's self-defensive pessimism.

Neil reads a letter from a twenty-one-year-old student called Hiroko, who says she studies international relations. '. . . I enjoy "Rent", "It's A Sin", "Left To My Own Devices", "It's Alright", "Opportunities" because they offer me a sense of tension and reminds me that I have something to do – such as my fighting against the violation of the human rights in the world that'll be my life work. That's why I've really been affected by your beaming voice and witty words . . . Thank you for being excited me . . .'

This sincerity and idealism is rather sobering.

They study some drawings. 'It makes you a hero if you've got big eyes,' says Chris. 'That's why they draw us with big eyes.'

One drawing shows them sitting in the same car, both with a steering wheel, facing each other.

'We're going in different directions so we don't go anywhere!' whoops Neil with delight. '*Very* symbolic.'

You seem very ambivalent about the idea of a 'Pet Shop Boys fan'. Sometimes out of their earshot, you can seem very heartless about them.

Neil: Do you think? I don't know. Chris has a very different attitude to me. Chris has no interest in what the fans think. I think he disregards them all. But we don't really agree with the fan worship kind of fan, and we try not to encourage that kind of relationship.

But you can't stop it, can you?

Neil: No, you can't.

Do you think you expect a response from your fans that you could never get?

Neil: Well, I want them to treat us like you would treat an actor or an actress. You might like what they do but you don't hang around their house. We don't get a lot of that, but we do get some. Actually because of our approach we get people wanting to be our friends. People write and say, 'All my friends like such and such but I hate that and like the Pet Shop Boys and I really like the B-side to such-and-such and I've written these interesting poems . . .' I quite like that. It's an aspirational thing, and it's exactly the sort of person I was when I was sixteen or seventeen. I was kind of snooty and I didn't want to be like anybody else.

But you glamorize that side of your fans – the poetry-writers, the sincere intellectual outsiders. Obviously the majority aren't like that.

Neil: No, they're not.

I've read a lot of your fan mail and most of it is 'Why are you called the Pet Shop Boys?' or about how they fancy you.

Neil: Yes, that's probably true. (*He sighs.*) I don't know.

And you want to believe that your fans are as different, in terms of fans, as you want the Pet Shop Boys to be different in terms of pop music, don't you?

Neil: Yes, I think that's true. Well . . . your fans don't always live up to your expectations. Maybe it's naïve of us. I think maybe the Pet Shop Boys perceive the Pet Shop Boys totally differently to anyone else. To everyone else we're two quite nice people and they come to see our concerts just like they go to see Elton John, and they don't fundamentally perceive any difference.

Chris, you do have a strange attitude to the fans, don't you?

Chris: Not specifically to our fans, but I find it bizarre: the glory and the adulation for someone on-stage. Particularly rock audiences going through their semi-religious gestures . . . the peace signs, the hands in the air, the lighters . . .

Do you just think it's naff?

Chris: Obviously I do think it's naff but also I always find it funny when a lot of people do things at the same time together. I naturally don't want to do it.

But you're always saying that you want to be 'One of the Crowd'.

Chris: Yes, I know, but I think that's fighting against my natural instincts.

You can be cruelly rude about the fans.

Chris: Really? But I'm just joking.

And you can be cruel when they give you presents.

Chris: I like getting nice presents. When I got that Armani t-shirt I was genuinely thrilled to pieces. But cuddly toys . . . I just don't know what to do with them.

You're supposed to appreciate the sentiment anyway.

Chris: I do. (*Hoots with laughter.*)

'He says, laughing.'

Chris: It makes you feel quite good but I always think, these people wouldn't treat me like that if I was any other person. They only do that because I'm one of the Pet Shop Boys. So it doesn't seem very real.

Yes, but the Pet Shop Boys are real. You're not any other person. You're one of the Pet Shop Boys and that's a real situation. That's as much a part of you now as your height.

Chris: Yes . . . it's true, but I sort of detach myself from it.

But that's just an excuse, isn't it?

Chris: Oh, I don't know. I think the fans can be a bit pathetic really. I got my first letter today from a girl who is a manic depressive suicidal: 'Without your music I'd chop my arm off . . .'

What do you think about that?

Chris: It's depressing. I don't think anyone should hold anything that dear to them.

Don't you hold anything that dear to you?

Chris: I don't think it's good to hold things that dear to you. That's probably why I'm not religious. I think it's a weakness in character to depend on anything.

Does that just hold for music and religion, or do you think one shouldn't hold anything at all that dear?

Chris: Mmmm. (*He considers.*) I think everyone would be a lot happier if they didn't.

Monday, *10 July*

We meet in the lobby at 7.30am. Becker has won the tennis final and Ivan tells me that the British chart position is number five. Neil appears, then Chris, who gives him a present and a card with 'my usual kind of droll witty useless remarks inside'. He apologizes.

'Oh Chanel, *hello*,' says Neil opening the present.

'The packaging is a triumph over content,' defers Chris.

'So it *should* be,' says Neil. 'This *is* the eighties.'

We get in a car.

'I'm officially middle-aged now,' Neil sighs. He is thirty-five today. 'It had to happen. You can't be a teenager for-ever.'

'I don't know,' says Chris, adding, sarcastically, 'how old is Mick Jagger?'

'Put the air-conditioning on "mega", please,' asks Neil.

'That's what the controls should say,' says Chris. 'From "bugger all" to "mega".'

It is only now, on our way to the train station, that he bothers to ask, 'What is the chart position?'

'Five,' says Neil.

'Who said it would be number five? *Told* you,' says Chris, more or less triumphantly.

They begin what will be an obsession of theirs throughout this long day of travel: customs paranoia.

'I'm going to declare my stuff,' says Chris. 'Mind you, to get caught would be good publicity for the tour, wouldn't it?'

In the train station café they open yet more presents. Neil has a large parcel. It includes a Japanese screen and a museum catalogue.

'It's an art package,' says Chris disdainfully.

'I don't get it,' says Neil, puzzled as to why exactly he has been given this.

Chris surveys the gifts. 'That, Neil, is an incredibly dreary present.'

'I think it's smashing,' says Neil, defending the fans *in absentia*. It is a loyalty that doesn't endure. 'Lawrence?' he asks, 'would you like a screen for your mother?'

They discuss whether Mr Udo will show his face at the airport. He hasn't been seen for several days and they rather think he will turn up.

'I think we're beyond making up,' says Neil. 'Actually I'm bored by the whole idea.'

Kaz has tried to find out whether there is a fundamental, secret problem and failed to uncover anything; now everyone genuinely seems to have lost interest. It has become merely last week's promoter drama. Chris mutters that in retrospect the week-before's promoter drama – Mr Bull's shenanigans with Levi's and censorship – seems hardly anything: anyway, compared to Mr Udo, 'He was a diamond geezer, wasn't he?'

On the station platform something about the way we stand round self-consciously as A Group leads Chris to reminisce about school trips to London when he was little. 'We used to practise in the playground, crossing the road, holding hands in twos.'

'Choreography,' says Neil.

As the train glides away Neil is singing 'I'd Rather Jack' by the Reynolds Girls. We pass the dome of the Nagoya hall.

'We've played it!' shouts Chris. 'We've done it! It was half-empty!'

The food trolley passes, piled high with sushi.

'I'd like a full English breakfast with tea,' says Chris.

'I wish they had trains like this in America,' says Neil.

'Well,' sighs Chris, 'America's not what it was.'

'We're seeing America at its worst,' he amplifies. 'The fifties was the time. Even the sixties were *quite* exciting . . .'

Pete produces, with a flamboyant 'I've got you now' gesture, a sack of fan mail with SAEs to be dealt with. Dutifully they begin to work through it.

The first few letters all mention Chris's dancing as a highlight. 'We've talked of nothing but your dancing' is typical. Neil pretends to be narked.

Chris writes back to one of them 'thanks for the presents and the accolades'. 'She'll need a dictionary for *that*,' he laughs.

Neil reads out: 'My heart was dancing with pleasure . . . both sound and words have special ability. Isn't it wonderful?'

They both like the last sentence. 'Yes, isn't it?' Neil agrees.

He opens a letter from someone who, inside, explains that they make prefabricated houses for Panasonic. 'They're all older than they look,' he says.

'Yeah,' agrees Chris. 'You treat them like they're about ten and they work in the City.'

Neil reads: 'I am envious of your uninhibited life.' 'Except,' he says, 'she's put "uninhabited".'

'We know what you mean, dear,' says Chris.

More reading: 'I recover my presence of mind listening to your music . . . when I quarrel with my parents . . . about Britain, is it always foggy . . .?'

Chris joins in a conversation in the next-door seats about astrology.

'We're supposed to get on worst,' he says, meaning him and

Neil. 'Librans and Cancers.' He says that he read about Librans in 'that famous book . . . Linda Goodman's Star Sign book. It described me to a tee.'

What did it say, I ask?

'It says I'm promiscuous.'

Oh, I say.

'Unfortunately, I'm not.'

More reading: '. . . with hearty congratulations on your success . . .'

'*Straight* from the textbook,' sniggers Chris.

'Twenty-five years out of date,' says Neil. 'Hearty congratulations, old boy.'

And: 'I love your everything very much, your winkle, your voice, your sad blue eyes, your posh fashion . . .'

'I think she means "wrinkles" . . .' says Neil.

And: 'Thank you for the great show tonight. That was really gramorous . . . sometimes it seems to me that your song is my friend who is so much cool and freaky and a bit shy.'

'This girl went to the same school as Yoko Ono,' Neil observes reading another letter.

We pass Mount Fuji. It looks just as it does in the famous photos, or in the formalized drawing in the film of the same name; a volcano with a ragged, sloping top jutting out above a smooth layer of cloud.

'It's amazing,' says Neil.

'I've never seen a sight like that in my life,' says Chris, though moments later he adds by way of qualification, 'It's still not like the Lake District.'

Carroll Thompson is reading a thick, semi-raunchy novel.

'Neil?' she asks. 'Do you know what a "curlicue" means?'

'What's the context please?' he says, as if he has three or four very precise definitions at hand and just wants to select the most appropriate. She reads him the context. He laughs and says he doesn't know.

'Where do they get those words from?' she asks.

'A dictionary,' grunts Chris.

He reads more letters. 'They've all seen *It Couldn't Happen Here*,' he points out, somewhat surprised. 'This one's seen it *three* times.'

'I sometimes put it on the video,' says Neil, 'but I can never get past the first ten minutes. It's a bit impenetrable. One of the hardest things we've *ever* done is to try to invent a logical spiel to explain *It Couldn't Happen Here* to American journalists.'

The fan mail takes them about an hour to finish. Then they fall asleep.

Your career is quite often talked about as if it's been a continual triumph, blotted only by one disaster: your film It Couldn't Happen Here. *Is that how you see it?*

Neil (to Chris): Go on. You're a great defender of this film, Chris.

Chris: Well, only so much as I think every now and again I might watch it. But I don't.

You both joke about it and put it down a lot.

Neil: I'll tell you why that is. I think we're both embarrassed that so many people apparently didn't like it, whereas when we saw it for the first time – I remember we were doing 'Always On My Mind' on *Top of the Pops* – we thought it was dead good. *Dead* good.

Chris: It's certainly got some very good moments in it.

Neil: Of course Chris and I have never been bothered by not understanding something. I think that is one of the reasons we're popular in Japan, in that we have a similar mentality.

Chris: I couldn't understand that this was what most of the criticism was about. We watched it several times and not once did I stop to think, 'What's it all about?'

That's funny, that, isn't it? It's like the Simon Frith piece. You'll be fascinated by it, point other people towards it, but still claim you don't understand it.

Neil: But that's why the Simon Frith piece interests me. I read it again when it was in the programme and thought, 'What *is* this about?' I like that. Anyway, back to the film: Jack Bond wrote the script and he read it to us over a bottle of wine and we loved it. We said, 'Fine, let's do it.' And it was fun making it; the most enjoyable time we've ever had, even though we had to get up at the crack of dawn. (*To Chris*) We had a laugh, didn't we?

Chris: Also it looked so good as we filmed it. Where it's 'West End Girls' it was four in the morning, the windswept sea front, with the flags with the sea projected on to them. It was incredible.

Neil: That was the night we appeared at the Palladium. We had to go back to Clacton and film that afterwards. To return to the great 'pop strategists' argument, it's always assumed that we have this incredible control over our career – which of course we *do* have – but at the same time if we like someone they can do anything with us really. We just do it. And at the end of the film we rather liked the result. Then everyone else hated it.

I think people don't like it because it simply doesn't work as a narrative film, does it?

Neil: I just thought it was a picture of the Pet Shop Boys. A lot of the fans like it. But we knew we had a problem when Krysia (*a friend who also used to run their fan club*) saw it and said it was terrible. And Murray was in defensive mode about it, trying to lessen the impact of the disaster, which he's very good at doing. We then realized it was going to be a rough ride, which it was.

In what sense?

Neil: It's very difficult doing something that gets slagged off. It's hurtful, and sometimes it annoys you because you think it's unfair.

Did it hurt you, Chris?

Chris: It was nothing but one big hoot, the film. I can't remember being hurt at all. I just remember laughing a lot.

Neil: Yes, there was a sense of 'how come *us*, of all people, famous for being boring, have got a film opening in sixty-four cinemas across the country?' We are the only pop stars this decade to have done that, I think; a feature film, not a rockumentary. We put a lot of effort into the promotion of it, which was wasted really. We went to New York and in the end it didn't even get shown there, so that aspect was humiliating. But it got some good reviews. It's a very sixties film . . . like *Magical Mystery Tour*. A couple of the reviews mentioned *Oh Lucky Man*. I think the mistake we made was telling Jack Bond we didn't want a lot of dialogue.

People often assume it was part of some much larger strategy.

Neil: There was a reason: that we knew we weren't going to tour. Originally we were going to have it shown in cinemas for one night only and it was going to tour, like a tour. That would have been quite interesting. But anyway it was the number ten film one week in the country. I remember hooting with laughter about that. My father wouldn't believe it.

Do you think the film said much about you?

Neil: I don't know really.

Because Jack Bond says that the taking-off point for the ideas in the film were the discussions he had with you about your lives.

Neil: Well, Jack Bond saw what we were like on television and he put that in a film. Then he filled the film with characters from songs like 'It's A Sin'. Also I think he thought we had domineering mothers, so he put domineering mothers in. In fact he probably, though he was too polite to say it, thought that psychologically Chris and I were moving away from dominant mother figures. It was set at the seaside because of our childhoods. It was originally going to be shot in Blackpool and Newcastle but it was too expensive. I think the seaside is quite important to us. Chris is forever talking about Blackpool Pleasure Beach. Chris has got very much a Blackpool world view. He comes from a city which is entirely devoted to leisure pursuits.

And all my Catholicism is in the film. Having a guilt complex about more or less everything. Another thing – and I've only just realized this this second – is that you (*he looks at Chris*) were probably telling him you were scared of being murdered. You have a *major* problem about that. So we get in a car and there's a psychopath at the back of the car. It's a major Chris Lowe phobia, that. Every time Chris goes back to his flat by himself he looks in every room to make sure there's not a murderer in there.

Chris (*defensively*): I think anyone who *didn't* do that would be mad. How could you *possibly* go to sleep not having checked? How could you sleep?

Neil: I never check. You'd hear them.

Chris: But they wouldn't move when you walked in. I lock all the doors in all the rooms, switch the burglar alarm on and I have the phone with me.

Neil: You see? He's a nutcase! Anyway, the film is quite an accurate reflection of what we're like.

Do you regret making it?

Neil: No! (*Chris nods in agreement.*) I have no regret at all. We regard it as some kind of achievement really. Matt Goss said to me, 'You've made a *movie*!' He was *totally* impressed. He's probably never *seen* it, but . . .

Chris: . . . the fact is, you've *made* one.

Leaving Tokyo central railway station we walk past the American rock band Living Colour. Neil and Chris don't recognize them.

'Do you want to meet them?' offers Ivan.

'No,' they chorus.

'I want to hear "Pet Shop Boys and Debussy",' announces Neil and we get into the minibus that will take five of us to the airport. (The rest of the entourage is now in a coach.) 'Pet Shop Boys and Debussy' is a tape a fan has given him this morning, inspired, no doubt, by the mention of Debussy in 'Left To My Own Devices'.

It begins with a spoken birthday message to Neil which they talk through.

'I'd like to do different songs in Britain,' mentions Neil. 'I'm sick of some of them. I think we should have done "Suburbia".'

The tape's birthday message is followed by all seven minutes twenty-three seconds of their 'I'm Not Scared'.

'That's a funny thing to do,' comments Chris tartly. 'To send you a tape of your own records. As if we haven't already got it! What are we supposed to do? Think, "That's good! Why don't we make records like this?"?'

'Let's have a bit of Debussy then, dear,' says Neil to the tape-recorder. 'God, this is a long track, isn't it?'

As expected when it finishes it is followed by some classical music.

'I've *never* liked Debussy,' complains Chris. 'Is this *La Mer*?'

'*La Mer*'s all orchestral, isn't it?' says Neil.

'I don't know,' says Chris. 'I just know I don't like it. I hate it when' – this next bit spoken with particular venom – 'composers try to *paint a picture*. "This is a windy forest . . ." tinkle tinkle.'

'Rent' begins.

'This is *such* a dreary tape,' says Chris. 'Throw it out the window, Neil.'

Neil takes no notice. Next is the song 'It Couldn't Happen Here'.

'Why aren't we doing this?' asks Chris. 'This is a good one for the lighters.'

'It's a serious scarf-waver, this,' Neil agrees.

Then an odd thing happens. After the chorus plays on the tape – 'you said it couldn't happen here' – Chris sings along an extra line: 'just before it did'. I presume this is just a pedantic joke, but it's not. 'It's the original lyric,' says Neil. It turns out that originally the chorus did run 'you said it couldn't happen here – just before it did' but that Chris refused to take it seriously.

'He kept singing it in a Preston accent,' explains Neil, obviously still not entirely amused by the affair, 'so I took it out in a mood.'

'"Did" is a funny word,' justifies Chris, 'especially at the end of the sentence. I was creasing myself laughing . . . legs in the air.'

'I had a *major* mood,' remembers Neil.

Hearing the song brings their thoughts back to the film of the same name.

'I might watch the film when I get home,' says Chris.

'I wouldn't if I was you,' says Neil.

The tape meanwhile has meandered back into some Debussy.

'Key change,' observes Neil, listening.

'You've got to have something to tart it up. That's why most people have key changes,' says Chris.

'It's certainly why we do,' says Neil.

'What's this one?' Chris asks him.

'*The Gollywog's Cakewalk*,' says Neil confidently.

'You can't have that!' snarls Chris. 'Haven't they renamed it?'

The rediscovery of the missing chorus line from 'It Couldn't Happen Here' inspires a discussion of other lost lyrics. Neil says that 'One More Chance' was supposed to have a couplet that went 'You, you're so extreme/your silk-screened life shot through with bullets'. Pete reminds them that in 1987 when they recorded 'Rent', a song they had written years before, the Elton John rent-boy scandal had just broken.

'Yes,' says Chris, 'and you didn't want people to think the song was about him.'

Neil nods. 'It originally went "You phoned me in the evening on hearsay to tell me who you are/you took me to a restaurant on Broadway and introduced me to a star". It became "You phoned me in the evening on hearsay and bought me caviar/you took me to a restaurant off Broadway to tell me who you are".' A few days later on-stage in Britain Neil remembers the original lyric again and substitutes it.

Then, he says, there's the first verse of 'Nothing Has Been Proved', which was intended to be the middle bit of another song they are yet to record called 'This Must Be The Place I Waited Years To Leave'. Then he explains how Che Guevara had been someone 'I'd been wanting to put into a song for a while' and only found his way into 'Left To My Own Devices' after being shunted out of a verse of 'Domino Dancing' that went:

A threat of distant thunder
The sky was red
And Che Guevara hung
Above your bed

'It was meant to suggest that a communist revolution was threatening – hence "the sky was red" – but I thought it was corny.'

The final phrase it found itself in, 'Che Guevara and Debussy to a disco beat', came from a remark of producer Trevor Horn's. They were talking about inserting into the song a long orchestral passage with drums and he said he's always wanted to make a record of Debussy to a disco beat.

On the tape the Japanese girl talks again. This time they listen and Neil says that they'll sample her voice for a song.

'I must watch *Spinal Tap* before our British tour,' threatens Chris.

'Oh no, Chris, *don't*,' says Neil.

Somehow we find ourselves earnestly discussing the failure of technology to deliver the sparkling seamless modern world we were promised when we were young.

'It never really happened, the space age, did it?' tuts Chris. 'It started well, but . . . we were meant to be having holidays on the moon by the year 2000. And we're nowhere near going to other planets. Of course it turns out that earth is the only planet that is inhabited.'

'I always said that,' announces Neil proudly. 'Nobody listened . . .'

This spirals into an even more unlikely discussion about whether time should be correctly considered the fourth or the fifth dimension.

'Hence the group, the Fifth Dimension,' says Neil, rescuing the conversation.

'Hence Eighth Wonder,' says Chris.

There follows one of those silences that comes when everyone has been talking too much but is very tired. It is broken by Chris who, out of the blue, turns to Neil and says, '*Why* did Japan get involved in the war?'

This is the sort of thing Neil knows and to begin with he answers seriously, in fulsome detail, describing the supersedence of a right-wing clique in Japan in the thirties, painting a picture of their burgeoning expansionist motivations. After a while he spots a less rigorous, more entertaining path . . .

'. . . and so you had Singapore, which is supposed to be impenetrable, and so you have lots of TV series with Japanese guards – one of them had a heart of gold, of course – and women in flowery dresses – "Oh, but we *must* have quinine, we *must*" – and meantime Alec Guinness is in *Bridge over the River Kwai* and David Bowie is kissing Ryuichi Sakamoto and . . .'

Chris stops him then. 'He didn't turn up, Ryuichi Sakamoto, did he? Or Issey Miyake.'

'Or Jason Donovan,' says Neil. 'It was a major un-star-studded event. We were blanked.'

'You had the people from *Motormouth*,' Pete points out mis-chievously.

Neil sings the Four Seasons song 'December 1963', then chants over and over the first verse of a seventies disco song: 'She was born in a theatre . . .' It is 'Rock'n'Roll Baby' by the Stylistics, though right now this is a fact that eludes us all as we frantically hum it through trying to work out what the chorus is.

As we draw up at the airport there are fans waiting. Chris recognizes one of them. 'It's the one who always says, "Do you remember me?" They're *so* self-obsessed . . .'

While someone checks in the baggage they talk to the fans. Ekko is there; Neil hands her an envelope he has clearly had ready for her. The girl who went to Yoko Ono's school is there and introduces herself. She is fifteen, lives in Cairo and is now going to school in Eastbourne to do A-levels.

'What subjects are you doing?' Neil asks her.

'History, English and economics,' she says.

'I did that!' says Neil, surprised. Naïve maybe, too.

'I know,' she says. 'That's why.'

He looks slightly startled. 'I failed economics,' he says, 'so that's not a good one . . .'

We go through passport control and compare passport photos. Neil's is cut out of a larger Pet Shop Boys photo from a professional photo session. Chris's is from before their success.

'You look quite good,' says Neil. 'You look like a thug.'

'I'm a student,' says Chris. 'I look like Den Watts.'

'Who's that?' asks Neil.

'Dirty Den,' says Chris.

'Oh,' says Neil.

Through passport control, as Chris said, we see the fans again, waving from the rail above. Almost to a girl they are in tears. They wave and wave and wave. Neil and Chris have a perfunctory skim round the Duty Free shop, waving back every now and then. After about ten minutes of this, though there is still a while before the flight, they decide to go through the security check and wait at the flight gate. Neil stands in the queue and Chris joins a few yards behind. The waving from above goes on and on.

'They want you to wave, Neil,' says Chris.

'I am waving,' says Neil.

'It's not enough,' says Chris.

'It's never enough,' says Neil, sadly.

On the moving walkway down to the gate Neil stares out the window, looking extremely thoughtful. I feel as though I'm intruding on something personal just by being there. 'I always feel a bit sad leaving Japan,' he says. 'It gets a bit traumatic.' Then silence. Then, 'Mind you' – getting louder, brasher again – 'they probably do it for about fifteen other groups.'

In the departure lounge he and Chris fight over the presents, though not perhaps as you might imagine. Chris tries to give them all to Neil; Neil tries to give them all to Chris.

Neil unwraps a package. It is the autobiography of newscaster Sandy Gall, entitled *Don't Worry About the Money Box*. He is understandably perplexed. Why? *Why?* Eventually he decides that it must be because he too used to be a journalist.

He flicks through a book of photos of them taken by a fan of their Japanese trips. 'There's the transition,' he points out, comparing photos again. He labels their three visits – their three life stages – as 'young and innocent', 'fat' and – this one – 'international businessmen'.

'I think you looked nicer then,' he says to Chris, pointing to his 'young and innocent' phase. 'Before success got hold of him and made him bitter.'

Neil then announces that 'of course' he has been given two books of poetry and then unwraps a copy of *Lolita*. 'A jolly good read,' he proclaims. Dominic hasn't read it so Neil gives it to him. 'It's dirty as well,' he promises.

Aboard the plane there is much conspiratorial muttering between Chris, Ivan and the cabin staff. Eventually, as we fly over Siberia, everyone is ushered into the first three rows of economy seating. We are stared at by bemused Japanese travellers and glared at by irate members of the road crew who want to sleep. The entourage is travelling split between first, club and economy: 'A hierarchical system,' says Chris, 'much as I disapprove. But,' he adds cheerfully, 'this is the eighties, after all.'

A cake – 'Mr N. Tennants' written on it – appears. Champagne flows. Neil, who has earlier slipped down a valium tablet to usher himself into the world of sleep, is brought through. We all sing 'Happy Birthday'. The wardrobe department present him with a rather fine pen.

'My homework was always returned,' he reminisces, 'because you couldn't read it. "What am I supposed to make of this? How do you expect to get to university?"'

'And you said . . .?' I cue him.

'Sheer talent,' he guffaws, and repeats the often-told story of the school report he got which read, 'On what does he base his claim to superiority?'

'That's one of my favourite quotes about me,' he says, before wandering merrily up and down the aisles singing 'I am sixteen, going on seventeen . . .'

Quietly there are a few stern words being spoken. Two of the crew have sat themselves without tickets in club rather than economy, a response to a longstanding argument with Ivan. Probably correctly he takes this as a challenge to his authority and is busy firmly dressing them down. Dark looks speed around.

Meanwhile some Japanese passengers watch and assume that all this fuss must be in honour of Pinkie, who, as usual, in remarkably flowing pink finery and impeccably made up, is the only extraordinary-looking person on offer. They come up and ask to have their photos taken with her, and she gracefully obliges. But one Japanese man clearly twigs that there is more going on than this and, sidling up to Pete, asks him which singer is on board.

'Stevie Wonder,' says Pete.

'Oh!' he cries, deeply impressed and delighted.

When I leave the airport Neil and Chris are standing with trolleys, queuing with itemized lists and patient but slightly resentful expressions in the customs Red channel at Heathrow airport. The foreign half of the tour is over. We have been away for a fortnight. The cliché about touring is that every place is the same – another hotel, taxi ride, soundcheck, concert, restaurant, club – but that's not quite the point. We've all had plenty of time free to us: a few have made concerted attempts at sightseeing or more. But mostly we've not moved from the world we've brought with us. Despite all the planes and all the miles, we've seen the bits of Japan and Hong Kong we've seen because they have travelled to us, not us to them. They've joined the world we've been in, a world that is one long strange conversation about the Pet Shop Boys on tour.

Returning to my flat, where I live alone, I throw all my clothes on to the floor and find myself vaguely irritated, a few hours later, that no one has picked them up when they've come in to turn down my bed.

Chapter Thirteen

Thursday, *13 July*

We meet outside the Holiday Inn. Neil says they've been 'not doing much'; this includes a meeting with Derek Jarman sorting out the concert film. Chris and Pete have elected to tour Britain in the Pet Shop Boys' car, an Audi Quatro. There are two coaches laid on – one double-deckered affair for the band and wardrobe, another for Neil and Chris.

Neil has been reading the press they have had so far. There have been some uncanny coincidences, including a piece in *Melody Maker*'s Talk Talk Talk section – a series of spoof captions (part of a long tradition of fictitious irrelevancies) in which Chris muses, eerily, whether or not he should dye his hair blond. An extremely unlikely idea, it must be said, unless you were one of the very few people who knew it was true.

Neil proudly carries onto the bus another magazine he has just bought, the latest copy of *New Statesman and Society*. On their cover they trail, alongside articles on food hygiene, the politics of water privatization and an interview with Marietta Higgs, the woman at the centre of the Cleveland child abuse furore, a piece on 'Derek Jarman and the Pet Shop Boys'.

It begins: 'For all his public introspection, the shy boy in Neil Tenant, the monotone-voiced leader of The Pet Shop Boys, is aching to break free.' The second paragraph moves on to say, 'There is part of him that wants to exorcise the pimply middle-class schoolboy and revel in a hedonist, even sexual presence . . .'

This draws Neil up. 'It kind of is true really,' he says. 'I'm surprised she's noticed it.' This approval is tempered seconds later by the realization – accompanied by severe huffing, puffing and profanity – that 'She's spelt my name wrong!'

He reads on.

'It's quite good, in a pretentious way,' he murmurs as he turns to the second page.

It finishes by stating that the Pet Shop Boys' way will never be the big, uninhibited, declarative way of a Tom Robinson or a Bronski Beat, but that they 'long to follow a fey, flamboyant tradition stretching from Noël Coward to Elton John, rolling in English eccentricity and overblown vaudeville'.

'The big declaration bit is quite true really,' he mutters as he puts it down. That finished, he studies his surroundings.

'Isn't it *exciting*? I'm on a real tour bus! My *own* tour bus! The last time I was on a tour bus was with Depeche Mode. Before that it was with Kajagoogoo, sitting next to Limahl.'

Across the aisle is make-up artist Lynne Easton, who has joined the British leg of the tour. She has just come from a twenty-four-hour shoot for the latest Transvision Vamp video 'Landslide Of Love'. There is a school of thought that says that their singer Wendy James, self-styled glamour rebel, is one of the horrible people of pop but Lynne insists she was very nice. Neil chips in to agree, and explains how he met Wendy James on *Saturday Superstore*. She did a phone-in and when a caller asked her what her hobby was she said 'getting drunk'. Off camera, the programme makers freaked out – they said that this was an irresponsible message to give to a young audience and insisted she came back on camera and apologized. As Neil tells it she was ready to give in but Neil told her not to be so silly. Sarah Greene, one of the presenters, chipped in and agreed with Neil.

'So there you had Wendy James, our greatest rock'n'roll rebel,' laughs Neil, 'being told by Sarah Greene and Neil Tennant how to rebel.'

They talk about Bros. Lynne repeats a tip she has been given: 'You can tell them apart by the colour of their Porsches.'

Ivan briefs Neil on the latest in the Courtney Pine at Folkestone Town Hall fiasco. Ivan has told Courtney, 'If you don't turn up I'll be so upset I can't accept responsibility . . .'

Neil says that if necessary they'll simply replace him. 'Even though,' he adds, 'he's irreplaceable.' Eventually the Pet Shop Boys will agree to pay £5,000 compensation for cancelling the concerts.

During the two days off Neil has finally seen Sonia, the Stock Aitken Waterman singer who has leapfrogged them in the charts. As with all new pop sensations he already has a firm opinion. 'I don't like the look of her,' he says. 'She's very cheesy. If the Reynolds Girls were one person it would be her.'

Stock Aitken Waterman have, at least in success terms, dominated British pop music for the last three years. At last count they've written and/or produced about eighty Top 75 hits: Kylie Minogue, Jason Donovan, Rick Astley, Mel & Kim, Bananarama, Dead Or Alive, Hazell Dean, Pat & Mick, the Reynolds Girls, Samantha Fox, Ferry Aid, 'Ferry Cross The Mersey', Sinitta, Mandy Smith, Brother Beyond, Donna Summer, Princess, Sabrina . . . and now Sonia. Their philosophy is simple, and unusually direct for the world of pop music. Pop music is for entertainment – that's all. The most entertaining things are simple and happy. The most important virtues are love, happiness and ambition. A song should have one simple theme, usually something to do with love, and should stick to that theme, expanding on it throughout the song. As Mike Stock, the main songwriter, once said: if you write a song about a girl with blue eyes then that, and that alone, is what the song is about. You don't write about her hair, you don't write about her clothes, you don't write about where she lives and you most certainly don't – he was triumphantly adamant on this point – write about which political party she votes for. She has blue eyes. That's it.

Another golden rule of Stock Aitken Waterman pop is that if you chance upon something people like – an idea, a rhythm, a look – you keep it until it stops being successful. Most pop stars pride themselves on change: 'This album is a real progression blah-de-blah . . .' Stock Aitken Waterman ask why you would possibly want to change something that is tried and tested and successful.

The Pet Shop Boys are ambivalent about them. They cheer the attack Stock Aitken Waterman have made on rock snobbishness. Chris likes a lot of their records: Neil a few. They also have reservations.

Neil: A lot of people are morons and like moronic things. What I think about Stock Aitken Waterman a lot of the time is that it's like *1984* when all the proles have that ghastly cheerful music. It's written for them – either by a computer or by a special department; I can't remember – and it keeps them all happy. (*To Chris*) You said yesterday that it was like music hall, which I thought was interesting.

Chris: The tunes are right back to music hall. You can just imagine the singalong when they get to the chorus. And you could really imagine if there was another war . . . Kylie becomes Vera Lynn. You can just picture her entertaining the troops.

In a sense you're only saying what they say anyway – that music should be made exactly in that precise way which will make people happy.

Neil: Yes, but you see we have the opposite strategy. Stock Aitken Waterman always know it's got to be cheerful. The Pet Shop Boys have always set out to make something fundamentally not-cheerful into something that has mass popularity. That's why we never used to smile, because we don't believe there's much to be cheerful about in the first place. You're being a wally and deluding yourself if you think there is. And therefore we are making pop records that fit in with that ethos.

So to your mind Stock Aitken Waterman records are reinforcing the contentedness of those who live in a fool's paradise?

Neil: Yes, that's what they're intended to do. They'd say, 'We're just making records for people to have a good time to.'

They are utterly and totally Thatcherite and their records are utterly and totally Thatcherite records. In which sense they are perfect pop because they are totally records of their time.

You plainly don't want to make records like that, but don't you think that to a lot of consumers Stock Aitken Waterman records are genuinely ecstatic pop records?

Neil: Oh, that's true. There's no two ways about that. But I don't think they're effective that often. Maybe about ten of them.

Even if it's only ten, then ten brilliant pop records in three years is pretty good going. Not many other people have done that in the eighties.

Neil: There's not many people making pop records in the eighties, concentrating on it. To be quite honest there's only really ourselves and Stock Aitken Waterman who have any interest in it. Incidentally one of the things I like about Pete Waterman is that he's a huge enthusiast. Consequently he's a bit of a prat, but he's a huge, huge enthusiast.

He's one of those people who makes you feel while you're in the same room, that anything can be achieved, isn't he?

Chris: I love people like that.

Neil: I just don't like the way they say things like, 'I don't like Morrissey – he's so miserable.' That's a pathetic thing to say, because Morrissey's made records that are actually funny; he's got a *fantastic* sense of humour. And what *really* gets me is when they're on the television and say, 'we give everybody what they want.' I regard that as an absolutely despicable attitude. It's patronizing and it denies any artistry whatsoever – which they possess sometimes. I don't think when they make a record they make any attempt to make it *fabulous*. Good pop music has got a sort of *magical* quality to it, a *fabulous* quality. Stock Aitken Waterman do not have that. Their videos look cheesy – Sonia and that dancer look like a bad pub turn on a Sunday afternoon making a *spectacle* of themselves.

Chris: I think you can separate the records from that aspect.

Neil: But I think they often sound cheesy and cheap.

Chris: Well, the thing I always like is the songs. They write such good hooky choruses. Actually I quite like the way their songwriting has developed. I like listening to their key changes into the choruses, their new tricks. I've been listening to Donna Summer's LP and that's definitely not cheesy.

Neil: But their videos are terrible and they're a sign of what Peter Waterman thinks the public wants. He wants everyone to be hideous and naff and have a jolly good time. It's like the whole world is a Radio One Roadshow twenty-four hours a day; that is their world. I feel excluded from that. It's not a world I am really part of.

Why have they been so successful?

Neil: They write good tunes.

Chris: And they have a good groove as well. You see, I don't like them *because* of who they're appealing to, I like them despite that. I judge a record on the basis of the record, usually the twelve-inch record, not on any other idea of the artist.

Neil: That's a very unusual way of listening to records. Most pop music is not just about music, it's always been about who the record's by, what they look like, how they sing on television, the clothes they wear.

Chris: But I still think the public primarily buys a record because they like the record, regardless. I think Sonia's number one despite what she looks like. They rely on their songs.

Neil: Mmmm. I think they're targeting the lowest common denominator because the lowest common denominator does consume music in the way you're talking about. Perhaps, with them, the artists are becoming irrelevant. But there is nothing remotely aspirational about their records. It's totally Thatcherite. The *Sun* is the same thing – it's the idea that you laugh at anything out of the ordinary and isn't it great? Everybody's totally *normal*, everybody's a 'good bloke' and they like a few pints and they want a nice car and they want to go on holiday and there is *nothing else to life*.

If that's their attitude, does it necessarily devalue their records?

Neil: It's what they're about. It's the function they're playing in society.

But the records don't espouse those ideas themselves. It's not intrinsic to the records.

Neil: It is.

So what is the difference between Rick Astley's 'Never Gonna Give You Up' and your 'Heart'?

Neil: Actually there's very little difference, but 'Heart' is a one-off for us.

But they're both brilliant pop records.

Neil: Actually I think 'Never Gonna Give You Up' is better than 'Heart'.

So does 'Heart' also presuppose this Thatcherite, Sun*-loving 'nothing else to life' world view?*

Neil: Well, all our records aren't like 'Heart'. It's a one-off cheerful love song. But there's also a difference. To me 'Heart' is like a Madonna record. I think that 'Heart' sounds sincere. Rick Astley sounds sincere too, I agree, but I don't think Sonia's record has any sincerity at all. If the person who sings it is interesting the record can be interesting but otherwise it's just a brainless fantasy of the way life is.

There are many 'How could we have let Chris drive?' murmurings as we head up the motorway to Birmingham, and already Neil and Ivan are bickering over which of them is to blame for his expected late arrival, but when we pull up at the National Exhibition Centre Chris and Pete have already been there a while.

'He was dead shy,' the fans already waiting outside tell us. 'He wouldn't speak to us.' They ask Neil, 'Are you really wearing pyjamas on stage?'

'You're not going to believe it,' he nods. 'I can't believe it.'

Inside Chris is trying on his new cap. As Neil predicted

Giorgio Armani didn't have time to make a leather cap – though they have apparently offered to make some special clothes in the future – so Ivan and Alan have arranged for a fake to be knocked up; a snip at £300.

He sits down, and Leonard, the hairdresser on the British tour, shaves his hair even closer than before. Lawrence photographs this.

'I don't have photographs like this,' announces Chris.

'It was good enough for Elvis,' counters Lawrence.

'Oh,' says Chris, acquiescing. He surveys his haircut in the mirror. 'My mum will loathe this. She is not going to like it at all.' The last time he had his hair cut very short – years ago – he tells me that his mother simply went 'Oh no! oh *no!* oh NO!' and ran indoors.

His parents are the first of a flood of Pet Shop Boys family who will see the British show. Their first visit is tonight, then they will come again on Saturday with his maternal grandparents. His grandfather, as the shortest Chris Lowe biography will tell you, used to play in a vaudeville jazz group called the Nitwits. Most people assume that the Nitwits were of no significance whatsoever and, indeed, this is always the impression Chris has given, but it is not so. Recently he made a remarkable discovery. In a lull during recording with Liza Minnelli, he mentioned his grandfather and – more out of politeness than anything – she asked him the name of the group. Both were flabbergasted. When she was young the Nitwits were her favourite group. She liked them so much that once when her mother, Judy Garland, flew her home from boarding school she arranged for the Nitwits to play on the tarmac as Liza stepped down off the plane at Las Vegas airport. Chris's grandfather had, of course, never mentioned this, but when Chris asked him whether it was true he simply nodded and said, 'Oh yes, that's right. I'd forgotten that.'

Chris tells us about the fans who greeted them, the ones he was 'shy' to.

'You know how all the younger girls like me and the middle-aged ones like Neil?' he laughs. 'Well, when I got here there was a middle-aged woman and, sure enough, she said, "Where's Neil?"'

Neil returns from a visit to the arena. Instead of piped classical music, the support act in Britain is a modern classical string quartet called the Balenescu Quartet. He has just been watching them rehearse.

'Well,' he says, 'the string quartet sound like a string quartet.'

'Horrible?' asks Chris.

'No,' he snaps, '*fantastic*.'

'Do they need music stands?' gloats Chris. He already knows that the answer is yes. 'As predicted by the classically trained member of the group,' he sniggers.

On the portable phone they get through to Mark Farrow, who is at the office in London. They have decided that the end-of-tour party will be called Bingobangobongo in honour of the Japanese club where Chris had raved madly and Neil had waltzed with Janet, the club where we had our best night in Tokyo. They want Mark to design the invitations, so Neil dictates the exact punctuation required in meticulous detail. As usual by now there are quite a few people milling round the dressing-room. Once Neil has finished on the phone he calmly, deliberately throws a strop.

'I'd like *everybody* to get out of the dressing-room *now*, so I can have a shower and concentrate on being nervous,' he says in a tone of voice that implies we're all idiots not to have left ages ago.

'I didn't know you'd become a Buddhist . . .'

The first words spoken by Chris's mother are, as he feared, not words of loving maternal greetings but a comment on his haircut. She is not impressed. Nevertheless pleasantries are exchanged and they go to join his sister Vicki in the arena, watching the Balenuscu Quartet, fifteen minutes through their forty-minute set.

'Twenty-five more minutes of this and I think people will leave,' says Vicki. She sees me note this. 'Don't even dare *think* about printing anything. I'll sue you.'

Both the Tennant and Lowe families, I shall be learning, have been well trained in dealing with the press.

The show is more animated than any of the Japanese shows and the audience is considerably louder. Mr and Mrs Lowe look on with anxious pride until Chris dances in 'Paninaro'. From then on they're beaming. For 'It's A Sin' – even though the penis, alas, against all instructions, is out – they cheer uproariously. Neil and Chris look thrilled. In a rather charming revision of stage etiquette, Neil bends down to sign autographs for the front row while singing the last verses of 'Always On My Mind'. Not to be outdone, Chris signs some more during the introductions. 'It's Alright' now ends in a jamboree of large silk flags, all different colours, waved by the dancers; a decision made because the previous jollity has been deemed 'too naff for Britain'.

Back-stage Neil and Chris look extremely chuffed. 'It's *much* better performing in England,' whoops Chris. His parents appear.

'Brilliant,' says his mum. 'Brilliant. Absolutely *super*, love.'

'We've got some champagne,' says Chris apologizing 'it's only Bollinger.' Leonard is standing a few feet away. 'Mum!' he says heartily, 'this is the man responsible for my haircut.'

Mrs Lowe frowns.

Neil is smiling but complaining about his back, which is hurting. Still, he decides, it's only to be expected: 'I am thirty-five. Tonight was definitely the real thing,' he says. Upon reflection he has decided that 'Japan isn't quite real'.

A nearly blind fan is brought back-stage and Neil chats to him. Then Harvey Goldsmith, the last of the three promoters, arrives. Neil asks him how he thought it went.

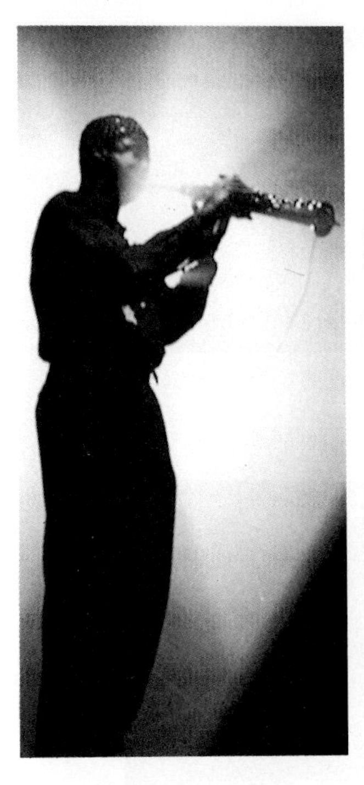

Courtney Pine

'Love Comes Quickly'

'Heart'

'Later Tonight'

Waiting to film 'Nothing Has Been Proved'

'Nothing Has Been Proved'

'It's A Sin'

'Shopping'. (Left to right) Casper, Courtney (between Casper's legs), Tracy, Dominic (wearing helmet with light on) and Chris

'King's Cross'. Chris in front of film of himself originally shot for the 'Rent' video

'Domino Dancing'. Neil, Robia and Casper

'It's A Sin'

'Shopping'. Neil and dancers

'Domino Dancing'. Robia, the bank of sequencers and samplers, Chris and Neil

'West End Girls'. Cooley's backflip

'Heart'. Neil in front of one of the dancers from Derek Jarman's accompanying film

'Paninaro'. Cooley and Chris

'It's A Sin'. Neil's famous twirl

'West End Girls'. Hugo (with moustache), Cooley, Tracy (with arms raised) and Robia

Pet Shop Boys

Neil Tennant

Chris taking his applause

'They were confused for about four numbers . . . stunned,' he says.

He suggests that they need some street noise to cover up the few seconds while the string quartet sneaks off-stage under cover of darkness before 'One More Chance' begins, a suggestion that is immediately taken up and used for the rest of the shows. He says he wasn't sure about the classical music: 'To me, you could have lightened it up.'

'*They* wanted to play John Cage,' Neil points out.

Harvey then says he thinks the middle section, 'The Sound Of The Atom Splitting', is too long. Neil disagrees; in London, he suggests, 'People will go berserk.'

Murray, the press officer, appears.

'What did the press think?' asks Neil. A coach load has been brought up from London. All the major national newspapers and the music press are represented.

'Pretty good,' says Murray. Days later Neil will claim he knew right then exactly what that meant.

Linda Duff, now a journalist on the *Daily Mirror* but once a colleague of Neil's on *Smash Hits*, arrives back-stage. 'I was in hysterics most of the time,' she tells him, though it's not quite clear whether this is meant as a compliment. When his back is turned, she asks Murray whom the big bouquets lining the wall are from. Murray says he doesn't know. 'No one will mind if I have a look, will they?' she says and leans over to read the labels.

Neil and Chris go outside to sign autographs.

'Neil!' screams one fan. 'You're absolutely gorgeous. I want to marry you.'

'Well you can,' says Neil matter-of-factly. 'Name the day.'

'Margaret Macdonald is my teacher!' hollers another. 'At the Crescent Theatre on Saturday morning.'

Neil perks up his ears. Margaret Macdonald is an old youth

theatre friend of his. Indeed her sister Frances is part of the public Pet Shop Boys legend as the person Neil used to kiss in the broom cupboard at school. 'We used to get caught,' he once said, 'but I think that was half the point.' He sends Margaret his love via the pupil.

'Chris! Can we have your cap?'

'No,' says Chris, outraged. 'How cheeky can you get?' He pauses. 'And I've only got ten of them,' he lies.

'Can I have a kiss, Neil?'

'No, all my kisses are gone.'

'But I've got the same birthday as you,' pleads the fan.

'What day?' asks Neil, suspiciously.

'10 July.'

'Oh,' he concedes, 'in that case . . .' She gets kissed.

The security man holding the gates open just enough for fans to trickle through sees me taking notes and wanders over, good-humouredly whispering in my ear, 'Put that security is waiting to go home.'

Neil mutters that he's decided to avoid kisses from now on. He says his reason is that 'I'm always scared I'm going to catch a cold. Major disease paranoia.'

We walk away. 'Do you know, we're obliging,' he chuckles.

Then they laugh about the way they've taken to raising their hands in greeting as they come on-stage.

'Have you noticed?' says Neil. 'We do Bros.'

'I think I'm Luke,' says Chris.

Back in the dressing-room Vicki and Chris argue about dancing.

'I taught you all your moves,' she says.

'I taught you the Saturday Night Fever dance,' counters Chris.

'Jane Tyson taught you that,' says Vicki, 'in the back room of the South Shore Tennis Club.'

'She never did,' says Chris. 'I learnt it at Man Fridays. You tried to teach me the Cabbage Patch . . .'

And so on. Chris puts on his Valentino hat.

'Oh, I like *that*,' says his dad. More than what's underneath anyway, the suggestion seems to be.

Susan, Neil's sister, worries about what Neil's parents will think. The general opinion is that Chris's parents would be quite hard to offend and would probably keep it to themselves if they were. The same general opinion says that Neil's parents won't be. She suspects they'll hate Neil wearing a fur coat during 'Rent'. And as for 'It's A Sin' . . .

On the bus Neil immediately mentions to Ivan that the sound was poor tonight – 'I don't need to say anything; he knows,' says Ivan. That over, Neil is content to bask in the glory of it all.

'The best bit was when they shouted "Chris, take off your glasses!" and he did! . . . It was really interesting to see what the audience is like. I was expecting the front row to be a lot younger . . . I was surprised people listened to the string quartet. They weren't supposed to listen. Anyway, it establishes an attitude . . .'

Ivan mentions the huge bouquet of flowers that Rob sent to wish them luck. Neil knew nothing of it. Earlier I had seen Tom stop someone bring them into the dressing-room, telling them they were to go in his car.

Chapter Fourteen

Friday, *14 July*

In Japan *Smash Hits* had faxed to ask if Neil and Chris would do an interview for the *Smash Hits* yearbook. They'd said yes, as long as they were guaranteed one of the photos on the cover. Since then they've been putting it off, but agree to talk this afternoon on the way to the venue. It's a style of interview that *Smash Hits* delight in: teasing out a mixture of quite trivial and very serious thoughts together. They simply have to chat about a number of fairly abstract topics . . .

Travel, I say.

'Is that the first thing?' says Neil. 'Are we going to talk sort of stream of consciousness? . . . Is a pot of coffee made? . . . Well it bloody well should be.'

Pete says he's no good at coffee.

'Pete. I have *every* confidence in you making me a cup of coffee . . . I can't think of anything to say about travel. Well of course the first thing about travel is actually the travelling . . . There is something romantic about it . . . As I was saying to you yesterday I don't think travel's necessarily good for people. I think it makes people dissatisfied. I've never been convinced that travel broadens the mind. I think it makes people kind of glib in their attitudes to things. I think it's very difficult to go anywhere and really experience it. I often feel that when we go places – I go places – we don't really find out much about it . . . one time you used to go places and it was all different but now the shops are the same everywhere . . . there's all the same things everywhere. So that's me on travel.' He looks to Chris. 'It's you on travel now.'

'Is it a monologue?' asks Chris.

You don't need to do that, I advise. You can just discuss it between the two of you.

'Oh,' says Neil. 'I thought we had to do a monologue.'

No, you can interact.

'Oh, well, I've done a monologue so you' – to Chris – 'can do a monologue.'

'Let's bicker instead.'

'That's a great one! They bicker about various subjects.'

I think that's the idea.

'Oh,' whoops Neil. 'You *sneak*.'

'. . . perhaps you could ask us what places we'd like to travel to. Are there places you haven't been, Chris, where you'd like to go to?'

'Yes,' says Chris. 'I'd like to go to Sicily. I quite like Italy. I just like the things I've heard about it. They cycle past and nick your bags in the street! They're *that* bad!'

'Chris, you should go to Brazil in that case, if you want to get your bag snatched.'

'It's too far. You want to go to Russia, don't you?'

'Actually I would like to go to Russia. I'd like to go to Leningrad actually. I don't know why I haven't been – it's incredibly easy to go.'

'We could arrange some dodgy promotional thing to go there.'

'Well,' sighs Neil, 'alas they don't release our records there, though as we *all* know we are the most popular group in Russia. Which I've never ever believed.'

Who told you? I ask.

'I can't remember. However it doesn't stop me telling people all the time. Actually I'd love to go to Leningrad. I've been interested in Russian history since I was quite young. You know, it's where the Russian revolution happened and all the rest of it, the Winter Palace . . .'

Chris, sarcastically, 'It's where the French revolution happened . . .'

Neil, exasperated, schoolmasterly, 'There's a lot of Russia where the Russian revolution *didn't* happen in. Perhaps I'll talk about the Russian revolution rather than love . . .'

Love?

'You can talk about love, Chris, you're better at that sort of thing than me.'

'Well,' says Chris, 'Love is a double-edged thing.' Laughs. 'Love . . .' He bursts into song: '. . . the power of love . . .'. 'There's been a lot written about it, trying to put their finger on what it is, but I don't know if I feel love so much as kind of intense urges.'

'Oooo!' exclaims Neil. 'We, the reader, have started paying attention at this point. And perhaps you could illustrate exactly what you mean. "Oh no,"' he coos, pretending to be someone reading the finished article, '"It's Chris Lowe talking about intense urges . . ."'

'Well that's about it really,' says Chris. 'Have I ever been in love . . .?'

'That's just made me think of that song by Cutting Crew with the worst lyric of all time,' interrupts Neil, '"I've been in love before . . . the worst time is when you're in it." We've always wanted to do a Greek version, when, after "the worst time is when you're in it", and a voice goes "innit?". Actually I think it's "the hardest time is when you're in it".'

'There's that sense of love that you have with people that you're close to but I never think of that as being love. I always think of love as being that intense feeling you get which is kind of an aching in the region of your heart where you go all flittery and go a bit doolally.'

'You feel a bit sick,' agrees Neil.

'But then again,' wonders Chris, 'is that love or just one of my intense urges?'

'No,' says Neil authoritatively, 'that's not an intense urge.'

'Well,' demurs Chris, 'I think mine tend to overlap a bit.'

'That's the whole point of love,' says Neil.

'. . . showing love,' says Neil, 'is very difficult. It's a bit soppy, isn't it?'

'It's a bit girlie,' says Chris, roaring with laughter.

'It's more than that. It's very exposed. It opens you up.'

'Also,' says Chris, 'unfortunately when I say something like "I love you" it sounds really really insincere.' He hoots with mirth. 'You know when you're writing a birthday card to someone? Even when I'm writing I always think it's insincere. But it isn't necessarily . . .'

Food?

'Well,' sighs Neil, 'of course the Pet Shop Boys are famous for liking food . . . for us dinner is often the main event of the day. If we're doing a promotional trip a major issue all the time is dinner: what time, where it's going to be, what kind of food, what you have to wear . . .'

'Sometimes,' says Chris, 'we even have to compromise our dress sense for the kind of food we want to eat. Can you believe that, fans? Sometimes fashion and food are incompatible and – though sometimes very reluctantly – food always wins.'

'You do find people for whom food isn't a major issue,' acknowledges Neil, 'but for us it's *completely* a major issue.'

★

'In the recording studio,' says Neil, 'we're famous for: it's half past eight, the Pet Shop Boys have completely lost interest no matter what's happening because we're thinking of the restaurant around the corner.'

'I've always liked skiving off,' says Chris. 'There is no greater feeling than skiving off something you're supposed to be doing.'

'People always say, "Why don't you produce your own records?" and really, ultimately, it's down to *dinner*.'

Money?

'You're the breadhead of the band. You'd better talk about that, Chris "it's not enough money" Lowe,' says Neil.

'It's not that,' defends Chris. 'It's just that if you're being offered a certain amount of money you know that you could be offered double it so why aren't you getting it?'

'I think Chris's attitude to money was summed up when he was asked in that *Star Hits*' – an American version of *Smash Hits* – 'psychological quiz, "If someone offered you one hundred thousand dollars would you walk a block of a city street naked?" to which Chris answered, "It's not enough money." He thought about it for a couple of minutes, probably toyed with the rights you were selling for that money and decided it wasn't enough . . .'

'I never really imagined having any money,' says Chris. 'I was always in debt.'

'You were hopeless with money,' Neil agrees, 'absolutely hopeless.'

'Even now I don't look at my account just in case it says overdrawn by loads. I dread that.'

'When I first knew Chris he was a student and he had a five-thousand-pound overdraft. In 1981! I could not believe it.'

'I just accumulated it.'

'And you know how he paid it off? He became a pop star.

So if *you've* got an overdraft become a pop star! It's a bloody good job Chris did . . .'

Neil makes a long speech: 'There's no point pretending money's not important but . . . journalists often think that people in pop music do everything for the money and I think people very rarely do things for the money. At the same time everyone has the same thing: they don't want to be ripped off, because the whole music industry is based on the idea of ripping people off. People used to get 100 per cent ripped off, now they probably only get 50 per cent ripped off . . . Pop music's never really got away from that fairground huckster kind of image, conning people . . . We've never really maximized our profitability . . .'

Are you well off? I ask.

'We are well off but only very recently, in the last two weeks, when we received a huge amount of money from EMI for the first time.'

Religion?

'I've got nothing to say on religion,' says Chris. 'I was brought up Church of England . . . I don't really think about it.'

I ask if he ever prays.

'No.'

'Not even on aeroplanes?' asks Neil mischievously.

'No,' says Chris. 'On aeroplanes I don't like to have . . .' – laughs – '. . . certain thoughts.'

'This is quite interesting, this is, actually,' says Neil. 'Chris doesn't like to think about sex on aeroplanes in case it makes the plane crash. That is a fact.' Chris is almost crying with laughter at this revelation. I ask him to explain.

'I can't explain that,' he says.

'It's because he thinks it's a sin,' says Neil. 'It's true, isn't it?'

'I don't like to talk about it,' insists Chris. 'I suppose it must be.'

'I'm a sort of vaguely religious person,' says Neil.

'Lapsed Catholic and all that,' says Chris.

'It's never left me totally. I'm not an atheist, though funnily enough I would quite like to be an atheist. But I just can't be. I'm sort of in thrall to the idea of God . . . I like the feeling of religion . . . the idea of being good has always attracted me. When I was a little boy I used to want to be a saint. I admired saints because they were so good – like St Francis of Assisi, who was a rich man and gave away all his money. I've always wanted to be a good person. Thought-out wickedness and selfishness always shocks me.'

A silence.

'I find it a turn-on,' says Chris. 'I think it's closely related to sex.'

'But you think sex is bad,' says Neil. 'It's a Christian guilt thing, associating sex with guilt. I think I do that too.'

Housework?

'. . . I have someone who comes round twice a week,' says Chris.

'*Twice* a week?' exclaims Neil.

'Does yours only come round once a week? Tttthhhh. I'm sorry. One up *there*, I'm afraid.'

'You're messier than me,' says Neil. 'I'm tidy. I always make my bed first thing.'

'You make your own bed?' laughs Chris.

'Every morning. I can't bear coming back to the house with the bed unmade.'

'You don't have a quilt, that's why. One fluff and mine's ready.'

'I don't like duvets,' objects Neil. 'I'm sorry, they're either too hot or too cold. That is *literally* a fact. Don't anyone dare deny it. Say a duvet is not either too hot or too cold and I'll call you a liar. At the hotel at the moment: too hot . . .'

'Well, it's because you like to be tucked in. I prefer that loose-living feeling that you get in a duvet . . .'

'I cook quite a lot,' says Chris. 'Actually I prefer to eat in than eat out because we eat out a lot during work. At the moment I tend to eat things like grilled lamb chops, new potatoes and veg. Simple food for simple people.' Laughs. 'When everything's nice and perfectly done I think it's fantastic. You just get the pure flavour of what you're eating. Otherwise I'll just do one of Neil's brown rice dishes where you basically just bung in a load of vegetables and stuff and then add a load of soy sauce. I do a chicken version of that . . .'

'This,' announces Neil proudly, 'is what is known as a Grim Stir Fry. When someone phones up and says, "Are you not going out?" you say, "I'm staying in for a grim stir fry." I almost invented the grim stir fry, when you have brown rice with broccoli and nothing else.'

'That's very grim, that one,' frowns Chris.

'And actually it's one of my favourite meals. Yours isn't very grim.'

'Mine has: you fry the onions and the bits of chicken . . .'

'Immediate salmonella panic for me there,' says Neil.

'Free-range, freshly cooked chicken.'

'Oh. That's OK.'

'Free-range chicken from Marks & Spencer. It costs the earth. It's cheaper to go out to eat.'

'That *would* appeal to you,' says Neil, 'knowing that you could have spent less at a restaurant.'

Clothes?

'Well, you know . . .' says Chris, drifting into silence.

'When you get up in the morning, Chris,' says Neil, taking over the interrogation, 'how do you decide what you're going to wear? What's your kind of thought process?'

'Well, I wish I didn't have to think about it at all because I hate it. Quite often in the morning I'm sitting on my bed in despair, knowing that I'm already half an hour late for a meeting and I've got nothing to wear. I've got all my clothes stacked up and I don't like any of them. All my favourite clothes are dirty. I wish I didn't care. I'm happiest when I've got a load of really nice t-shirts and I like all of them and I've got a load of new underpants and socks and I've got my favourite jeans.'

'Clothes are like a major major issue,' observes Neil. After chatting a bit more he mentions, 'I've always liked wearing a tie and a jacket.'

'I've never liked wearing a tie,' says Chris.

'Also I quite suit wearing a tie,' says Neil. 'But, as it happens, in normal life I very rarely wear suits.'

'Neil!' objects Chris. 'When we're in Sarn West' – a recording studio – 'you'll often come in in . . .'

'That's when I'm going through one of my "if I've bought these clothes I may as well wear them" phases, so I arrive in a Yohji Yamamoto suit.'

'The best thing,' declares Chris, 'is when you're on holiday and all you're doing is going to the beach and all you have to do is put a pair of shorts on. And one thing for me is having a happening pair of training shoes. You've got to have a happening pair of training shoes.'

'You see,' Neil disagrees, 'I don't like training shoes.'

'I hate shoes,' says Chris. 'I absolutely hate them to death.'

'Chris has never worn shoes,' confirms Neil.

'Apart from at school and I hated them. You can't bounce in shoes, can you? You can't bowl down the street.'

'You like to *bounce* down the street and I like to *stomp* down the street,' says Neil. 'I like the stompy feel of shoes.'

Chris laughs. 'You like to goosestep with your boots on.'

⋆

Politics?

'Where does that footpath go?' says Neil, looking out of the bus window. 'I think that's one of your architectural cock-ups.' The footpath ends in mid-air.

'It's called Lemmings Leap,' says Chris. 'Neil's a member of the Loony Left.'

'Yes,' says Neil. 'I don't know that I am really.'

'I'm very . . .' says Chris, 'if someone's arguing one point I automatically think the other point of view, which is rather unfortunate. I don't really like party politics. It's too pathetic, isn't it?'

'Politicians are a bit pathetic,' Neil agrees. 'There's no two ways about that.'

'I always find it easier to go for a personality,' says Chris. 'I used to love Ken Livingstone when he was the head of the GLC because you could tell he was doing a lot for London. You felt part of a city and whatever he said sounded like complete sense. I haven't voted for the past two elections. I hate Mrs Thatcher.'

What most about her?

'Her children.'

'That's a fair answer,' says Neil.

'You can tell a lot about her,' says Chris, 'by Carol and Mark.'

'Of course *I'm* very interested in politics,' says Neil, beginning a long speech. 'When I studied history I did a lot of political history and I've always been interested in British political history, Gladstone and all that. I read books about it . . . as you get older you get more disillusioned with politics because it's such a lot of bullshit and PR and nobody talks the truth any more. Actually in my opinion all of British life has been screwed up by the way newspapers and television – in particular newspapers – report things, because everything in Britain has become a fantasy. People *pretend* to be shocked by things. There's always people pretending to be shocked by things that aren't remotely shocking and it's just gone absolutely nuts. It's actually very difficult now to discuss politics because so many subjects are taboo – the entire Labour Party's policies are governed by how they will appear in the media rather than by what they actually are. Whereas the Conservative Party has, in my opinion, always had, since 1979, a completely secret agenda of things they're going to do, like use unemployment to destroy the unions, but you can't say that. They have the backing of a supposedly free press to build up the fantasy around them . . . likewise the royal family are regarded as apolitical and they're *totally* political. They're fundamentally right-wing.

'You can always destroy someone by saying they're a loony . . . in this country people hate intellectuals and there's an enormous distrust of ideas, as against a sort of generalized pragmatism . . . You can see what a great administrator Ken Livingstone was by what a shambles London is now. London Transport, for instance: since the King's Cross disaster, which I think Mrs Thatcher should be held responsible for because her policies caused it. Mrs Thatcher does not care about personal safety against the cost of something. She thinks that if it's going to be cheap but less safe then that's tough bananas.'

After last night's success today's soundcheck is perfunctory and relaxed – Neil spends most of it improvising keyboard parts over the songs and Chris decides to play percussion. Afterwards they adjourn to the hospitality room for supper. Neil sits down on a table with about twelve people and says, 'This conversation is going to be strictly in Latin' (a reference to Dominic, who studied classics at university). Meanwhile, on another table two members of the road crew – one English, one American – debate which is the most barbarous race.

'You crush each other at football matches,' says the American.

'You sit on freeways and shoot each other,' says the Englishman.

'Only in Los Angeles,' says the American. And so on.

On the Pet Shop Boys table the talk is of dirty words.

'I looked up "shag" in the dictionary when I was about eleven,' Chris recalls, 'and it didn't say anything dirty. I thought, "*What's* this shagging business if it's"' – his eyes widening – '"*not in the dictionary!*"'

'You used to laugh at words you didn't know,' remembers Neil. 'You'd laugh at a joke about "a period", say, and you've never *heard* of them . . .'

He mentions that last night he watched ten minutes of the hotel blue movie. 'It was useless. It was made in the sixties,' he informs us, adding approvingly, 'The clothes were good.'

Chris mentions that his mum carries on a correspondence with some of the fans. 'Can you believe that?'

On the TV above our heads in the corner of the room is a programme about the French revolution. This week is the 200th anniversary of the French revolution and all the programmes on TV are about it.

'The bloody French revolution,' grumbles Chris. 'I wish it had never happened.'

'They only killed 17,000 people,' points out Neil, displaying the factual grasp he seems to have of all matters historical. 'Stalin killed 25 million. Besides that the French revolution is nothing. In Napoleon's army they killed a third of the male population of France.'

'Anyway,' sighs Chris, going all metaphysical, 'what is human life anyway? It's worthless. There's too many people on the planet anyway.'

Someone mentions the Iran–Iraq war and that it finished some time ago.

'It's finished?' says Chris, alarmed. This is news to him. 'I'm amazed that's finished. I used to watch *Weekend World* and that was one of the ones that Peter Jay said would *never* finish because it was too complicated.'

The conversation turns to TV programmes from their youth . . . *Hector's House* . . . *Bill and Ben* . . . *Rag, Tag and Bobtail* . . . *Tales from the Riverbank* ('that used to be great,' sighs Chris) . . .

'You know,' says Neil, 'telly used to be better.'

'We had the *best* programmes,' agrees Chris.

'There's no innocence any more,' says Neil, his pudding arriving.

Someone mentions *How*.

'A woman called Bunty,' hoots Neil.

And Johnny Morris.

'*Zoo Time* was naff,' insists Neil. 'He'd pretend that all the animals were talking.'

'I *liked* that,' says Chris, a little defensively.

For a dressing-room they have two rooms. Neil disappears into the far one to rest. He is worried about his voice. In the near one I interrogate Chris.

'It's a life of ups and downs,' he scoffs, 'a rollercoaster ride. I did come from Blackpool.'

This is how he tells it: He was cheerful at school when he was little. On his first day he didn't cry; he just bounded into 'the playroom with the jugs of water on the side', ready to have fun. At junior school he was good at sports and had to choose between being a prefect or house captain (he chose the latter). 'I suppose I was what you could call a bit of a hero.' Then he failed his eleven plus. Big drama. He now puts part of the blame down to the fact that they were the first year to study Modern Maths, which he thought was stupid: 'Making a computer out of a cornflake packet,' he scoffs scornfully. His parents, particularly his mother, didn't want him to go to the local secondary modern school where most of his friends were headed.

'They realized that if you went to the secondary modern school you'd basically just had it. There was such a difference in the standards of achievement. If you went there you did CSEs – they didn't expect you to do anything else. If you went to a fee-paying school you did O-levels and A-levels.' He took the entrance exam for a public school called Rossall. He passed but the fees were too expensive. He also took the exam for Arnold School and that's where he went. Because his parents were paying a lot of money for him he felt duty bound to work hard. 'So I turned into a swot.' It just seemed obvious that he had to make an effort; it never crossed his mind that lots of other kids didn't try even though their parents were paying the same fees.

At the age of eleven he decided he wanted to be an architect. He was even practical enough to check the precise qualifications he would need later in life. 'It's pathetic, isn't it?' He thinks the interest came simply because the Lowe family moved house so often and he had seen so many different types of houses. 'I think my dad would very much like to stay in one home but my mum is always looking for somewhere else to move to.'

At senior school he became more introverted and opted out of most sports. He remembers loving homework. He had a small circle of friends who were all brainy as well; they helped each other. He remembers daydreaming for hours in his room. His main cause of anguish was spots.

'I was *furious* about spots. I couldn't *believe* doctors couldn't do anything about them. I went to the doctor's but they don't even regard it as a problem. They're mad. When you're a teenager the smallest thing like that is a big deal. What they do is give you a cream. A *cream*! It's a well-known fact that cream doesn't do anything . . .' Eventually he went to a skin specialist who prescribed antibiotics and the problem more or less cleared up.

In the school cadet force he'd go abseiling and play the side drum in the band. 'I like rhythm. I used to do some funny ones, like your Max Wall ones where you want to do a silly walk.' He got his O-levels and then couldn't believe how hard A-levels were. By that time he had begun to sneak out to the pub and *Saturday Night Fever* was on release.

'It's a difficult time. You want to have a good time because all the parties are happening, the sixth-form dances, but it's quite a strain because you know if you don't do well in your exams you can't do that thing you want to do.' Some summer nights he couldn't sleep. It would all keep going round in his head: 'A-levels . . . spots . . . things like that.' During the day when he wasn't at school, he'd walk the family dog, Judy, for miles along the Blackpool sands. 'Just normal adolescent trauma.' He loved dancing. He says he's always found that when you're under the most pressure that going to clubs and dancing is the most fun: as a *release*.

Did you try to stand out at school?

Chris: Not at all. I've never wanted to stand out. I want to be one of the crowd.

You say that, but you've become a pop star, and hardly in the most invisible fashion.

Chris: Well, I think one of the reasons I want to be one of the crowd is that I've never been one of the crowd. Not of the sort of crowd I imagine myself being part of.

What do you mean?

Chris: When I think of a crowd I think of Liverpool, where you have this working-class situation where you've grown up with everybody and you have about a hundred close people. Whereas I've always felt more detached than that, even with my close friends. I've always had *one* very close friend. Actually, really, you don't need more than that. When you've got one I don't see how you've got time for others. But I'm kind of contradicting myself. When I say 'one of the crowd' I've always liked to be part of the same fashion as everybody else. I've never wanted to make a statement or stand out. I wasn't a punk or anything because I've never had any desire to dye my hair orange and make a statement walking down the street. I've always been completely unmemorable. I was the sort of person at school no one would notice.

But you've become a pop star?

Chris: Yes, but I don't see that as being me, really. I'm manufacturing something.

But you have to live it.

Chris: Well, yes, during this tour, because I'm putting on my Pet Shop Boys persona.

Which is . . .?

Chris: Kind of, a bit cheeky . . . as it said, 'impish' . . . moody. Actually I'm impish and moody anyway. But the thing that annoys me most about being called moody is that I'm only ever moody for a reason. Often I don't tell anybody why I'm in a mood, so that makes me in a bigger mood because I expect people to realize why I'm in a mood.

But on-stage or in videos you always look moody.

Chris: I've got one of those faces. If I'm not smiling it's moody.

But, whereas most people would be embarrassed into smiling in those situations you dogmatically refuse to be. It seems you'd rather bear the pressure to smile than to do something that doesn't fit into your area of how you feel you should act.

Chris: That's true. I can't expand on that. Just put that as my quote.

Chris Lowe learned to play the piano and the trombone and he played the latter in the school dance band. That year 'There were at least six of us who were really good musicians.' They'd play at dances for teachers and parents: some trad jazz, some old pop songs like 'Moon River'. Seven of them formed an offshoot band, the 'wittily' named One Under The Eight. They'd use some of the school dance band's music and dress up in white shirt sleeves: 'basically the school uniform with different ties'.

They took it seriously, joining the Musicians' Union and playing at formal dances: the Conservative Club, the local masonic lodge. They were paid union rates. They performed standards like 'My Way' and 'La Bamba' and also this 'hilarious thing called "The Jazz Twinkle"'.

One Under The Eight had always been spoken of in Pet Shop Boys interviews as Chris's only previous group until he mentioned in a recent article, to everyone's surprise, that earlier on he had also played keyboards in a school rock band called Stallion. 'I wasn't in it for very long.' They would 'jam' for hours. 'I can see the enjoyment of groups doing that. I just don't think it's very good for the person who has to listen to it.' They played one concert, at a local youth club. For the first half of the concert they were fronted by two girls who sang pop songs like Freda Payne's hit, 'Band Of Gold'. Then the girls stepped away and it became 'a heavy metal jam sort of thing . . . a bit tragic, really'.

At home he'd play the piano but he'd never remember anything that he played. He used to imagine that one day he would invent a computer that would remember what you have just played: 'I thought that was the only way I'd ever do anything musical.' (Now, of course, such machines are commonplace.) Even now, though, he will just play things and it will often be Neil who has to remember them and who will structure them into songs.

'I'd play for hours at home and my dad would keep banging on the wall because the piano was in the dining-room and they'd be watching television in the living-room and I'd be getting excited and banging really hard. This was from the age of eleven until eighteen when I left home. And as I once said in *Smash Hits* I used to pretend I was whoever it was . . .' (December 1985: 'I used to pretend that Tchaikovsky could compose through me, and it worked!') '. . . and I literally did. It's amazing what state you can get your mind into. But it was never recorded; and I never used to structure anything into a song.'

He looks surprised when I ask him if it crossed his mind that anything he was playing might be valuable, might be worth keeping, and answers, 'Not at all. I just enjoyed it. In fact my mum used to come in and say, "That's nice – what's that?" and I'd stop immediately and walk out.'

When I ask him why then, several years later, he suddenly started writing songs with someone he looks perplexed and eventually answers, 'Well . . . we just kind of did.'

Chris: The thing we've always been interested in, more than anything else, is writing songs. So when you ask us what else we're trying to do – what we're trying to express through sleeves or whatever – it's secondary. They're because they have to be done. They're not the reason for doing it in the first place. The reason you form a group isn't to design a sleeve, is it?

But you always claim that you didn't write songs before.

Chris: No, I didn't, but that's why I do it now.

So why is it important for you to write songs now?

Chris: Because it's the Pet Shop Boys. That's what the Pet Shop Boys *do*.

That's not a reason. That's what you've made the Pet Shop Boys do. The Pet Shop Boys could play golf.

Chris: Actually we probably *could* play golf. I've got a set of golf clubs.

Neil: It's quite a good title for a song: 'Golf'.

Chris: But when we met Neil didn't have a set of golf clubs, he had a keyboard.

Neil: Chris, if there'd been a paintbrush we'd have been painters. (*They collapse in hysterics.*) That's Gary Kemp's quote: "I just happened to pick up a guitar. If I'd picked up a paintbrush I'd have been a painter."

Chris: That's one of my favourite quotes, that. That went into heavy rotation in our European interviews.

So why write pop songs?

Chris (*mimicking the question*): Why do it? (*Sighs.*) It's that 'why' again.

I just find it odd that never having written songs you could start at the age of twenty-one for no reason.

Neil (*to Chris*): And you've got two Ivor Novello awards. (*Laughs.*)

Chris: Someone might have started when they were two and not have written a good song yet.

Is it the most fantastic feeling?

Neil: It is actually.

Chris (*grumpily*): It's all of those things and more. It's just . . . good.

Neil (*to Chris*): When I first met you you were thinking of buying a synthesizer.

Chris: Was I?

Neil: Yes. That's how the whole thing came about. And you obviously weren't going to play other people's music because you would never bother to, so you were obviously going to write your own.

Or just doodle.

Neil: Yes, he'd have doodled, like he always has done.

Chris: It's difficult to say why.

Neil: He just does it because he does it. When I first met Chris – in fact I still think this – I thought he was a natural talent, like North Sea gas really. You could just drill into it and it would all come out. It's true. It was like that and it still is like that. If the Pet Shop Boys broke up tomorrow it's quite likely that Chris would just do nothing. (*To Chris*) Isn't it?

Chris: Quite likely.

Neil: He'd probably be quite happy as well. Really, I normally provide the motivation.

Chris: And the structure.

Neil: I am the drill, basically, though I'm not just the drill. But Chris can just sit there and make up music, just like that. I have to go, 'Oh good, we'll put this, this and this and we'll call it that and it'll be great, let's do it now . . .'

Chris, what do you make of that?

Chris: Well, I'm very flattered. I hope I don't start running out of oil.

At Liverpool University Chris joined the school orchestra for a term but hated it. After this his final appearance on-stage before the Pet Shop Boys was when the English National Opera visited Liverpool. The head of his Hall of Residence asked if anyone fancied being an extra – Chris and his friend volunteered. They were toreadors in *Carmen*: 'the triumphant toreadors in these amazing costumes with these women throwing themselves at our feet'. They simply had to walk across the stage at the Liverpool Empire: 'Anyone could have done it.' They were, nevertheless, thrilled. One night after their appearance they went to the pub, still in costume. 'I felt dead embarrassed about that.' For the rest of the term they marched round singing the tune from their scene out loud.

The next year he had his work experience in London. To begin with he stayed outside London with his brother's god-parents, commuting in each day. He was poor and fed up. At weekends he would also go into town and wander round the shops, entranced by it all. Then he saw an advert in a newsagent's window for a bedsit in Sydney Street. It was painted blue and orange but he took it anyway. He had a little electric one-ring stove to cook off so he lived on sausages and beans. He would boil eggs inside his kettle.

'I've never liked living alone. I've got to have someone to say goodnight to – "Goodnight, I'll see you tomorrow" – or otherwise I'll think, "God, I don't know anyone. I'm the loneliest person in the world. No one will know if I die in my sleep."'

He began making friends. Then he met Neil. He remembers

one of the first songs they wrote being about Wardour Street. One of the next went 'Life's hard/it's all you've got/and all you get/is a broken heart'.

At the end of the year he moved back to Liverpool. It wasn't so good this time. Lots of his friends from before had been on shorter courses and had left. The people in his house were studious and he and his friend used to feel guilty tiptoeing out to have fun. Meanwhile the Pet Shop Boys started doing well. 'I didn't really think anything but "worra laugh". I still am amazed really. It just seems strange as if – and I've always thought this – as if it's not my life. It's a very strange feeling. It just seems so incredulous that anything like this could have happened to us. It's a bizarre situation. I didn't ever think of it in terms of making it my life or anything.'

At the end of his course he didn't start work. He fancied a rest, so he signed on the dole and dossed at a friend's house in London. He knew that Neil had told Tom that if he, Neil, could earn as much – £13,000 a year – by making pop music as he was being paid at *Smash Hits* he would give up his job there. Perhaps surprisingly, Chris's family were quite enthusiastic at the prospect of his trying to make a life from music.

'My family, particularly my mother and grandfather, have always wanted me to do music. They've always thought I'd be mad to do anything else. My grandfather made his living out of the trombone and he used to say to me, "I don't know why you're doing all this studying – you'd have a great time as a musician." He used to work for an hour a day in Las Vegas. He used to say he couldn't understand why anyone would want to do anything else. It was the opposite of most parents. I was studying; they were saying, "Concentrate on your music." I thought, "There's no way I'm doing that." I knew people who did music were often struggling.'

One day he played them a demo of 'It's Not A Crime' and they were thrilled. He was chuffed too, because he asked them what they thought of it without hinting that it was anything to do with him. It was his grandparents who lent him the money for the flight to New York to record with Bobby O.

Chris has talked for about an hour and a half. He sighs as if to say, 'It's a funny life, isn't it?' Tom Watkins bundles in. 'Here she comes,' says Neil. Chris slips next door to get ready.

Starting to do a pre-show autograph-signing Neil says, 'I think we're too nice'; then 'It's a bit organized having a pen in our hands, isn't it?'

The first fan is Scottish.

'Why aren't you going to the show in Scotland?' asks Neil.

She says she couldn't get tickets.

The show in Scotland is far, far from sold out. 'There's loads left,' says Neil. 'I know someone who's got 3,000.'

'Neil,' says another. 'You should dance.'

'Don't be silly,' he chides. 'I can't dance.'

'I've written sixty letters to you,' says the next.

'Aaaah . . .' he sighs politely.

Chris receives endless plaudits for his dancing.

'I'm not doing it again,' he announces. 'It's proving too popular.'

They return to the dressing-room. Neil's hair is coaxed up by Leonard.

'That hair is so happening,' compliments Chris.

'It's a disaster for the ozone layer,' says Neil.

From the hall comes the sound of the string quartet, then a pause, then applause.

'They're not supposed to clap at the end of a movement,' says Neil. Then he adds, 'I think I've got a cold. I'm worried I won't get the high notes. Actually,' he says, 'I never do anyway.' He threatens to turn the whole show into a rap, and practises by rapping 'Love Comes Quickly'.

Chris sees someone carrying a plastic bottle of Harp lager, the alcohol on sale out front to the public. He isn't impressed. After all the meticulous care to make everything on-stage extraordinary it seems a little sad that the fans drink the same dull, unattractively packaged drinks as they would at any old rock concert. 'They should have little bottles of champagne.'

Back-stage, afterwards, Chris's family are everywhere.

'All they talk about is my hair,' he complains. 'There's no mention of the show.'

'I say,' shouts his grandmother. 'Chris . . . *topher!*'

He darts over but by the time he arrives the family are deep in conversation. He stands there, ignored. 'I can't get a word in edgeways,' he says, loud, though no one is listening. 'I only haven't seen you for months.'

Someone mentions Jason Donovan. 'He dances like a cowboy,' says Chris, dismissively. 'He's not in the same league as Chris "Fred" Lowe.'

I meet a woman called Bridget who explains that she worked with Neil at Marvel Comics. She recalls how one day he brought in a review of David Bowie's film *The Man Who Fell to Earth*. 'I was really impressed. He just said, "Here's what I wrote . . .".'

Her friend tells me he knows Tony Jasper, the person who wrote Cliff Richard's recent biography, and says he liked the way the Pet Shop Boys walked on-stage out of rhythm: 'The juxtaposition of that and everything else . . . it sets off the dancers.'

Bridget mentions one night in the early eighties when Neil played her a Pet Shop Boys tape. 'I asked to borrow it for a party I was having – it was really good dance music – but he said no, he needed it, for . . .' – she shrugs – '. . . whatever you need them for . . .'

There are more autographs to sign.

A girl says to Chris, 'I love you.'

'You don't even know me,' responds Chris.

'You were in the front row, weren't you?' Chris says to one bloke.

'Yeah, how did you *know*?' says the boy, overwhelmed.

Dainton lets some more fans through. 'Let's put Birmingham on the map,' he growls. 'Even if they are in the Third Division . . .'

Someone hands a mirror to be signed. It is unlicensed unofficial merchandise. Neil signs it 'Unofficial. N. Tennant'.

A t-shirt is offered to be signed.

'Even Ariel won't get this out,' he tells the owner.

More kisses are demanded.

'You know, I think at garden fêtes they charge for kisses,' says Neil.

'If anyone wants a kiss,' says Dainton, 'it's half a bar for charity.'

A fan holds up his programme.

'Sign it "to Jimmy",' he says. Then he dictates 'from Neil Tennant'; as if otherwise there was a real danger Neil would have signed it 'from Jason Donovan'.

Neil asks the fans who else they like. 'Erasure' is a popular answer.

'We're from Norwich,' declare two fans.

'I've never met anyone from Norwich before,' says Neil.

Another fan screams, 'You're the best group in the world.'

'You *know* I made him say it,' laughs Dainton.

'I know what he means though,' says Neil.

Dominic stomps over from the band bus, waiting inside this huge hangar for the signing session to finish. He complains about being kept waiting. Afterwards Neil will splurt, 'Cheeky bloody Dominic. I nearly hit him. Do they think we're doing it for fun?' It turns out that Dominic does at least have a reason. He is anxious to get back to our hotel in the centre of

Birmingham where his fiancée is expecting him, and as they have been sitting on the coach Juliet has just read out everyone's horoscopes. His says that he is going to have a problem with his love life and keep someone waiting . . .

Soon they leave. In the coach, Neil reads a report in the local newspaper about the Pet Shop Boys' '£60 shirt horror'. A hooded sweatshirt they had designed costs, unbeknownst to them, £60.

'It's outrageous,' agrees Neil, adding, 'I quite like that sort of thing.'

They enjoyed tonight: 'One of the greatest nights of my life,' says Neil, 'without being corny . . . You dance more now, Chris, don't you? That Bobby Brown thing? You didn't do that in rehearsal, did you?'

'No,' says Chris. 'I believe in spontaneous performances.' This is a fib – one of his most repeated spiels on the tour is of course that the show is theatrically rehearsed because they despise the myth of rock'n'roll spontaneity.

He says his gran asked him tonight, 'How do you enjoy show-business?'

'The first time I met her she asked me that,' says Neil.

Pete tells some complicated sex story involving Steve, another friend who has joined the security posse for the British leg of the tour. Everyone roars and roars and roars.

'Oh,' gasps Neil at the end. 'You *nastiness* . . .'

'You've heard that a thousand times,' says Pete.

'I never get tired of it,' says Neil.

They talk about the fans.

'The Women's Institute organizes coaches for your fans,' jibes Chris at Neil.

Neil sings, 'Why can't a woman be more like a man?' from *My Fair Lady*. 'That's such a camp song,' he realizes.

Back at the hotel, the reception they received on-stage tonight is still sinking in. It all seems rather new and very, very real. Perhaps it's not surprising they are suddenly so struck by it.

Rarely can a group have become so famous without confronting their audience until so late in their career and it is obviously a lot to take in at once.

'The thing is,' confesses Neil, 'I don't think I believe all these people *like* us.'

Chapter Fifteen

Saturday, *15 July*

The first reviews are not good.

The *Daily Telegraph*'s Tim de Lisle is lofty and a little snide. The Pet Shop Boys, he concedes, had worthy ambition but their limitations were too obvious: 'They are wooden and their sound is tinny.' He manages a few compliments, comments that Courtney Pine's saxophone solos are 'a pneumatic equivalent of the lengthy guitar solo purveyed by the sort of groups the Pet Shop Boys disapprove of' and says 'but these are peripheral matters – all you need is stage presence and Tennant, with his tentative walk, nasal voice and endearing shiftiness, hasn't got it.'

Nevertheless he is kind compared to *The Times*' David Sinclair. The show was so bad from the perspective of *The Times* that it required a full half-page of indignation. The headline is the clever-clever 'Missing the point of a live performance, actually'. The caption underneath the live photo reads: 'Left to their own devices: Neil Tennant and Chris Lowe evinced stage personalities that were as engaging as a blank sheet of paper'.

The piece itself nailed its colours to the mast immediately, beginning, 'It looked bad from the start.' The hall, he observed, was 'drastically undersold'. The string quartet 'bravely sawed away in the face of embarrassing indifference from the young, chattering crowd.' He declares to the Pet Shop Boys that part of the aim of live performance is 'for the musicians to reveal something of themselves to the audience through the performance of their art, to make flesh and blood that which otherwise exists only as a series of electronically coded and stored impulses.'

He describes Neil as having 'a daft series of costume changes', 'looking like a waxwork version of the comedian Julian Clary' and describes the limitations of his 'glum, adenoidal voice'. Chris is merely 'utterly impassive'. The films were but a 'game effort to fill the spaces' and Courtney Pine, whom he seems to approve of, was for the most part 'boxed into a tight corner by the unsupple, metronomic rhythms'.

Widening his aim he explains that the Pet Shop Boys are creatures of the eighties and have 'reflected both the glamour and the hardness of their era'. He talks of 'a disconcerting hollowness at the centre'. To emphasize the shortcomings of most of the set he heaps slightly barbed praise on to 'a majestic version' of 'It's A Sin' (including, he tells his readers, 'mildly *risqué* shots of sensuous-looking young men'). After that, he concludes, 'Normal service was, unfortunately, quickly resumed.'

That afternoon I call Courtney Pine's room. He is there, practising as usual. I tell him it is the Man with the Book, as that is the name with which he has christened me and by which he recognizes me (he claims he is going to write a song with that as its title). He invites me down and we sit on his bed, him cradling his saxophone, listening to Inner City's 'Paradise' LP playing quietly in the background.

He attributes his collaboration with the Pet Shop Boys to fate. He had been considering buying a Fairlight computer-synthesizer and, knowing that the Pet Shop Boys used one, he bought a cassette of 'Actually' at a motorway service station to listen to the sounds. He knew little of them as a group. A month later he was called and told they would like him to play on a song (Dusty Springfield's 'Nothing Has Been Proved'). He turns down most session work but, to his mind, fate was involved here, so he said yes. Anyway, he slyly confesses, he wanted to look at their equipment; he is fascinated by modern music technology.

His impression of them beforehand had been vague, built up from a few TV performances. 'They looked really boring,' he laughs. When he saw them on Live at the Palladium playing 'Rent' in their inflatable Issey Miyake suits he noted that 'These guys are really trying in a different way. They're not going to jump up and down to get your attention. They're doing it in a different way.' He noticed that, in that sense, it worked: 'Even Jimmy Tarbuck had to say something.'

He turned up at the Dusty Springfield single thinking 'it was just another session'. Sessions tend to be a muchness to him. He turns up, whoever's in charge will ask him if he's heard a solo by someone else and ask him to do something like that and he will get quietly narked. 'I've spent the last five years trying to sound like me.' True to form Neil mentioned something about 'a Stan Getz kind of sound'. 'I had my session man's face on: "Oh yes, I can do that. No problem."' Courtney says he knew from the first that the song needed a soprano sax solo but Neil asked for tenor so he did eight takes with that, then tried the alto. Finally he turned to the soprano. That's what they used.

He was surprised to find them 'very warm and friendly. I thought they'd be really cold and that I'd be in and out, "hello" and "goodbye".' They called him again to play on Liza Minnelli's LP but he was uncontactable. His agent finally tracked him down and told him to be at the studio within an hour, so he 'packed up some equipment, got down to the studio, had a couple of jokes and then into the office again'.

Then they asked him to come on tour. He imagined that it would be like the reggae and funk concerts he'd played before – in other words normal performances but less hard work than at jazz concerts because there'd be less complicated things to play. 'I thought it would be a challenge to see if playing jazz has helped me to play this music.'

He's a little overawed by the size of the organization and the size of the crowd. In the beginning he was also upset at being separated from his instruments in transit. He's also been worried whether he's been playing too little or too much, and has been getting frustrated at having to play over exactly the same backing track at every concert. 'But it's another challenge.' He says his favourite song is 'Rent' because it reminds him of the early eighties synth pop boom, music like Depeche Mode that, surprisingly, he loves. And he likes 'Shopping'. He hates most of 'Opportunities' – 'a Bananarama kind of thing' – though he loves the bridge.

'I can't really relate it to jazz.' He explains that the Pet Shop Boys tour is the world of the C major chord; he's more used to the world of 'a C augmented chord with 13th and 15th extensions'. In pop music, 'People want to hear a very melodic line that you can sing. That is a challenge, particularly when you've been going the other way for five years.'

I ask, mindful of the flak Branford Marsalis drew from the jazz world when he played with Sting, whether some people might think he was cheapening himself by playing with the Pet Shop Boys.

'Nope,' he says. 'You see, for me, I'm trying to get my instrument to sound like a voice, so, just as a singer can sing a lullaby or a nursery rhyme, or sing something very complex like an opera, I'd like to have that flexibility, just to turn anything on at any time. I don't find it a compromise because that should be in my weaponry as a musician. If I can play jazz music – which is the ultimate music in the world – then why shouldn't I be able to play some that doesn't require as much effort?'

So this doesn't?

'Not in the same way. In this, sometimes I can make a tune round four notes. There is a challenge in making a tune round four notes, whereas in jazz music you use as many notes as you can.'

Which, I admit, is what I'd always imagined to be going on in jazz. Why do people do that in jazz?

'Because so much has happened in jazz that for you to be

relevant you have to do something different and it seems that's the only way to go.'

So, I confirm, jazz only makes sense in terms of its own history?

'Yes, for me it does. You have to be a part of the history. You have to come out of that history. You can't suddenly arrive and say, "I'm improvising. This is different, it's got nothing to do with jazz history but it's jazz music." That doesn't make sense. You have to have a knowledge of the history of jazz music. That is, if you want to.'

That's the usual way?

'Yeah.'

I ask him more about the Pet Shop Boys. He says he's been trying to work out what goes on but can't really. He says that they seem to work a lot of the time 'by cancelling each other out' – one says one thing, the other another and it's the compromise that works. To begin with he assumed that Neil just handled the lyrics – 'I just thought he was some guy who had some lyrics, found a keyboard player, went off, did some records and got lucky' – and was deeply impressed to discover that he was a musician as well. He mentions several times how astonished he was that 'that substitution in the chorus of "Always On My Mind"' (a B♭ chord is added) was done by Neil. He was surprised to watch them in the studio and to see that they didn't even operate the Fairlight themselves. 'They were like the commanders, directing the stuff.'

Chris, he reckons, is quite stern, but he was very impressed by the way Chris talked to him after the first night's concert in Hong Kong and admitted that at the end of 'Left To My Own Devices', where Chris rotates the chords of the chorus and Courtney solos over the top, that 'it was horrific for him', just trying to keep the rhythm. He says that most people he's worked with would rather have said, snootily, 'I liked what you are doing, all that *out-of-tune* stuff', or said, 'Don't take so long a solo – don't fuck me up.'

I ask about Neil, and he is not the first to make the observation that 'I think he'd be a good schoolteacher . . . it's strange how someone can stand on-stage and not jump about and attract so much attention. He has a persona . . . this charisma.'

He supposes people like the Pet Shop Boys because 'they're a very English band'. He puts that mainly down to Neil. 'He just looks English.' Then he reconsiders. 'Chris is like the rebel of English society and Neil could pass as one of those country gentlemen. He's always wearing those blazers. I think they show two sides of society. It's like, one you'd see down the Wag Club and the other at some Conservative ball. Well, maybe not Conservative. I don't know if that's a conscious thing they're doing.'

I ask him about Folkestone Town Hall and he chuckles. He claims that he'd always said he was touring a solo tour simultaneously and that he might have to play his own concerts on some nights. He sounds as though he believes it. He says it looks as though he'll miss Wembley because he's booked at a jazz festival.

'It's just one of those things.'

I suggest that it's a bit more serious than that.

'I've got people working on it,' he says, breezy and cheerful.

Maybe the reviews fire Neil and Chris up, for tonight is the best performance of the tour. The crowd are younger, and noisier, than the previous nights and there is feeling of pure exhilaration in the air. The performance is impeccable and afterwards no one has to confer – they all know it was very special. At the end of 'Always On My Mind' Neil stands, bathed in applause, at the microphone stand.

'Thank you,' he says. 'Good night . . . *I love you*.'

During 'It's Alright' Chris agrees, for the first time, to say the line 'it's gonna be alright' as he does on the record (though, with typical perversity, he refuses to say it until he has taken the microphone from Neil and is holding it himself).

★

'Did you hear Neil say "I love you"?' gasps Chris back-stage. This simply isn't the sort of thing that is supposed to happen. Not at all. 'I'm going to have to stop the tour,' says Chris.

'I thought, "I've just said I love you,"' agrees Neil, no less surprised. 'I couldn't *believe* it.' He says the two girls in front of him were holding up a flag that said, 'Neil, you're a Sex God.'

We leave quickly. Chris and Pete announce that they're staying in Birmingham tonight and going to rave; they insist that the *whole point* of touring is to rave in different places. They are heading for a rave that has been all over the local papers since we've been in the area and which the police are expected to bust; Ivan quietly worries that Chris will end up behind bars.

Neil jumps on the coach and we draw through the waiting crowd. Fans are everywhere, screaming, hitting the coach, waving, shouting . . . we pull away.

'That was just like being Marc Bolan there for a minute, wasn't it?' says Neil, delighted. Later he reflects on how preposterous being a pop star is. 'Sometimes it's a nice kind of preposterousness. Like the fans chasing. I enjoy that, but I only enjoy it once or twice. In our whole career we've only been mobbed about six times. Each time I've enjoyed it because it's *like* being a pop star.'

We are heading for Scotland and we quickly discover that on this coach there are only four of us: Neil, Lynne, Ivan and myself. 'We should be on the happening coach,' says Neil, imagining the wild rock'n'roll debauchery and cavorting that must be going on among the band. The drivers communicate by radio and a couple of miles down the road we pull up and change coaches.

We expect a wild welcome, climbing on clutching bottles of champagne. In fact our arrival is greeted with a complete lack of interest. Downstairs the English contingent are watching *Gremlins* on the video and have no intention of letting anybody's party mood get in their way. Upstairs most of the

Americans are tucking themselves into their bunk beds for a kip. Wild and crazy it is not.

Courtney, at least, will talk for a little while. He reminisces about his first tour, a fresh-faced senior prefect and school goalkeeper in a world of drug-taking jazz musicians. At seventeen he had left school because his music teacher said he should: 'You're not going to get to university so leave now.'

We settle in a small seated alcove upstairs at the back: Neil, Danny, Carroll, Mike Lynch, Juliet, Lynne, myself.

'How long is the journey?' asks Lynne.

'Only five and a half hours,' answers Neil. 'Like flying from Tampa to Los Angeles.'

Understandably Neil is lambasted for this. 'Tampa to Los Angeles' isn't the everyday benchmark by which most of us measure 'quite a long time on a bus'.

He makes a few gentle inquiries about tour morale and about the rumours that spread. 'It's like Chinese whispers,' he says. 'I can see how factions would start after a month. It's like school. After a month there are people you'll never really talk to your whole time there.'

He returns to his earlier 'I love you' outburst.

'Tom thought it was hilarious,' he says, 'because that's what Matt always says. But at that moment I did mean it. They were all so sort of *there*, weren't they? . . . these sweet girls in front waving their stupid balloons . . .'

They talk about Chris, and Danny mentions that when Chris played the percussion at the soundcheck on Friday, 'on my drum riser going doolally' he said 'he'd rather be up there doing that'.

'Chris sometimes programmes a drum pattern in his Fairlight at home,' says Neil, 'and just listens to it.'

They laugh about 'It's A Sin'.

'It'll probably be in the hymn book in the end,' says Neil.

'The "Morning Has Broken" of the nineties,' says Carroll, somewhat spookily.

'I wanted to be a priest,' reflects Neil. 'Actually I wanted to be a cardinal because I liked the clothes.' He mentions a priest he knew when he was growing up who'd come from the Far East and had a huge wardrobe. 'I also wanted to try on those happening vestments,' he admits. 'He owned a rubber plantation as well.'

'Driving through the night, it's so exciting,' sings Neil under his breath, another self-quote. 'And I was *right*,' he exclaims.

Then Bros are discussed. This week they have been on Wogan.

'It was fascinating to someone of my age,' pontificates Neil. 'Bros, Kylie and Jason talk about things as if they're marketing people: "Yeah, we've probably lost 30 per cent of our fan base" (as Luke said). Wogan asks, "What is your new music about?" and they say, "It's about longevity." And you want to say, "Yes, but what is it *about*?" Everyone thinks about longevity but that's not what it's *about*.'

Carroll mentions that she has turned down a chance to be one of Bros's backing singers at the Wembley Stadium concert next month. 'I'd feel very weird,' she says, 'like I was cradle-snatching.'

'Bros,' sighs Danny. 'We're like chalk and cheese.'

'That's a real Bros song title, "Chalk And Cheese",' observes Neil. He begins to imagine how it might go: 'We're chalk and cheese/you don't know how to please/put me at my ease/we're chalk and cheese . . .'

'I thought their worst song was "Cat Amongst The Pigeons",' says Carroll.

'I like it,' says Neil. 'It has the weirdest lyrics: "There's a cat amongst the pigeons/there's a pain in her chest." I think originally it was "there's a baby at her breast". It's about teenage pregnancy.'

He surveys the assembled company. 'It's the alcoholics' corner,' he deduces.

'Can we have far too much to drink?' suggests Danny.

We open a bottle of champagne.

'Why did you stop being a lover's rock person?' Neil asks Carroll. In the early eighties Carroll had released two lover's rock LPs and been very highly regarded. She talks about the boredom and the lack of money and some of the gangsters involved. 'I didn't really understand that world,' she says, a little sadly. 'Most of the people who have remained in that world still don't make any money and talk about changing the world . . .'

'Here's to lover's rock,' says Neil, raising his plastic cup.

Mike asks what lover's rock is. Someone else mentions, by way of example, Culture Club's first hit 'Do You Really Want To Hurt Me?'. Neil says he tried to sing that once in a Japanese Karoke bar. 'I thought it would be quite easy but it wasn't.'

'So what *is* lover's rock?' asks Mike again.

'It's slushy reggae, basically,' defines Neil. 'Does anyone want a sandwich?'

There are no takers.

'It's smoked salmon.'

Danny moves in.

'You like your luxuries, Danny, don't you?' he says. 'Smoked salmon . . . champagne. I'm a bit like that. You didn't get that in the North. We never had champagne. I only had smoked salmon about ten years ago.'

Someone mentions the reviews. Neil says it was stupid to invite the press to an added, unsold-out show. 'They all had to gleefully mention it wasn't full, but no matter. It was a major PR mistake but to be honest,' he laughs, 'tough bananas.'

'A lot of people went home very happy and that's what counts,' says Carroll. 'It's very expensive. They make a choice sometimes between buying the tickets and paying their bills. It's a great honour.'

This is said with such honesty and feeling that you can sense everyone present drawing breath, taking stock, storing this away.

Neil reflects on the *Daily Telegraph*'s comments. 'It was written from Olympian heights. It was so patronizing. They're jealous. And of course the reason is because I'm a journalist . . .'

'Tossbag,' mutters Danny, succinctly.

Carroll begins once more. She says that these people are stupid, that they've no idea why people do these things. They're always looking for stupid motives. 'They think you do it for the money or something. The reasons are obvious,' she declares. 'You do it for entertainment and self-expression.'

This statement, casually tossed out to a half-drunk, back-of-the-bus rabble, makes a lasting impression.

Why do you care so much about your record sleeves?

Neil: Well, we've always been a bit of a luxury product. The first sleeve of 'West End Girls' we wanted to look like a Chanel perfume bottle. We wanted our records to be bought because there was an intrinsic worth about them, not for any begging reason.

But it's just another way of making them seem desirable?

Chris: Well, we're making it desirable to ourselves more than anyone else. (*Neil nods.*) We're doing it because in our record collection at home it's got to look good.

Neil: I quite often look through our records and think how fantastic they look. Every now and then there's one that displeases me, like the second 'Opportunities' sleeve. I'd almost like to bring it out again in a different sleeve. I always rather felt it sullies the whole thing. You want to make the record something *special*. It's not just nothing – the sleeve. I personally think it's as important as the music. You're buying an object, so you want it to be a beautiful object. I also think a sleeve should give you things to wonder about. You can get the 'It's Alright' sleeve and spend hours wondering about Chris's glasses.

Does it pay off commercially?

Neil: I don't think it makes that much difference. It gives you a sort of aura. It says this is something unique. It is a new Pet Shop Boys record. It only bears a relation to the previous Pet Shop Boys records.

And why is that important? Why don't you want your records to bear any relation to most other pop records?

Neil: Because we're not just light entertainment. Most pop groups would go on *Opportunity Knocks* if they were asked. We wouldn't. (*To Chris*) Your parents once suggested we went on *Opportunity Knocks* – do you remember? Having an aura means that you are something unique. Most pop groups are nothing unique – they are *anything*. Consequently no one *really* likes them. Whereas the Pet Shop Boys are unique. You can recognize one of our things immediately.

If what you do isn't light entertainment, what is it?

Chris: Heavy entertainment. (*Laughs.*)

Neil: It isn't *not* light entertainment but it's also meant to be, to some extent, a statement. It's an act of self-expression. As Carroll Thompson said, it's for entertainment and self-expression. When people buy our records they get something which has been very carefully put together and is a kind of statement about something – although it sounds incredibly yukky to say that – and always has some kind of meaning.

So what's that meaning for? To change the world? To change people?

Neil: I don't know if it makes any difference really. I want people to know this is something we, or I, think.

So are you just showing off your creativity?

Neil: Well, why does anyone do anything creative? They don't just do it for the money, because they do it anyway if they don't get any money. They do it for entertainment and self-expression. And ultimately that is the purpose of everything we do – entertainment and self-expression.

★

Do you agree, Chris, with what Neil says: that you do it all for entertainment and self-expression?

Chris: Mmmm. (*Is silent for a long time then laughs nervously.*)

You always stop talking at times like this. Why?

(*Silence.*)

Do you not like talking about why you do things in this way?

Chris: Yes, I suppose that's it. I just don't enthuse on this level. (*Shrugs.*) I don't like intellectualism.

So why are you spending your life doing this? Have you thought about that?

Chris (*clarifying the question*): Why are we doing the Pet Shop Boys?

Neil: Yes.

Chris (*mumbles*): Because it came about.

Neil (*a little exasperated*): Why do you carry on doing it?

Chris: I'm not the sort of person to *stop* doing something . . . (*They both burst into hysterics.*)

So it's just pure casual momentum that makes you carry on, is it?

Chris: Well, because I enjoy it. (*He raises his voice, almost angry.*) I'm not doing it to change the world or anything. I've got no kind of manifesto or great reasoning for doing anything. I don't know. I don't like self-analysis.

Neil: It's true, Chris hates self-analysis. Chris doesn't like facing up to the facts, or the truth, about anything. In fact there's a way that you could see Chris's approach to the Pet Shop Boys – which has largely determined the approach of the Pet Shop Boys – as a way of being in a pop group without shaming yourself. (*To Chris*) That's got a lot to do with it, hasn't it?

Chris: Yeah.

Neil, do you think that, silently, Chris has the same motivations as you?

Neil: Not necessarily. But maybe he agrees with my motivations. Or doesn't disagree, I mean. I never know, Chris never tells you anything. Chris's mother used to phone me up to find out what was going on in the Pet Shop Boys because Chris didn't talk to her. I learn things about Chris in interviews that I never knew. Chris never told me he was in a group called Stallion. He's one of those people, he doesn't tell people things. He's not fundamentally a gossip. Mainly because he's not interested in other people.

Do you recognize this person, Chris?

Chris: It might come from my mum and my grandma, who are right chatterboxes. We'd go round to my grandparents' home and I'd want to watch the television and I'd be distracted by conversation all the time. Once something's happened it's been and gone really. It just seems incredibly tedious to recount things. I'm most interested in what I'm doing now. My memory for the past is non-existent. It's gone.

Whereas you, Neil, are very interested in the past?

Chris (laughs): Neil and his history.

Neil: Yes, I think you learn from history. You know, Chris and I think in different ways and I suppose that's one of the strengths of the Pet Shop Boys.

The buses roll north up the motorway. The Pet Shop Boys bus is empty, except for Ivan catching up on paperwork. On the band bus *Gremlins* has finished and they've put on *Robocop*. Upstairs, the hardened drinkers move on to red wine.

Neil muses about America. 'A lot of it has a dreamy innocent quality. They say, "England? Is that near Germany?" At the same time you get people who like Marc Almond.'

Danny goes downstairs. Neil asks him to sort out the air-conditioning.

We talk about money. Neil remembers the time when he saw the Police play Shea stadium and their manager Miles Copeland flew back to England in economy: 'A masochist,' thinks Neil. 'He was making some serious point.'

'People who become rich,' he generalizes, 'are normally

seriously mean. And they also have to be very interested in money.' Which, he says, he isn't. 'Our money sits in the bank, basically. I always imagine that one day maybe it won't be there any more.'

The childhood nostalgia of yesterday's supper returns. *Bewitched*, Neil murmurs, is 'my sort of programme': 'Margaret Macdonald used to be able to do the nose thing,' he says without explaining to anyone who Margaret Macdonald is.

The Beverly Hillbillies . . . *Katy, the Farmer's Daughter* . . . 'We weren't allowed to watch *The Addam's Family*.' He reminisces about when *Dr Who* and *The Monkees* would be on one after the other on Saturday night. 'Chris was saying the other day how much he hated the Monkees.'

'I forgot about the air-conditioning,' confesses Danny.

Neil responds with some remarkably convincing heavy metal band oaths, totters to his feet and staggers downstairs to tell the driver himself.

'Where are you from?' asks Mike when he returns.

'Newcastle,' says Neil.

'Are you a contemporary of Bryan Ferry?' asks Mike.

'He's forty-four!' splutters Neil, outraged. 'Actually a lot of pop stars come from Newcastle. They're always pretentious. We are to a man.'

He starts singing *The Beverly Hillbillies* theme. 'I'll tell you what – someone could have a hit with that now. It's the sort of thing Radio 1 would find amusing.'

And on . . . Flipper . . . Skippy . . . the Skippy Girl, Lisa Godard, Alvin Stardust's wife . . . the Whirlybirds: 'They were in helicopters,' summarizes Neil, 'and it all seemed terribly exciting' . . . Marmalade's 'Reflection Of My Life' . . . the Tremeloes' 'Call Me Number One' . . . 'I love it when teeny groups go credible' . . . '"changing" and "rearranging" . . . the worst rhyme ever' . . . 'one of the Tremeloes married Anthea from *The Golden Shot*' . . . 'Flippy' . . . 'Flippy?' (it's a drunken mistake . . . Skippy and Flipper again) . . . 'I rather like Flippy

. . . that's what the Pet Shop Boys will be reduced to, singing old TV themes' . . . the Casuals . . . 'the Slimcea advert' . . . '"Jesamine/a butterfly child/so free and so wild"' . . . 'I missed out on Ry Cooder and the Eagles' . . . Bread: 'I used to play those songs on the guitar. Obviously I knew "I'm Not In Love" as well.' . . . 'Neanderthal Man' . . . 'It's the same as the Strawbs' "Union Man"' . . . 'Pilot! I love them. They were on EMI . . . hence they had no career' . . . *Grease*: 'I hate it. Olivia Newton John was like Kylie' . . . 'I get this ruthlessness vibe off Kylie: "Bette Davis plays Kylie Minogue"' . . . *Thank Your Lucky Stars* . . . Brian Matthew . . . Peter & Gordon . . . 'Hand On Your Heart' sounding like an old song that goes 'I don't want to go to the party tonight' . . . 'Lift-off with Ayshea' . . . Pan's People . . . *The 39 Steps* . . . *The L-Shaped Room* . . . *Poor Cow* . . . *The Family Way* . . . *Kes* . . . Susan George . . . Wayne Fontana And The Mindbenders . . . 'Tapestry', 'the biggest selling album of all time – for a while' . . . James Taylor: 'I used to like that song "Fire And Rain"' . . . Amen Corner . . . 'I've just started to like Simon & Garfunkel' . . . 'I Only Have Eyes For You' . . . 'my favourite Stevie Wonder song is "All In Love Is Fair"' . . . 'I often think of getting "Songs In The Key Of Life" on CD but it's so expensive, £26 or something' . . . 'Japan seems like a strange dream now' . . . the next Dusty Springfield single: 'I think it'll be number one. If it's not I'll be *extremely* upset. I think it's one of the best songs we've ever written . . .'

Slowly even the alcoholics slip away to sleep. There is only Mike, Neil and me, half asleep, silently talking notes.

'It's a new experience, touring,' reflects Neil drunkenly. 'It's like having sex for the first time – sort of exciting and frightening at the same time.'

The sun is coming up. Sometime in the next few minutes both Mike and I fall asleep. Neil is left, a little disgruntled, wide awake with no one to talk to. We pull into our hotel, Airth Castle, at 5.30 in the morning.

Chapter Sixteen

Sunday, *16 July*

Airth Castle sits on a little hillock in the Scottish countryside. There is a glorious view of the Scottish lowlands, spoilt only by a dual carriageway, a series of small pylons and what appears to be a power station.

After lunch Neil and I decide to go for a walk. Most of the entourage have already headed on out, to go clay pigeon shooting. At the bottom of a long lane we find a tree; hanging from it is a ragged piece of rope knotted to the centre of a small wooden plank. Neil, whose general demeanour doesn't suggest athleticism, jumps on to it and swings. He explains that he used to like climbing trees. Beyond the bottom of his garden when he grew up there was a field with two trees. They called them the Big Tree and the Small Tree.

We find a small row of houses, immediately christened the 'Bill Forsyth row of houses'; drab, grey stone, children playing outside next to bashed-up old cars. Guiltily we try to peer through the windows, nosing at their front rooms, examining the decor.

Neil mentions his mother, how she sometimes gets upset by his lyrics. 'I was a lonely boy/no strength no joy', for instance, from 'Left To My Own Devices'. 'When I look back upon my life/it's always with a sense of shame' from 'It's A Sin'. She takes them as a criticism of his childhood, of his upbringing. They're not, he insists. He was a happy child.

Neil: I realize that 'Left To My Own Devices' is partly autobiographical. I'd been to see my parents just before we wrote it and my mother had said to me that she worried that when we were children we had a corner of the garden each – mine was the top left-hand corner – and I used to spend a lot of time there and I had all these toy soldiers and I used to make caves for them there and bury them with twigs over the top, and leaves and then soil, so that they were secret caves and only I knew where they were. This was when I was about eight. And I used to pretend to be, not a roundhead soldier as it says in the song, but actually a cavalier. I used to jump round the back garden pretending I was on a horse, as you do when you're young. In the garden Susan had top right, I had top left, Philip was too young and Simon had bottom right. My father grew a few things like mint in the bottom left. People often do it like that, don't they? So that you can grow anything you want in your part of the garden. I used to like it that I had a big bush in mine and when it rained I could sit under there and you didn't really get wet. There was a field behind with cows and I used to sit there for hours and hours and hours playing with my toy soldiers. My mother used to say she worried that I wouldn't have any friends because I'd sit there and live in a fantasy world. When she heard 'Left To My Own Devices' she was very depressed, she told my sister. But I wasn't remotely lonely. I've never been a lonely person. In the song I was pretending I was because my mother had recently mentioned that she used to worry I would be. But she was quite upset, piecing together my childhood from my song lyrics.

He reflects on the wider Tennant family's perplexed disapproval that the Pet Shop Boys won't jump at chances to meet royalty, then recounts a story Ian McKellen told him about meeting the Queen at Buckingham Palace. He was admiring one of the pictures on the wall when the Queen came up and said, 'If I ever have to leave here in a hurry, that's the one we'll take the wire cutters to.' We agree this makes her sound rather nicer and funnier than we'd imagined.

Once we have wandered down several lanes, dodged the dual carriageway, greeted a horse in a paddock of showjumps and been frightened by a dog or two, we are a long way from Airth Castle. As we have walked in a long arc I suggest we cut back across the country. Somewhat reluctantly Neil agrees, declaring that it's only a matter of time before we get lost and he throws a strop and shouts, 'I told you so.' It's a long trek and as we edge round one field we hear noises from the tall grass. Neil, who is closest, leaps back, stifling a scream. First he thinks what he sees is a cow then, a fraction of a second later, when he recognizes human flesh, thinks it's a dead body. It's not. The courting couple's red car is parked about quarter of a mile away by the side of the lane.

We find a way cross-country and arrive back at the 'Bill Forsyth row of houses'. There, an ice-cream van dawdles along the street and pulls up. We are delighted. This is *just* like a Bill Forsyth film. Neil has a vanilla cone ice cream but is very disappointed: 'It looks nothing like in the picture,' he mopes.

Back at Airth Castle, Chris has arrived. In the end, he says, they didn't go out raving. He has just read their latest review, this one in the *Sunday Times*. Robert Sandall is the first of many critics who will quote something Neil had said at the party after the 1988 BPI awards (reprinted in the tour programme), that 'It's kind of macho nowadays to prove you can cut it live. I quite like proving that we *can't* cut it live. We're a pop group, not a rock'n'roll group.' Robert Sandall interprets this as being a sincere 'act of faith' at the time and suggests that the Pet Shop Boys have only now played live because precedents in terms of theatricality have been set by Prince and Michael Jackson, and because they needed to cover up the embarrassment of the 'extraordinarily inept feature film *It Couldn't Happen Here*'. He says he likes Derek Jarman's films but that Neil 'raising his arms to the admiring fans looks like a fagged-out traffic policeman' and that Chris 'essayed a few tentative dance steps' and 'looked inhibited as only the shy English can when required to shake a leg'. It ended, patronizingly, 'The moral of the show was clear: performing live in a big venue is a skill and it needs more practice. Big hits, big budgets and big ideas are not enough.'

Chris's mood is defiant. 'I know it's the best live concert there's ever been,' he says, 'so I don't care what some jerk from the *Sunday Times* says.'

'Tom wants revenge,' says Neil.

They talk over a row from the night before. Ivan had, or so the tour party Chinese whispers have led them to believe, complained about how many friends they had put on the guest list.

'We can do what we want to do on *our tour*,' says Chris. 'Neil said, "If we want to cancel the tour tomorrow we will." People forget who we are. We're the *artists*.'

'We're too nice,' sighs Neil.

Two British fans called Mel and Sue, who often hang around the Pet Shop Boys in London, have checked into the hotel. They too have, by chance, had the day's schedule pushed under their door, telling them to meet in the bar before dinner. It is decided that they might as well join us. 'Those are the only two fans we've got,' says Chris. 'We can't blank them.' They wander up to where we sit on the grass outside and offer to buy us a drink.

Neil looks up at the castle turrets and muses, 'I'd like a home like that.'

'I don't know why you don't,' says Chris.

'Neither do I,' admits Neil.

Chris surveys the countryside. 'Why aren't we in a town?' he scowls.

'Shut up, Chris,' says Neil. 'It's beautiful here.'

'You can't get a pizza,' complains Chris. To the best of my knowledge Chris hasn't eaten a pizza all tour.

At about 6.40 I mention that I'm going to my room to hear the final part of the new chart run-down. Neil and Chris wander off too. One of the fans shouts after them, 'Let us know how many places the single has gone down.'

We meet in the bar. The single is down two to number seven; holding up quite well. Sonia is at number one.

'It's rubbish! Balderdash! Poppycock, this country business,' says Chris as we move through for dinner.

'But you look so healthy,' says Juliet.

'With a nuclear power station out there?' says Chris, gesturing through the window.

Neil starts humming an old tune Carroll wrote in her lover's rock days: '. . . sing me the love song . . .'. He says he'd like to get Dusty to do it. Carroll doesn't seem to take this as more than a whim, but he mentions it over and over and the week after the tour she will come down to the studio and show him the chords and they will record a rough non-reggae version, her singing, him playing piano.

The Pet Shop Boys are trying to avoid getting too involved in Dusty's LP. They must make their own and, anyway, 'Doing a whole album with Dusty would probably give you a nervous breakdown,' says Neil. He explains how perfectionist she is: 'She sang "Nothing Has Been Proved" one syllable at a time. It took two days.'

'"I love you",' sniggers Chris down the table, reviving Neil's on-stage outburst. 'I'm going to say "God bless" when Bros are there,' he laughs. 'God bless!' is one of Bros's favourite sayings; at the time of speaking Tom thinks they should use it as the title of their second LP (imagine the posters 'God Bless: Bros') though unfortunately this later changes to the more ponderous 'The Time'.

Bros stories begin. Someone tells about the Exterminate Bros society – Craig fans who have leafleted record shops asking them not to stock Bros records; the time Luke bought Shirley a large stuffed animal then flew it back from France next to her in its own seat – first class; the time Bros were having a medieval banquet in a Northumberland hotel and the hotel sold the extra capacity to Bros fans as 'Have dinner with Bros' – Bros walked out; how they will say, 'too many people have eaten with this knife', and demand another.

'Bros,' says Chris. 'I think it's absolutely brilliant. It must be great being that loopy. Some people work all day at being loopy.'

Someone mentions Arthur Baker. A New York producer, he was responsible for some of the best early hip hop records, worked with New Order on 'Confusion' and 'Thieves Like Us', and is now making his own solo LP with guest singers. He has also remixed a couple of Pet Shop Boys songs.

'Bobby O told me,' says Neil, 'that he always wears the same underwear to mix his records.'

The wine arrives.

'Would it be *totally* pretentious,' asks Neil, 'to say, "Have they got any proper wine glasses?"? These are sherry glasses.'

Suddenly Neil jumps, startled. Outside the window the power station has bellowed out huge black clouds of smoke. 'I thought it was a Chernobyl-style disaster,' he says, calming down. 'It's just the greenhouse effect, happening before your eyes.'

Carroll and Neil talk about the creative impulse.

'When songs come . . .' says Carroll.

'Yeah,' agrees Neil. 'Sometimes it's almost annoying, because you'd rather relax, and you've got to write this song.'

Another guest in the hotel comes in and asks them to sign something.

'Put "From Neil Tennant and me, Chris Lowe, the Pet Shop Boys – I love you",' sniggers Chris, ridiculing all of Neil's on-stage patter in one go.

Neil slaps him.

Neil: There is my famous tendency to hit people. Like when I hit the managing director of Canadian EMI because he was saying what a super place South Africa was. I told him to shut up and slapped him in the arm. The Tennants have always slapped each other. I don't think of that as violence, but Chris Lowe is always quite shocked when I do that, when I hit people and tell them to shut up.

They examine a preliminary guest list for their party. One section is of 'trendy people' whom they don't necessarily know but who will give the party the desired atmosphere. The other section is of pop stars.

Neil looks at the pop star list. 'The 'Narns are coming!' The 'Narns are Bananarama. 'Depeche Mode are coming! Morrissey is coming! He's making the trip specially.'

They open more wine.

'Pete,' says Neil, 'can drink on the understanding he doesn't mention the word "Arsenal".'

They talk about the concert film. Compromises have started – it is now to be shot at Wembley. Hiring a separate venue is too expensive.

'We could call it *It Happened Here*,' says Neil.

'And in America,' says Chris, 'it can be called *It Didn't Happen Here*.'

Neil splashes some wine over his Italian shirt.

'Neil, you need a bib,' says Chris.

Neil hits him again. 'You're not too old to be slapped,' he says.

More wine comes, but it is in a screw-top bottle and isn't what we'd ordered.

'Give it to the other table!' says Neil, gesturing to where some of the band are.

When it is brought over to them, Dominic peers at it with utmost snootiness.

'No,' he decides loudly, deadpan. 'Throw it away. Into the moat!'

Earlier, whispers Chris, Dominic was doing a mime of someone posh and English breakdancing on the lawn.

'He's in the wrong century,' says Neil. 'He should be Governor General of Calcutta.'

Chris begins to get depressed about their reviews.

'It's the final nail in the coffin of our credibility,' he laughs morosely. 'The less effort we put in, the better it goes. The more you put in, the more it gets slagged off.'

They discuss the sound. Everyone is unhappy about it, is the only conclusion.

Richard III is on the TV later. Neil Tennant, the historian, jumps upon this fact.

'It's a brilliant film, but *can* I point out – it's historically inaccurate. He *didn't* have a hunchback. He *didn't* lock the Princes in the Tower. In *fact* he did some very boring administrative reforms. There's a Richard III Society to defend his reputation.'

'So Shakespeare's just tarted it all up?' asks Chris.

'It was propaganda,' explains Neil. 'Henry VII discredited him. Shakespeare based it on Tudor propaganda.'

'So how do we know?' asks Chris.

'Because historians – *we* historians – got together and sorted it out; and there you go!'

Spooky things start happening. We have already been told that there is a ghost, Mary, in room ten. First someone hits something, I knock my bowl and Neil knocks over his wine glass, all within a fraction of a second. Then we notice the musak is a spooky instrumental version of 'I Go To Sleep': 'I go to sleep and imagine that you're there . . .'. Then we notice that the number of the table, 6, is not actually a 6 but an upside-down 9.

'I'm totally freaked out,' says Neil. 'And 999 is the Number of the Beast.'

Er . . .

'No,' he realizes, 'that's the police.' He considers this. 'Same thing.'

Chris announces that he's going down to the pub in the village.

'You can come,' he says to me, 'if you don't bring your notebook and wipe your memory banks.'

By the time we have got outside, played football in the dark on the lawn and wasted another hour all this has changed; we are going to a club in Falkirk, about ten miles away. A convoy of cars heads off.

The Club House, as it is called with admirable literalism, at first seems just the job. It is packed and the music – a mixture of slightly trendy current dance-floor favourites and seventies disco – is perfect. But then, though nobody seems to recognize Chris, our party is identified as, anyway, *unusual* and the DJ dedicates records to 'the Highbury posse', 'the London boys', 'the people from America'. It doesn't go down too well. One of the local toughs faces up to Steve and tells him in a 'this is the way it is' manner that we shall all 'be got' when we leave.

We leave.

When I wander back in, alone, a few minutes later to check whether we've left anyone behind, the DJ is announcing, '. . . Well, it's true! The Pet Shop Boys were here! And we *didn't notice*!!'

The taxi driver matter-of-factly tells us, 'The night I wouldn't want to be in there' – and he waggles his finger back towards the Club House – 'is Sunday. There's the highest percentage of arseholes there on Sunday.'

*

We congregate outside on the steps of the Country Club, a hotel annexe converted from stables. Chris rationalizes what has happened. 'All animals protect their turf,' he says earnestly.

That he should be saying this in all seriousness as we sit, drunk, in darkness, having fled Falkirk, is seen as fairly amusing by everyone present. Apart from him, that is. He snorts at the hilarity he has provoked.

'Read your Desmond Morris,' he snaps haughtily.

We begin swapping ghost stories. Pete thinks he saw one in a Miami hotel. Jay says he once 'felt a presence'. Chris is sceptical.

'Think how many people die every minute,' he reasons. 'There can't be a ghost for each.' He has, he explains, a policy on things like this. 'I made a decision that I wouldn't believe in things like this, and it made my life easier. I know what I was taught in science, and I'm sticking with that.'

Inside, in the lounge, a little light pre-bed drinking session is under way. Dominic is holding court. 'I'm half-Irish in case anyone wants to lampoon me,' he offers, for no obvious reason. Then he begins, uninvited, to tell a story with the unpromising words 'Have you ever been to Cornwall? It is a *marvellous* place . . .' Partly because of his delivery – archaic, *deeply* self-important and rather slurred – and partly because throughout everyone is exchanging searching looks as to say, 'What is the point of this story? Why is he telling us this?' the tale is quite unforgettable. 'Like an Alan Bennett play,' says Neil after. In short, Dominic and some friends went to stay at Porth Nevas in Cornwall. They drank a lot. One night they stole a stone brown owl from a nearby house, just because. The next day, hung over and remorseful, someone was charged with taking it back, but they mutinied; it could later be seen, half-covered by waves, on the beach.

After this it is somewhat hard for the conversation to regain any momentum. Danny murmurs something incoherent.

'What *are* you saying?' asks Strugger.

'About what?' asks Danny, bewildered. This is not a query that Strugger is ready for. He considers.

'Er . . . about *anything*.'

Monday, *17 July*

Ivan and Chris are out on the lawn, sitting in old metal chairs in the sun at lunchtime.

'These seats probably give you piles,' says Chris. 'Don't metal seats give you piles?' He announces that he is 'on a big downer'. It is the reviews.

'I feel it was a really big mistake to tour in the first place. I feel very exposed. I don't like having our failings exposed. Especially,' he adds, 'when I can't see them.'

He quotes by memory today's review in the *Guardian* by Adam Sweeting: '"The very dull 'Paninaro' was tarted up . . ." I feel like not playing it tonight.'

He takes some joy however that the country is being hit by a growing wave of strikes: train drivers, underground drivers, bus drivers, dockers. He reminisces about how much fun the early seventies were, with the three-day week and power cuts. 'It's been ages since we've had a general strike. It'd be great to have a summer of discontent. Of course,' he smiles, 'if there were, I'd go abroad to Italy until it was all over.'

Ivan phones Amanda in the record company office in London and Chris goes over the latest party invitations. Dusty Springfield ('It'll be all over by the time she's done her hair'), Duranduran ('new spelling!'), Morrissey ('as if he'll come . . .') . . . 'Marilyn would be good.'

He complains that Elton John isn't on the list. 'Elton John sent us a crate of champagne when "West End Girls" was a hit and it was like "Welcome to the club" . . . all the stories we've heard; he just sounds such a laugh.'

'He's in LA', says Ivan.

'Well? *Why's* he in LA?' asks Chris, as though it's Ivan's fault. He reels off a list of people who definitely *can't* come.

Philip Salon is on the list.

'Do we want him?' Chris considers. 'He did stop us getting into the Mudd Club once.'

'It's great, isn't it?' laughs Ivan. 'Getting your own back?'

'Let's invite him,' Chris decides, 'and not let him in on the door. Is Ian McKellen on the list? There's all our actor friends! Barbara Windsor. Gareth Hunt. Margi Clarke . . . Neil Dickson . . . Jack Bond . . . Patsy Kensit . . . Michael Caine . . . Roger Moore . . . Lionel Blair . . . Frank, Liza and Sammy, of course . . . Joss Ackland . . .' He laughs. 'Of course I probably won't go. I'll go to a rival do somewhere . . .'

Neil appears after his morning swim. Juliet has been teaching him the breast stroke. They were interrupted by an old judge who lives locally who informed them with considerable pride that 'the most good people in the world live in Airth' then told them they shouldn't sing pop music but something good like 'Over The Sea To Skye'. So, there and then, that's what the three of them sing.

Chris tells him that Tom has phoned up David Sinclair from *The Times*. 'I'm furious with him. He said, "*We* have tried to put on a show to please intellectuals and it went past you . . ."'

Ivan asks them if they'll do a short TV interview tonight for a show called *The Garden Party*.

'It sounds useless,' says Chris.

'I don't like daytime TV,' says Neil. 'Also, we don't need it.'

'A local radio interview?' asks Ivan.

'To be honest, we don't need it either,' decides Neil. 'The single's going down and we won't sell any more tickets now.'

'The tour is a flop,' grumbles Chris. 'We don't want to publicize it any more. Tour?' he says, feigning innocence. 'We haven't done a tour.'

'We should spread a rumour,' suggests Neil, 'that the reason the Pet Shop Boys are so boring on-stage is because it wasn't them, it was stand-ins.'

Over lunch Chris reads the latest synopsis for this book; still impossibly vague. He nods. 'But most importantly,' he smiles, 'it is going to be edited by the Pet Shop Boys *themselves*. All the interesting bits are going to have been taken out.'

'*Being Boring* is the title,' says Neil. 'Or *Yawn!* with an exclamation mark, like *Shout!*'

Neil reads the *Guardian* review and discovers that, despite Chris's gloom, it is actually quite good. Still, he sighs, 'They never mention the staging. I suppose he vaguely mentions that every number is staged like a Broadway musical. Well? That's *never* been done before.'

Chris complains that he had a full cooked breakfast at a roadside café this morning and is feeling poorly. He has foolishly swallowed – 'not sucked' – some Settlers and is now regretting it.

'Oh,' says Neil, 'cancel the gig. "We are sorry. The concert is cancelled. Chris has indigestion".'

They discuss how much money this book might be worth.

'How much did Bob Geldof get for *Is That It?*' wonders Chris.

'He's not boring,' Neil points out.

'Tom also said to David Sinclair, "You obviously don't like that whole Andy Warhol kind of thing,"' winces Chris. 'Having a bad review is one thing. Having Tom phone up the reviewer . . .'

'. . . only makes it worse,' chips in Neil. They are angry, but quite obviously in a funny way it is daftness like this that makes them like Tom so much. 'The best quote he ever gave,' laughs Neil, 'was when someone asked, "Would it have made any difference to their success if you hadn't managed them?" And he said, "No, but they'd have had a lot less fun . . ."'

*

Chris: Whenever we're doing something, Tom always says, 'Forget about that – you've got to think about what Edna from Huddersfield thinks.' The idea being that everything we do has to be for the benefit of Edna from Huddersfield. 'Forget all that fancy packaging and arty videos . . .'

Neil (also mimicking Tom): 'It's all very *well* . . .'

Chris: It's exactly what Stock Aitken Waterman think. I suppose it's fine if you want it.

I ask them to sign a page in an autograph book that *Smash Hits* is filling to give away in a competition. Fascinated, they riffle through the pages. Someone has written 'love and peace'.

'It's pathetic, all this "love and peace" stuff,' says Chris.

They pore over Kylie Minogue's signature.

'What's *this* all about?' muses Neil. 'A psychiatrist writes . . .'

Even stranger is Matt Goss's.

'A psychiatrist would have a field day with that. He's got lines all over his name, like prison bars. *That* is a deeply confused person.'

'How can you make "Matt Goss" that complicated?' wonders Chris. 'It's got about ten letters and you've got about eighty lines there.'

'You always get the smell of fruit on coaches,' grumbles Chris, on our way into Glasgow. 'That's *another* reason I hate them.'

During the soundcheck one of the backing singers warbles a line or two from a Queen song.

'Sorry,' lectures Neil, 'there's no singing of Queen songs at Pet Shop Boys soundchecks. It's in the rule book.'

When they rehearse 'King's Cross', Neil carries on singing after the end:

and there's still no guarantee
and the brown owl's in the sea

Back-stage they discuss whether Mel and Sue should be allowed into the concert free.

Chris suggests not. 'If they can travel round the country staying in top hotels . . .'

'I think their efforts have gone into petrol and hotels,' argues Neil. 'Also, they're no trouble.'

Chris concedes.

There is a problem over the party. They have decreed that strictly no press should be invited; nor people EMI would like invited from the world of radio and TV. But Tom has persuaded EMI to pay for the party – at an estimated cost of £40,000 – and obviously EMI are expecting some say as to who comes in return. On the phone to Murray in London they run through a list of press people they're prepared to allow, and Neil explains in graphic detail why tabloid journalists may not come: this is a party where they want to be able to do whatever they want to do. They want to celebrate and indulge as they like, not be part of some ghastly huge public relations exercise.

Murray obviously expresses a doubt that anything really reportable might happen. Neil persuades him otherwise.

Neil phones Tom. Meanwhile a young Swedish bloke enters; he tells them he is head of their unofficial Scandinavian fan club, about a hundred members so far.

'I don't think you should have talked to David Sinclair,' Neil tells Tom.

'This is the greatest day of my life,' the Swede tells Chris.

'He would say the job of a critic is not necessarily to be objective,' explains Neil, '. . . Tom . . . they judge me in a different way, as if I'm a former colleague . . . they gave us a huge space . . . most people just look at the photograph . . .'

The Swedish fan reaches forwards clumsily and gives Chris a

farewell hug. Chris looks embarrassed. They both sign his t-shirt.

'I'll never wash here,' he says.

'You'll get a bit smelly,' observes Neil.

He leaves. Somehow the conversation twists round to Cresta, a sweet drink of our youth.

'I remember that,' says Neil, shouting the catchphrase 'It's frothy, man!'

'Why don't they still have it?' asks Chris.

'They come and go,' sighs Neil, world-weary. 'It's like our party. It's all about marketing.'

Chris reflects on how the Swedish fan had been trembling. It seems to have unnerved him a little. 'Actually,' he says, perhaps trying to justify it to himself, to make it seem more normal, 'I was a bit like that when I saw Batman and Robin.' The Batmobile came down Blackpool Promenade when he was young. 'I think there was more than one Batman in town,' he chuckles. 'It was like going to see Father Christmas.' Suddenly he comes out with the strange observation, 'It was always sunny in my childhood.'

'It was always raining with the washing hanging out and something boring on the telly,' says Neil.

'It was always sunny in my childhood,' repeats Chris.

'We'd have ice on the inside of the windows,' says Neil.

Do you see yourselves as very different from each other?

Chris: Yes, there are two distinctive personalities that overlap. Neil is more intellectual . . . more studious. I tend to be a bit more . . . well, at least one side of me is more fun-loving . . . flippant.

But in a very controlled way?

Chris: Yes. The things I like to do I like to have them straight away. Neil has the ability to work at something. I'm probably more hit and miss . . . more spontaneous, possibly.

Do you think you come from similar backgrounds?

Chris: Well, we do both have fathers who are sales reps. (*Laughs.*)

Neil: No, we do have quite similar backgrounds. Our fathers basically did the same job and that does mean quite a lot really. For instance we both used to do the same things in the school holidays, i.e. sit in the back of our father's car in trading estates.

Chris: Go to the Little Chef.

Neil: And we've both got strong-willed mothers who've had a very strong influence. And we're both quite close to our brothers and sisters. But there's differences. The showbusiness element is very different, but it's funny – I'm more showbusiness than Chris is as a result of that.

Chris: I've always had a slight rebellion.

Neil: We used to argue among ourselves at one time – 'Are we in showbusiness?' I used to say, 'Yes, we are' and Chris would say, 'No, we're not.'

Chris: I think we've moved more into it.

Neil: And I think the problem we have is we flirt with showbusiness. One of the reasons we do that is that I have a genuine fascination for it, because basically I've always been stagestruck and would like to appear in something on Shaftesbury Avenue. Chris goes along with that. And because of that flirtation with it I think people sometimes see it as 'Oh, they want to be like that . . . they want to be middle-of-the-road . . . ensure longevity in their career . . .'

Another thing we have in common is that we both had the same reaction when faced with a musical instrument at an early age: we couldn't be bothered to play other people's stuff so we'd make up our own. That's what I did on the guitar, apart from looking at Beatles' songbooks to see what chord changes there were. It's kind of vaguely pointless playing other people's songs.

Chris: It's already been done.

Do you think that's unusual?

Neil: Actually it is. Most people learn either to get their exams or so that they can play at people's parties.

Chris: My dad can play by ear. He's never had a piano lesson in his life but he can play a tune just using the black notes. It's absolutely amazing. And my Auntie Vera can as well, but she plays on the white notes.

Talk turns to how, the last night in Birmingham, the crowd cheered wildly every time Chris appeared in the film accompanying 'King's Cross'. Chris says nothing.

'Didn't you realize?' asks Neil.

'Of course I did,' he grudgingly admits. 'I was thrilled to pieces, though I didn't show it.'

We discuss how odd it is that not one review has mentioned the costume with a semi-erect penis dangling from it. 'Let's face it,' says Neil. 'They probably thought, "*Very* clever, Tennant and Lowe, *very* ironic, the penis, it's so childish I won't mention it . . ."'

He mentions that so far he has been compared with Julian Clary, Liberace and Noël Coward.

'Let's face it,' he murmurs, 'I do want to be Noël Coward.'

He reflects upon the *Guardian* review, declaring war.

'So! The *Guardian* thought I wasn't camp enough. "Mildly camp," they said, I'll show them!'

Chris discovers that the dressing-room is on the street – peeping through the blinds he can see a shopping mall and their fans arriving. 'A mixed bunch, as usual,' he says.

'Our fans are poseurs,' decides Neil.

'They're beautiful people,' says Chris, almost straightfaced.

'I should say, "This one's for all you beautiful people,"' says Neil. 'I might talk some more tonight. Marc Bolan used to. David Bowie said, "This one is for all the strange people" and we all whooped and went mad.'

Two fans settle on a bench just feet away from Chris. He gives us a running commentary.

'They're *kissing*! Oh *no*! They're swapping food from mouth to mouth . . .'

'Oh, you *vilenesses*,' laughs Neil from his make-up chair. 'Actually when we were teenagers we used to do that with chewing gum.'

'It *is* chewing gum,' reports Chris. 'They're swapping chewing gum, French kissing and drinking Pepsi *at the same time*! Eurghhhhh! Eghhhhhhh! It's *horrible*! Aaaahh! They're in love, these two. Really in love. And look at *him*. Eurgh! He just pulled a silly face. Yuchhh!'

Some football hooligan types go past; Chris looks pleased. 'Our audience is so happening,' he decides. 'I think we should congratulate them. They're the sort of people who, if they didn't know who you were, would fight you in a club.'

On this tour the Pet Shop Boys get a *per diem*, spending money. 'I love having cash,' announces Chris, as if it wasn't his own money in the first place that he gets given each day. 'We may get huge cheques but we never have cash. Mind you,' he reflects, 'that's where Ken Dodd went wrong.'

For the first twenty or so minutes of tonight's performance things don't go too well. Whenever the audience try to stand, the security sit them back down again. They don't try too hard anyway and the response is distinctly muted. During 'Heart' a few make a determined effort, but by the end of the song they have been coerced back into their seats. Then 'Paninaro' starts. Elsewhere it has been popular; here, just as legend has had it, seems to be an anthem everyone knows. From the first echoing timpani rolls the whole audience has recognized it and is on their feet. In response Chris dances with more vigour than ever before. He sticks his tongue out. Near the end of his dance he turns his back to the audience and – 'scream! scream!' – wiggles his bum. From then on the mood is triumphant. At the end Neil, now beyond shame, says 'Thank you . . . we love you . . .'

'I know,' he says straight after, 'I've gone now. I was only a stone's throw from going . . .' and he mimes getting down on his knees. '"It's *awwwlrittttteee!!!!!*"'

I ask Chris about his bum wiggle.

'It was an ironic statement,' he bluffs. 'I did it with irony.' Later he claims it was a tribute to George Michael. The response that 'Paninaro' got he takes as some sort of vindication 'considering it is "a very dull record", as the *Guardian* said'.

It is agreed that tonight there were a disproportionate number of Chris Lowe fans, several in fake Armani hats. 'When the band breaks up,' says Neil, 'you'll be big in Scotland.'

Pete leads some fans into the dressing-room. Two girls have t-shirts that say The Girls Behind The Pet Shop Boys. He tells them that Steve Strange, one of the leaders of the early eighties new romantic club scene and figurehead of Visage, is outside.

'Oh, bring him in,' says Neil. 'We *are* the last of the new romantics.'

They are photographed with the girls. 'Very *Sunday Express*,' says Neil. Everyone nods as if this is a very sensible thing to have said. 'Whatever that means,' he says, and everyone nods again as if to say, 'No, we don't know what it meant either.'

Derek Jarman sails in. It is the first show he's seen. 'Wonderful,' he coos, spraying kisses.

'Hello, Derek. Did you see me wiggle my bottom?' says Chris, who seems to have forgotten the gesture's ironic overtones.

The girls stand to one side, drinking champagne.

'I can't believe this is happening,' says one. She surreptitiously picks up the champagne cork as a souvenir. The other points to a piece of used chewing gum on the floor. It has clearly been there for ages.

'It's probably Neil's,' she gasps, clearly wondering whether it would be bad form to pinch that too. Sensibly she restrains herself.

Chris chats to Steve Strange about how he used to pray he'd get into Steve Strange's nights at the Camden Palace, then tells him he wiggled his bottom because 'They weren't reacting so I thought I'd try the George Michael trick.' Steve Strange mentions Bros. 'Do you like Bros?' he asks.

'Well,' says Chris, 'I *know* Bros.'

Neil and Chris pose for some more photos with some boys in fake Armani gear.

'CD' they go as the photo is taken, their sarcastic music business version of 'cheese'.

'Rags to riches.'

'West Ham.'

The photo-session is interrupted by Ivan, barking, 'We've got to go.'

'Can't we sign autographs?' asks Chris.

'No,' says Ivan.

'He's a hard man,' says Neil.

'He could be called a little Hitler,' says Chris.

'Call me what you want, just get on the bus,' says Ivan.

The Polaroids develop.

'I look just like Gary Glitter,' says Neil. 'The *shame*!'

He gets on the bus. As we leave there is complete hysteria. It is Marc Bolan time all over again. The bus shakes with the fans thumping and it appears that we're going to hit some of them to get out.

'We only ran over three,' says Cooley.

'I know why people go on tour now,' reflects Neil, rather thrilled. 'It's because they like being pop stars.'

Chapter 17

'We're on our way to Wembley tara tara tara,' sings Neil, as we drive back to Airth Castle. Someone puts on Prince's 'Sign O The Times' album on the CD player. Everyone looks happy.

'Drinks are on room 21,' shouts Neil when we arrive. He is hyper tonight. 'I don't know why I don't live in a stately home . . . I suppose I'd burn it down like Jane Eyre . . . I like this t-shirt,' – the 'Down Boy' one – 'it was worth a whole Japanese tour . . .'

Tracy orders a Southern Comfort and lemonade. Neil tries it. 'You should have a scotch and coke. Ringo Starr's favourite drink, 1965,' he adds factually. Neil Tennant, 1989, has a hot chocolate. 'You *know* it's happening,' he says.

'Are you still at college?' he asks Sue, one of the two fans.

'I never was. That was her,' says Sue, nodding towards Mel.

'I'm an artist,' apologizes Neil. 'I can't remember these things.'

Someone says, 'I've got a brand new drink.'

'I'm sorry,' says Neil. '"I've Got A Brand New Drink" . . . It's a song title.' Then he says he wishes this tour was going to America. Mind you, he predicts, 'The next tour will be even more of a major production.' He mutters, 'Actually, we've got the idea for the next one . . . bamboo scaffolding . . .'

Tuesday, *18 July*

After much fussing over travel arrangements it is decided that Chris and Pete will drive in Chris's car, Neil, Dainton and I will take the morning shuttle flight from Edinburgh and everyone else will go on the coaches.

At breakfast Neil mentions he had 'a central-heating dream – that the central heating was going to explode' and then we discuss the rail strike. He tells me about the strike when he worked at Macdonald Educational. The members of the NUJ chapel staged a four-month sit-in after they were all sacked in a dispute over redundancies: they slept in the office in a rota. He was one of the negotiators. In the end Robert Maxwell bought the company – Neil attended one meeting with him. The dispute was resolved and they got their jobs back. He says it taught him a lot about the press. Journalists flocked to hear their story, many of them very sympathetic, but they all got it utterly wrong. The only one not to, oddly, was an old bloke from the *Daily Telegraph*.

On the plane we sit in a row of three: Neil in the aisle, me in the middle and by the window a deaf old lady who seems both shocked and surprised to be in an aeroplane at all.

'I bet you do this all the time,' she challenges us.

We both look a bit shame-faced because, of course, we do.

At Heathrow, Dainton points out that one of our fellow travellers is Steve Perryman, the football manager. He tells our car driver, 'I love that group.'

At the hotel Neil talks to Murray. There is a suggestion that they should talk to the *Sun*, to redress the balance of positive and negative press on the tour. 'They've got to have a strong angle,' agonizes Neil. 'I think I would be the Liberace of the Nineties. If Chris wants to do it I'll do it, but I'm not keen . . . the thing is, they are the most frightful people, really.'

Wednesday, *19 July*

The next afternoon the gloom that has spread since the first British reviews lifts. The midweek music papers have reached a very different verdict. *RM* is the first we hear of: 'The greatest show on earth,' says their writer Tim Nicholson. *Twice*. '. . . The most consistently exciting and splendiferous show that I, or any of the people I met afterwards, have ever seen. This was all too good to poke fun at. It has set a standard that every pop show will be forced to try and match, and few ever will.'

The *NME*, in a more roundabout way, is equally hyperbolic. Claiming that 'The Pet Shop Boys have never given a tinker's cuss for being understood. Adoration will do . . . nicely,' it declares. 'What we saw tonight was the best a pop concert can ever hope to be.' There is some typical over-analysis – the string quartet is 'a brilliant conceptual joke' and Chris's dancing is 'an orgy of self-referential wit' – but it concludes 'the greatest pop entertainment ever . . . "The Pet Shop Boys on Tour" overturns all the most wretched and sordid myths of big-event popular music . . .'

Neil and Chris don't choose for the moment to dig at the reason for such hyperbole. To the music press the Pet Shop Boys are a group they probably would have had to invent if they hadn't existed: the group that prove pop music can be modern, ecstatic, danceable, flippant and funny but also still be serious and intelligent; you can like it *and* theorize about it. For those magazines they are the group that you can praise and by doing so put down the rest of pop music.

Neil and Chris don't dwell on this for the moment, but then neither had they dwelt earlier on the reasons why the national press reacted in exactly the contrary manner. To those writers the Pet Shop Boys are the epitome of everything that has undermined *real* music in recent years – theatricality not virtuosity, wit not spontaneous passion, pop not rock, keyboards not guitars.

Right now the Pet Shop Boys simply revel in the praise. Chris rolls round the bed in Neil's room, reading out the reviews and laughing. Their good mood is added to when they learn that 'It's Alright' – the single EMI was confident no other country would even want to release – has gone to number eight in Germany. The *Sun* interview idea is quietly, but definitely, dropped.

As they talk Neil sews a button on to the famous blue shorts, Chris is amazed. 'Do you know how to do it?'

'Yes,' says Neil in an 'of course' voice. 'Are you *that* hopeless?'

'Yes,' says Chris. 'If a button comes off my shorts I throw them away.'

'Actually,' agrees Neil, 'I usually don't wear them again, but I like these shorts so much . . .'

Prince's 'Batman' soundtrack is playing on Neil's cassette player. He says he likes it, Chris says he doesn't.

'I sometimes think we should have done that She-Devil film,' muses Neil. They were offered the soundtrack for the film of Fay Weldon's *The Life and Loves of a She-Devil*, starring Meryl Streep, but after some thought they turned it down, deciding they should do another proper Pet Shop Boys LP next.

'I'm more into touring,' says Chris. 'We're a live band.'

Neil finishes his shorts. He does them up. They come undone immediately. 'Do you know what I've done?' he curses. 'I've put the wrong button on.' He is livid.

They are to do a short TV interview for Thames News. Neil arrives first and chats to the interviewer and a man called Malcolm from EMI . . . about *Scandal*, about how they shouldn't have fictionalized the court scenes, about John

Hurt . . .' We saw him at Madonna's birthday party. He was squeezing her bottom at the time. She was putting up with it. He's quite a famous respected actor in America . . .'

He paints a picture of the evenings in Japan – 'a gang of lager louts hitting Tokyo' – and complains about how a plate of biscuits here at the Mayfair Hotel costs £6.70. 'I couldn't *believe* it. Not very *interesting* biscuits . . .'

Malcolm mentions Paul McCartney. Neil says he likes one song on his new LP, the one called 'Distractions', but complains, 'It's a very lazy piece of lyric writing. "Distractions like butterflies are buzzing round my head."' 'Well? Butterflies don't *buzz*, do they?'

Chris arrives.

'I'm just going to ask you five questions,' says the interviewer.

'How we met. Why you're called the Pet Shop Boys . . .' says Chris sarcastically.

'What *is* a West End girl . . .?' joins in Neil.

And so the interviewer is warned off those, but it is a dull interview anyway.

On the bus to Wembley Chris puts on a video of *Ripping Yarns*. 'I hope it's Tom Brown Schoolboys.' (It is.) Ivan is in a bad mood. He has discovered that performers' contracts do not include a clause for an automatic buy-out of the video rights – he must negotiate it all separately – and he has just found out that he has been demoted from being Bros's tour manager. They are jealous of the time he has been spending with the Pet Shop Boys. Everyone is outraged, though Chris mutters, 'I can understand how they felt. I'm very possessive with the people we use.'

It is Amanda at EMI's birthday. 'I've sent her flowers on your behalf,' Ivan informs them, 'and she thanks you very much.'

Then: 'Courtney Pine wants a lot of money to appear in the film.' Long looks all round.

'Try to knock him down,' says Neil.

'And,' says Ivan, 'people are getting a bit cocky. People are taking it a bit easy.'

'Double the fines,' says Chris.

'You should have a word, Ivan,' suggests Neil. 'These are the most important gigs of the tour. I don't want people having a laugh.'

Ivan tells them that Wet Wet Wet's management saw the Scottish show: 'They thought it was very clever and funny that the audience didn't get it . . .'

'They can explain it to me,' says Chris.

'They thought it was subtle . . .' elaborates Ivan.

'Like when the boys kissed?' Chris inquires.

Are you surprised that there's been no moral panic, no big media fuss, about 'It's A Sin'?

Neil: You just can't outrage anyone any more.

Beforehand you were slightly worried, weren't you?

Neil: Yes, but I think we've realized over the years that if you want to do something and you want people to notice in that way you have to *tell* them you're doing it. We could have leaked a story to the *Sun* or had the *Sun* in to say, 'Isn't this outrageous? There's a naked penis. And people . . .' – however young they are – '. . . in the audience.' You've got to stir it up if you want that.

Chris: I don't think people care anyway.

Neil: To be honest I think if we'd taken all of our clothes off on-stage it wouldn't have got a mention in the paper the next day.

Chris: It wouldn't be a big deal anyway.

Neil: I don't think people watch the films, except in 'King's Cross'. Marcia (*a fan who writes to Neil*) said she didn't watch the film apart from that.

Chris: So what did she watch?

Neil: She watched us.

Chis: But I don't *do* anything.

Neil: She watched you not doing anything . . . *fascinated* by that. Half the audience just stand there looking at you thinking, 'God, there he is . . . like an Andy Warhol film.'

Chris: A really boring film.

Neil: Standing there picking your nose.

Chris: I do that. I started laughing because of the Raw Sex thing. (*A TV spoof of the Pet Shop Boys in which 'Chris' picked his nose through boredom.*)

Neil: I do it too. Make-up makes your nose itch.

And so there is a pep talk. We are all called into the production office and Ivan tells us how things are to be. He concludes, 'This isn't me bullying you, this is me *asking* you . . .'

Back-stage someone tries to give Chris a tape of a friend's band but he backs away, as if scared of infection. 'We don't take demo tapes. You only get sued later.' Oddly he's probably right – it is one of the occupational hazards of being successful in pop. Unknown songwriters who once sent a tape to you, or your management, or someone whom they can link with one of your cousins, sue you, claiming that your latest million-selling hit shamelessly rips off their undiscovered gems.

David Jacob, the recording engineer on many of their records and the engineer for the live video, appears after the soundcheck. He tells them bluntly what they have known deep down for a long time but which everyone else has been glossing over – that the sound isn't very good. In fact here in Wembley it is awful. They look miserable.

Pete disappears outside, where a tout will offer him £1,000 for ten back-stage passes. (He refuses.) Alan cleans Chris's training shoes with a toothbrush. Around him a debate about the sound rages. They discuss sacking the soundman there and then.

Ivan suggests they ask the man doing the on-stage sound to have a go.

Ivan looks worried, but then he has other problems as well. £4,000 is needed from somewhere, he has just been told, to pay for crowd lights for the live video. Neil and Chris say they doubt it's necessary, as they're not planning a clichéd live video with light streaming through outstretched adoring fingertips.

'Point number three,' moves on Ivan. 'Derek Jarman is refusing to wear a pass.'

'Good on him,' says Chris, instinctively approving of anything that involves disobedience.

'He says if you don't wear one he won't,' says Ivan. Ivan has told security to kick him out if he doesn't.

Neil adopts his peacemaker voice. 'He can have one in his pocket. That's the solution.'

'He'll still get stopped,' objects Ivan.

'Then he has that *great* moment,' grins Chris, 'when you get it out of your pocket and say, "Bog off".'

'Oh,' says Ivan. He looks furious. Nevertheless the next time Derek Jarman is seen he is wandering round cheerfully, a pass fixed to his overalls.

Ivan goes. Neil and Chris curse themselves for not trusting their initial instincts on the sound. To their minds if they hadn't been swayed by other people they'd never be in this fix.

They soundcheck some more, with Ivan and both mixing engineers on the sound desk, all long faces and scowls and sour words. Jim blames the quality of sound inside the Pet Shop Boys computer equipment. 'I don't think that's true,' snaps Neil. The other engineer chooses to back his fellow professional and simply swears blind that the PA equipment is wonderful. Little is resolved.

Neil storms off. A few minutes later, back-stage as the audience begin trickling in, he hears a middle-of-the-road soul record playing through the speakers.

'Why are they playing a Simply Red record?' he fumes. 'I do

not want our audience hearing a Simply Red record. I'm in a *totally* bad mood now.'

As it happens the record is 'Aja' by Steely Dan, but it seems a bad time to point this out. Just as he had on the first night in Birmingham, Neil returns to the dressing-room and throws everyone out.

Chris's parents sit in the hospitality room, enjoying a little light supper. His mum has just read the review in *Melody Maker*, favourable though not as over-the-top as the previous couple.

'I don't normally buy it,' she tells me pointedly, as something I must know, as if she had been talking about some National Front fanzine. 'I've never forgiven them for what they said about Diana Ross.'

She mentions her dancing days and how the dancing in the show takes her back. She says she keeps all the Pet Shop Boys articles in a scrapbook. 'I call it a scrapbook,' she laughs warmly, 'of course there's twenty-five of them now.'

She talks about the Pet Shop Boys' new portable phone – she's not impressed. She hates ansaphones – 'you can never get through to anyone, but you've made a call, haven't you?' – and to her portable phones seem even worse. She was outraged to discover how much the portable phone network costs to use. She called it from a friend's home, ADC, so that the operator would call back with the cost. It was £2.41. 'My friend said where did you call? Outer Mongolia?'

Gill Smith, once a journalist, now a record company press officer, turns up with Betty Page, another journalist, the first one to suggest the hamster derivation of their name. Gill laughs about the first big magazine feature they did, when 'West End Girls' was about to come out for the second time; two pages in *Record Mirror*. They followed the route of the song in a hired Daimler, drinking in the Dive Bar mentioned in the lyrics, then drove round the East End for photos and had an expensive meal in Chelsea. ('It seems incredibly fitting that our career started off with an incredibly expensive meal,' laughs Neil when asked about this.) Gill says in passing that she still has the interview transcript. It arrives in the post a few days later.

It's another death blow to anyone who believes that the Pet Shop Boys approached their career with cool calculation, with a keen sense of strategy and of image-creation. They get drunk – as is only too obvious from the photos, neither cosmetic nor 'film stills' – and Chris tries hard to sabotage his career throughout the interview, as if he couldn't really take seriously the fact that his opinions and views were being solicited on anything.

The received wisdom is that you control your press very carefully: who you talk to, when you talk to them . . .

Neil: It's almost true, but it only applies to Britain. In Britain, where we do less press then anywhere else, we do think carefully, just like we think carefully about where to put our adverts.

It's true, isn't it, that in a sense you have a British career – the one you're most proud of – and a messier, more compromised one out of Britain?

Neil: Yeah. Here the Pet Shop Boys are at their most authentic and pure.

Chris: It's very difficult to control it outside Britain. You can't do it. They tamper with your artwork. You don't know what the magazines are. If you say, 'Are you *sure* it's worth doing this radio interview?' they'll say (*puts on silly mid-European accent*), 'Yes, this is very important for North Germany.'

Neil: You see, we don't think promotion has any value. We always say we're most successful in places where we don't do any promotion because people are disappointed when they see us. I think there's a kind of truth in that. Early on, promotion may help, but normally what you're doing is cooperating with the record company in a territory so they will do as much to promote your records as possible. 90 per cent of the whole thing is to get your records played on the radio and available in the shops. I also think if a pop star comes from a different country, you like the fact that they're so distant. You can't believe they're real. When I was a boy I could never believe that Americans were real. I couldn't believe that the Supremes were flesh and blood.

We do so many interviews abroad and mostly what we do is defend pop music. I don't know why we don't get paid by Stock Aitken Waterman for defending them abroad.

Chris: You just want to hit some of the German critics.

Neil: (mimicking a snooty German voice): 'Don't you think the guitar is making a comeback?' I endlessly say, it's like when the man at Decca told Brian Epstein that beat groups were going out of fashion. People think that about synthesizer duos. We're here to stay. It's just a kind of music. Then they say, 'I think you're very interested in marketing.' And I always say, 'Obviously you get some groups who are based on a marketing approach . . .' – and they nod – '. . . for instance U2 . . .' – and they're nearly sick – '. . . because you can't deny what a brilliant marketing campaign they've done for "Rattle And Hum".' Then I say that our approach is more haphazard than people think, which it is. People always think because the Pet Shop Boys are a synthesizer duo that we have a monolithic marketing-based way of doing things. We don't, but in my opinion U2 are a *triumph* of marketing, to the extent where we once wondered whether we should ask U2's manager to manage us.

'Time,' sings Neil in the dressing-room bathroom, 'is waiting in the wings/he speaks of senseless things . . . Time in quaaludes and red wine . . .' It is an old David Bowie song, 'Time'.

'I didn't know what quaaludes were,' recalls Chris.

'My parents will be here now,' says Neil. 'They'll be dreading it.' Looking at me, he says, 'They don't talk to the press.'

'Don't let the fact that your family's here worry you,' teases Chris.

'On the *contrary* . . .' bluffs Neil.

But tonight there are problems. Chris has a substitute keyboard and it is set to a different key, so that at the beginning of 'Opportunities' everything is dramatically and terribly out of tune. During 'It's A Sin' half of the track simply doesn't play. The crowd is quiet and it is impossibly hot. Though by 'It's Alright' even Neil's mum is dancing, it hasn't been the best of nights.

'It was *crap*,' fumes Chris back-stage. 'Really *crap*.'

'I know it was crap,' says Neil.

'I didn't enjoy it,' says Chris. 'It was far too hot. I thought I was going to faint.'

It is time to meet people.

'I can't handle it,' says Chris. 'I'm not well. I want to go straight to bed.'

He won't, of course, and his very vocal despondency draws Neil back to acting out the responsible role: Neil must make sure that, with people to meet, small-talk to be chatted, their attitudes are presentable.

'Chris,' he says sternly, 'don't go out there with a major downer.'

Chris nods quietly.

'It was marvellous,' Mr Tennant tells Chris.

'Birmingham was better,' chips in Neil. 'The people were friendlier. Let's face it – southerners are snooty.'

Neil's mum tells him there was something wrong with the sound during 'Later Tonight'. She says, 'It sounded like a record put on backwards.'

'The volume of the sound takes away the character,' agrees Neil's father.

'Well,' muses his mother, 'the young ones like that. It's not made for fuddy-duddies.' And with this she looks at Neil's shorts, unimpressed in a way only one's mother can be. 'What brought *this* on?' she asks.

'It's my shorts,' says Neil, accurately.

'Oh *dear*,' says Mrs Tennant. 'You wear them for *comfort*, I presume?'

'What was the one after "Later Tonight"?' asks Mr Tennant.

'"Nothing Has Been Proved".'

'That was awful from where we were,' says Mrs Tennant.

As they leave Mrs Tennant grasps my arm with an unexpected, almost threatening firmness. 'You're not going to quote me,' she says. This is phrased not as a question or even as an instruction but as a simple statement of fact. Just in case she hasn't made herself quite clear she adds, 'Or I'll sue you.'

They are depressed. Neil rambles aimlessly on the coach about the first two groups he ever saw live: Jon Hiseman's Colosseum and Led Zeppelin. Chris simply says, 'I'm really fed up.'

They're angry at the performance, at the seats their guests were given, at the sound, at the venue. There is something else too, something they don't really articulate until later. Before this tour they had enjoyed three and a half years of imagining what Pet Shop Boys fans were like, without ever having to match their ideas up with reality. They knew one thing: whatever Pet Shop Boys fans were, they weren't the same as other fans. In Hong Kong and Japan they found an unremarkable mixture but that didn't matter too much. Then in Birmingham and Glasgow it was a little disappointing, though they were thrilled by the screaming girls in Birmingham and the football lads in Glasgow. But all the time there has been a belief that London is where the real Pet Shop Boys audience will be. London is where they would understand what was funny and what was serious and what was sad. In London they would understand 'The Sound of the Atom Splitting'. They would know that if no one is on-stage and lights cascade around the hall, then the response isn't to stand, bemused, waiting for the Pet Shop Boys to return but to turn Wembley Arena into a mad Acid House rave for eight minutes.

But it wasn't like that. The London audience was less remarkable than the regional audiences, just the normal Wembley Arena for a group like the Pet Shop Boys who straddle several markets. The faces may be different when Simply Red play but the overall crowd would look much the same.

You've always imagined that the Pet Shop Boys appealed in a very special way, haven't you?

Neil: Well, I hope we do, but sometimes I just wonder. I think maybe we just don't any more. I think people just think, 'Oh, it's the Pet Shop Boys.'

Chris: It was easy before, because we invented our own audience. We didn't have a real audience so we could imagine what our audience was like and confirm to ourselves that we were different. But when you see a real audience you realize that maybe you're not how you imagined.

What had you imagined?

Chris: That they were less conformist. The audience is very normal, a lot of them. Sort of *family* types. I always imagined that people who liked us were really quite subversive. I wonder how people see us. I think people probably just look at us and see two really nice normal happy-happy people who are totally unchallenging.

Back at the Mayfair Hotel they won't serve us in the bar because of – familiar problem – Neil's shorts. 'To top it *all*,' sighs Chris, though he does try to laugh it off: 'Actually, Neil, it's not the shorts that are the problem, it's your legs.'

So we drink in reception. Chris asks the barman for something to help him sleep and is recommended a Grand Marnier.

'Today has gone wrong,' states Neil.

'It's a disaster,' agrees Chris.

'Today,' says Neil, 'is the official Worst Day of the Tour.'

It is perhaps a good thing that just now they discover a proof of an advertisement for a Liza Minnelli single, intended for the *NME*, in Neil's pigeonhole. Despite everything that has happened (perhaps because of it), tired and fed up, they nevertheless pore over it, discussing every word, every punctuation mark, every black space. They decide it has to be redone. When I later mention that I was surprised they were so bothered, Neil retorts, 'It's so satisfying if it looks good and so irritating and *cheapening*, it makes you feel dirty if it's wrong. And look – you're given a page in the *NME* and you can do what you want with it. And it's not even *our* record!'

I say I don't think most pop stars bother.

'That's because,' he says, 'it doesn't occur to them.'

Chapter 18

Thursday, *20 July*

'It Bites?'

'No.'

'Cocteau Twins?'

'Yes.'

'Lizzie Tear?'

'I suppose so.'

On the bus to Wembley, Ivan takes the Pet Shop Boys through the latest party invitations.

At the venue there are more arguments about the sound.

'I've heard three things so far,' rages Jim, the soundman: 'Turn it up, make it clear and turn it down.'

Tonight the film crew is to shoot the performance. There are a few diplomatic gaffs to be ironed over. Derek Jarman has, against specific instructions to the contrary, brought his own hair and make-up people. He argues that the usual stage make-up is 'totally unacceptable'; what he quite clearly means is that he doesn't like it.

An hour and a half before the performance the Courtney Pine situation still isn't resolved. The Pet Shop Boys have reluctantly offered him £3,000 for being filmed, but his agent still insists on £5,000. As chance would have it, sitting in hospitality is a journalist from Radio 4; Neil has agreed to do an interview for a programme they're making about Courtney. Obviously he is hardly in the mood to pay fulsome tribute.

'Our price and Radio 4,' Neil tells Ivan wearily, 'or his price and no Radio 4.'

Ivan says he'll pass it on. 'Everyone else has agreed to the MU rate,' he says.

'How come we're getting so much, then?' asks Chris mischievously, 'Our fee far exceeds the MU rate.'

'Because we're the bloody Pet Shop Boys and it's *our* film,' snaps Neil.

'We're merely musicians,' claims Chris with insincere modesty. 'We're just a cog in a larger machine.'

Later Neil will talk to Courtney direct and he will agree to the lower fee with the difference to pay if the video recoups. 'He said, "As long as nothing gets in the way of the music . . ."'

The make-up argument reaches the dressing-room.

'I quite like my make-up,' objects Neil. 'I think I should have my panda eyes in the film.'

'It won't be the same without,' agrees Chris. 'It's the real you.'

'Yes,' laughs Neil, 'the real me. The whole thing came from me telling Pierre Laroche that I wanted to look like Dusty Springfield for a birrova laugh.'

He chortles about Chris's mum last night.

'She was being a bit of a pro,' he says, mimicking her: '"The problem was that we were sitting on the prompt-side, not the SM-side." It was a hoot. She knows I should know these things. She *knows* I'm pretentious.'

Some friends pop their heads round the dressing-room door.

'All we want to hear later,' says Neil firmly, 'is that it's fantastic. There will be no criticisms.'

In fact tonight goes very well until a kerfuffle at the end. There was a power-cut during 'One More Chance' which hadn't affected the on-stage performance but which had ruined the recording for the video soundtrack, so it is arranged that they will perform the song once more as an extra encore at the end. Neil comes back on-stage in darkness and is stranded there. No music, no lights. 'I felt like Rick Astley,' he fumes. Tempers are short.

'That's it!' screams Chris. 'Cancel the whole film. They've screwed up.'

In the end it's decided it can be patched up.

After a while they go out to sign some autographs at the gates to the back-stage enclosure, where fans are pressed up against a chain fence. Objects to sign are either hurled over the top or passed through gaps. As they sign, P.S.B. Riverside, a youth football team that includes Pete's brother and which the Pet Shop Boys sponsor, go by in their coach and wave. Chris jumps up and down and waves back.

'That's our football team, by the way,' he tells the fans.

It's obvious from their expressions that they don't believe him.

'Chris,' cries out one fan, 'what do you think of the new Armani shop?'

'I think the one in Milan's better,' chuckles Chris, being deliberately snooty. The fans jeer good-humouredly.

'Who cut your hair?' shouts another. 'Did you sue him?'

'Are you pleased Vince Clark didn't enjoy himself?' (Erasure were here tonight and – while I was watching them watching the show – seemed quite enthusiastic.)

'Has he ever enjoyed himself?' retorts Chris.

Someone asks Chris to sign a cigarette packet. He refuses on moral grounds.

'Can you sign my hand?' someone ask Neil.

'What's the point of that?' scoffs another. 'It'll wash off.'

'I'll have it for a bit,' says the first, rather sweetly.

'Are you going to put a live album out. "Lively"?'

'Actually,' says Neil, 'maybe that's what we can call the video: *Pet Shop Boys, Lively*.'

'Did you get pissed off at me waving at you?' shouts someone.

'No,' says Neil. 'I quite liked it.'

'Can you smile?'

'Why does everyone want me to smile?' scowls Chris.

'Because you look so miserable,' comes back the answer.

They walk back inside.

'You know the last time that was done,' says the security guard, 'was when the Jam were here, ten years ago.' They look surprised. Even though, as Neil points out, the Jam must have been here in 1982 – seven years ago – it hasn't struck the Pet Shop Boys that they've been doing anything unusually friendly or whatever. Their attitude has been more: well, it would be rude not to, wouldn't it?

Friday, *21 July*

This afternoon they must run through all the songs again for Derek Jarman to film close-ups and different angles. Neil chats to him in hospitality. Derek raves about Chris: 'one of the most minimalist performances'. 'Let's Dance' plays on the caterer's radio cassette.

'Poor David Bowie,' sighs Neil. 'He's invented rock'n'roll and did anyone thank him for it?'

For the filming Derek Jarman sits in his grey boiler-suit behind the camera monitors about fifteen rows back into the empty auditorium. He issues instructions through a hand-held microphone, his eyes bulging like an over-anxious headmaster. He confesses to being terrified by the technology involved here.

'I'm a technophobe,' he mutters. 'Why don't we do it on Super-8? It's totally ridiculous and mad. All these wires. There's no communication with the cameras. Soon the director won't even be there, he'll be editing it from the moon. Every year you get more and more divorced from things,' he sighs.

A friend, singer Robyn Archer, peers at the monitors playing back last night's shoot.

'You've got plenty,' she says, reassuringly.

'You'd be surprised,' he says. 'Plenty often isn't enough.'

After four songs we are way behind schedule.

'I chose to do it,' says Derek Jarman in a self-recriminatory tone. 'It's my fault.' He turns to a friend. 'You know how it is.'

As this frantic filming carries on, back-stage James McKay, the producer, drops a bombshell on Ivan. The schedule has been fixed for more filming next week against a blue screen of images which can then be dropped into the film. Now he tells Ivan this won't be necessary. As Ivan spent much of last night arranging this extra week with the cast, who have all cleared their diaries for it, he is furious. Now the Americans must be put – with barely a farewell – on the first available plane out after tonight. 'You might have told me,' he grunts through gritted teeth.

Something else is also becoming increasingly clear to Ivan. Two weeks ago the only one sure thing about this video was that it wasn't to be like a normal concert video. Little by little there have been compromises – shooting it in a special theatrical setting, filming staged scenes for some of the songs, filming extra footage to edit on top of the film next week – all of these have now gone by the wayside. And now? Now 'It's just going to be a live video,' admits Ivan.

By five o'clock complete panic has set in. Derek Jarman decides to skip several songs and go direct to 'West End Girls'. 'We'll come back on Tuesday,' he shouts, in a fluster, but of course that is out of the question. After 'West End Girls' they realize they have time to shoot one more song and choose 'Always On My Mind'. But as he is now taking the songs out of order it means that not only must the cast change back into a costume they have just changed out of but that a reel of film must be rewound: five more minutes wasted.

'I'm sorry if I've been irritable,' he apologizes through his microphone. He looks as though these have been some of the worst hours of his life. 'It's been a nightmare.'

Back-stage, nerves are a little frazzled. Neil and Chris ask for a Do Not Disturb sign to be put on the door and lie on the dressing-room floor on their backs, sleeping.

It does the trick. When I return they're much more cheerful.

Chris mentions that one of their long-held ambitions is to record a particular U2 song with Patsy Kensit.

'We could do it with the 'Narns,' suggests Neil.

'They'd see the joke,' agrees Chris.

'We'd make it hi-energy,' says Neil. 'Actually I think they're friends of U2.'

'That's why they had a bomb scare in Northern Ireland,' supposes Chris.

'We had a bomb scare the other week,' says Neil.

At this every jaw in the room drops. A bomb scare? This is the first most of us, including Chris, have heard of this. A mere bomb scare obviously hasn't been important enough to mention.

'I wouldn't have done the concert if I'd known,' says Chris.

'It was only a minor one,' reassures Ivan.

'I've only hidden a small bomb,' play-acts Neil, pretending to be a minor bomber. 'Don't worry about it. It'll only kill one or two people. It'll probably sound like an orchestra hit . . . '

The word keeps coming through of arriving celebrities. Holly Johnson is here. Ian McKellen is here. George Michael is here (and has asked for, and been granted, special permission to stand by the sound desk: 'Taking notes probably,' says Neil).

Outside, George Michael's assistant quietly curses that 'They've given us the naffest seats' as George and his sister Melanie share a drink with Holly Johnson. When the Pet Shop Boys come on, George Michael does in fact reveal himself as quite keen. Too much of a pop music fan to be totally cool, he sings along to the choruses of 'Left To My Own Devices' and all of 'Love Comes Quickly'. Bros are here too and Luke gives an impressed burst of applause to Danny Cummings's solo. It's the last concert of the tour and, especially after the problems of the previous two nights, it's a wonderful success.

The first people into the dressing-room are Bros, together with Luke's girlfriend Shirley Lewis.

'You clever bastards,' shouts Luke, then, to Chris, 'You cool mother.' Matt imitates Chris's dance while Luke and Chris swap car details. Neil says to Matt, enthusiastically, 'I like your record.'

'You look like Elvis,' Matt tells him back. 'There's a lot of stars here,' he adds, as if this is more impressive than anything else. And then the famous and the families stream in.

Tom talks to Neil's mum.

'I haven't had so much fun since . . .' he announces loudly, and you can see everyone turn, pause, and think, 'This is it, he's been so good and the tour was nearly over but now, as we feared, he's going to say something disgraceful' '. . . my Aunt Enid's wedding.' The sigh of relief is audible.

'Where are your shorts today?' asks Neil's mum, adding hopefully, just in case this should be seen as a mere casual inquiry: 'Have you given them up?'

And then behaviour starts loosening up.

As we walk outside it's raining. Chris starts dancing and punching the sky. 'I'm already grooving,' he shouts, 'and we're not there yet.'

Bingobangobongo. Westway studios. There are celebrities everywhere, rooms full of people dancing, a fairground ride. For the first time in weeks I leave my notebooks behind, but the party is later written up in the *Tatler* as the last great party of the eighties. Neil walks round in his suit, talking fast to his friends. All tour he's said that he'll probably just 'stay an hour', but he lingers for most of the night. Chris rushes round manically, dancing, jabbering away, a demented beam on his face. 'Isn't this just the most brilliant party?' he asks every time he passes.

At five o'clock, long after it has got light, the music stops. The few hundred people still here prepare to leave, Chris bids them to stay and asks the DJ to continue. It is six when everyone finally staggers out. Chris bounces into his car. Dainton tries to form us all into a posse to head off to more fun, but Chris says goodbye in the way that means 'don't try to follow' and joyously heads off: somewhere, he has been told, there is another party, just starting.

Epilogue

August 1990

The week after the tour I spend two days talking to Neil and Chris while they mix the soundtrack for the live video with David Jacob. Neil overdubs a couple of vocals but aside from that the music is left untouched. From discussions they were having, it became clear to me for the first time that they were planning not to renew their management contract with Tom Watkins.

After that they both went on holiday – Neil to Tuscany, Chris to Cyprus. They met in Milan to go shopping. During the rest of 1989 they did some more collaborating. They worked a little with New Order's Bernard Sumner and ex-Smiths guitarist Johnny Marr. Both of them helped write a song called 'The Patience Of A Saint' and Neil co-wrote the lyrics and sang backing vocals on a song called 'Getting Away With It', released as a single under the group name Electronic. It reached number twelve in the charts and in April, to their pleasure and somewhat to their surprise, began climbing the American charts. At the beginning of August they joined Electronic for two live stadium concerts in Los Angeles, supporting Depeche Mode. It was the first public Pet Shop Boys performance in America.

Despite their earlier resolutions Neil and Chris decided to work some more on the forthcoming Dusty Springfield LP. They recorded three more songs with her: 'Occupy Your Mind', 'Daydreaming' and 'I Want To Stay Here'. The first was based around the Acid House snippet that Chris had been playing on tour after 'Domino Dancing' and which they had first tried to make into a record with the people behind the Sunrise raves. The latter was the song Neil remembered travelling overnight from Birmingham to Glasgow, originally recorded by Steve and Eydie in 1963, which he was reminded of by Kylie Minogue's 'Hand On Your Heart'. They played Dusty the Carroll Thompson song, 'Sing Me A Love Song', but she didn't like it. 'In Private' was released as a single near the end of the year and, to their disappointment, only reached number thirteen.

Following the tour Carroll Thompson and Courtney Pine recorded together a version of the Diana Ross hit single 'I'm Still Waiting'. Carroll also had a hit single, 'Joy And Heartbreak', under the name Movement 98. Jay Henry sang on Dusty Springfield's 'Daydreaming' and Dominic was frequently called upon to work with the Pet Shop Boys in the studio.

Liza Minnelli's LP was released under the title 'Results', though no extra 'power woman song' of that title was ever written or recorded. It sold over 100,000 copies in the first week, the single, a version of Stephen Sondheim's 'Losing My Mind', reached number six and Neil and Chris appeared on *Wogan* talking and performing alongside Liza. Neil went to the London *Batman* première with her and the photo of them arriving together was larger than that of any of the many other celebrities in next day's edition of the *Sun*. Over the next few months three further singles were released, but they all fell short of the Top 40.

In October Pete organized Bingobangobongo 2, an all-night rave in Brixton Academy to celebrate Chris's thirtieth birthday. Frankie Knuckles was flown over from New York to DJ. Plans for another rave, to benefit the charity Crusaid and to feature a performance by Liza Minnelli, fell through when it proved impossible to put it on without losing money.

Since the previous summer the media ballyhoo about raves – to the media forever 'Acid House parties' – had grown. In the late summer the police began breaking them up and preventing them by setting up roadblocks. A pressure movement, the Campaign for the Freedom to Party, was set up to oppose government legislation engineered to delegalize most such parties. Chris attended their opening rally in Trafalgar Square in January. 'It's the one thing I really care about,' he told me, perhaps not quite truthfully, the day before.

In late September Massive Management issued the following statement:

> On October 31st 1984 Neil Tennant and Chris Lowe, the Pet Shop Boys, signed a 5-year management deal with Tom Watkins of Massive Management.
>
> Although they have enjoyed a remarkably rewarding and successful relationship with Tom Watkins and Massive Management, Pet Shop Boys have decided to set up their own management office, which will represent them, with effect from November 1st, 1989.
>
> Chris Lowe, Neil Tennant and Tom Watkins would like to stress that their relationship will continue as amicably as ever and, indeed, Neil Tennant is a director of Watkins' new venture, the Decorative Arts Group.

The Decorative Arts Group is a London gallery in St Johns Wood selling twentieth-century furniture, paintings and ceramics. Since the split Neil and Chris have seen Tom quite often and their relationship is friendly. In early 1990 Massive Management, under very different circumstances, stopped representing Bros (lawsuits flew in both directions). Meanwhile Massive also manage Electribe 1.0.1., who had their first hit in late 1989, a teenage girl trio masterminded by Tom called Faith, Hope and Charity and a heavy metal band called Richter Scale, discovered by Ivan and in development. Ivan, who still works for Massive Management, collected no fines during the Pet Shop Boys tour.

The Pet Shop Boys set up an office run by Jill Wall, head of Parlophone Records from 1985 to 1987 and marketing director at Polydor until the Pet Shop Boys offered her this job. They bought a property in Notting Hill Gate, and converted it into an office. Dainton has been employed full-time.

Rob Holden was not reinstated at Massive Management. In September he went to ZTT Records as general manager, but it didn't work out and they parted company in November. Since then he has acted as manager for several acts including dance duo Orbital and B.E.F. (Martyn Ware and Ian Craig Marsh) and was involved in new age fishing smocks before accepting an A & R job at Polydor records. He was not asked to sign a silence clause: as part of his leaving agreement he kept his Kawasaki ZXR750 motorbike but at the time of writing is banned from driving.

When Neil and Chris saw a rough cut of the film of the tour they were not at all happy. It had been filmed on video and didn't capture the show well. No Super-8 footage from Japan was included: apparently it didn't come out. Despite several attempts to re-edit the film the Pet Shop Boys have so far refused to approve its release.

None of the Christmas record ideas for 1989 was ever followed up, nor did Janet Street-Porter's Christmas TV special happen, although the Pet Shop Boys now talk of a new Christmas record ploy for 1990.

Songs called 'Backburner', 'Camp David', 'I've Got A Brand New Drink' and 'Golf' are yet to materialize. 'She's In Love With The Man She Married' is, as yet, unrecorded. There has been no move to record the 'Posthumously' LP.

The Porsche skiing glasses that Chris bought in Hong Kong

are yet to appear in a photo. When I recently mention his threat to go blond he dismisses the idea as simply a preposterous moment of madness. No one has yet worked out exactly what was done to earn Mr Udo's displeasure, though Neil now suspects that they drove too hard a bargain – a dishonourable bargain – in the first place.

The tour itself seems to have taken on a strange kind of legendary status, referred to – either approvingly or disapprovingly – as the most extreme and remarkable example of a theatrical pop show.

Jason Donovan was quoted in a magazine saying how disappointed he was to miss the Pet Shop Boys shows.

The Pet Shop Boys first saw some of this book one evening in October when I took rough versions of Chapters 6 and 11 to Sarm West studios where they were working on songs for Dusty Springfield's album. It was Chris's thirtieth birthday so they drank champagne and Chris read bits out. They kept laughing and saying, 'This can never come out.' Neil said it was not what he'd expected but he thought he liked it.

'It's just like we are,' hooted Chris. 'We're horrible, aren't we?'

Neil said he hadn't realized how much they had played up to being observed.

They were alarmed at how much they swear and asked for their swearing to be taken out throughout the book. They were far more adamant about this than any other changes, insisting that 'swearing looks very different written down' and that they simply don't like it.

On New Year's Eve I posted them a rough finished manuscript before going away for three weeks. The evening I got back I met them, by chance, in the street in the West End of London. Neil read the whole manuscript. Chris read about a third and laughed that he was horrified how horrible he was and that it had changed him as a person.

In March Neil spent about eight days going through the whole text with me on the word processor at my flat. Chris decided not to come. When he dropped round one day I asked him if he had finished reading the rough manuscript yet, but he said that the hadn't and he thought that the cleaner had thrown it away. He would read it before it was published.

Relatively few changes were made. Apart from the swearing, a few comments about other people, usually other pop stars, that were made in the heat of the moment and were either obviously libellous or just deeply offensive, were taken out. In a very few cases where the text was changed, people who would have been unfairly compromised by the book can no longer be specifically identified. Occasionally where I had misinterpreted or got wrong a factual matter it has been corrected, but generally the text has been left to stand as my interpretation of events, motives, intentions, feelings and so on.

In April they went to Munich to record their next album with German producer Harold Faltermeyer, taking with them copies of the final manuscript. Though they at first sent a message that any further suggested changes would be minor, two weeks later they sent over a manuscript with significant deletions, mainly of spur-of-the-moment pronouncements that, they feared, might easily be taken out of context. I visited them in Munich to discuss these and, and after some slightly heated discussion, reached a compromise on the material in dispute.

Not one of the book titles mentioned on the tour (*Yawn!*, *Being Boring*, *You* know *the Story* or *A Rant*) were ever seriously considered afterwards. For a while this book was to be called *Honestly! A Book About the Pet Shop Boys*, then for a while it was *Bingobangobongo: A Book About the Pet Shop Boys*. Neil and Chris lobbied strongly for *Pet Shop Boys in Print*. Eventually it borrowed its name from their fan club magazine *Pet Shop Boys, Literally*.

In May, the book received some early publicity, courtesy of the *Sun*'s latest pop music columnist, Piers Morgan.

'The Pet Shop Boys claim their new autobiography,' he wrote, already straying from the truth, 'is a "fascinating insight into the lives of Neil Tennant and Chris Lowe". Having had the misfortune to meet this dreary duo, I find it hard to believe there's anything fascinating about them.'

Neil and Chris were both amused and puzzled by this. To the best of their knowledge they have never met Piers Morgan. Nor do they plan to.